W9-BGE-719

# AMERICAN VILLAINS

American villains /
REF 364.109 AME
33534025086
OLD MILL HIGH

MAGILL'S CHOICE

# AMERICAN VILLAINS

## Volume 1

Joe Adonis - Jim Jones
1-298

*from*
**The Editors of Salem Press**

OLD MILL SENIOR HIGH SCHOOL
MEDIA CENTER

SALEM PRESS, INC.
Pasadena, California   Hackensack, New Jersey

*Cover photo:* The Granger Collection, New York

Copyright © 2008, by Salem Press, Inc.

All rights in this book are reserved. No part of this work may be used or reproduced in any manner whatsoever or transmitted in any form or by any means, electronic or mechanical, including photocopy, recording, or any information storage and retrieval system, without written permission from the copyright owner except in the case of brief quotations embodied in critical articles and reviews or in the copying of images deemed to be freely licensed or in the public domain. For information address the publisher, Salem Press, Inc., P.O. Box 50062, Pasadena, California 91115.

The paper used in these volumes conforms to the American National Standard for Permanence of Paper for Printed Library Materials, Z39.48-1992 (R1997).

Essays originally appeared in *Great Lives from History: Notorious Lives* (2007). New material has been added.

**Library of Congress Cataloging-in-Publication Data**

American villains / from the editors of Salem Press.

p. cm. — (Magill's choice)

"Essays originally appeared in Great lives from history: notorious lives (2007). New material has been added."

Includes bibliographical references and index.

ISBN 978-1-58765-453-4 (set : alk. paper) — ISBN 978-1-58765-454-1 (vol. 1 : alk. paper) — ISBN 978-1-58765-456-5 (vol. 2 : alk. paper)

1. Criminals—United States—Biography. I. Salem Press.

HV6785.A44 2008

364.1092'273—dc22

2008017122

PRINTED IN CANADA

# Contents

# Publisher's Note

*American Villains* covers 177 of the most infamous assassins, serial killers, frauds, gangsters, murderers, terrorists, thieves, and traitors of American history. These criminals are not generally covered in other biographical surveys; whereas works on "villains" abound, most define these as fictional figures—from novels, films, comic books, and video games—rather than the real-life individuals covered here, whose actions had an impact on the history of the United States at levels ranging from government and politics to law enforcement and criminal justice to popular culture. Taken from *Great Lives from History: Notorious Lives* (2007), these essays have been updated to reflect the latest on the status of the criminals and other infamous personages covered. Students of American studies, U.S. history, criminal justice, and sociology will find these essays of particular interest, filling gaps in the reference literature.

## Scope and Coverage

All individuals covered are from U.S. history, starting with the eighteenth century and extending to the present day. They can be classified in one or more of the following categories: Assassins (11); Con Artists, Cheats, and Frauds (7); Corrupt Politicians (2); Cult Leaders (6); Gangsters (37); Military Figures (3); Murderers (43); Outlaws and Gunslingers (19); Pirates (1); Political Rebels and Revolutionaries (3); Racists and Hatemongers (8); Scientists and Doctors (2); Serial Killers (20); Sexual Predators (7); Terrorists (4); Thieves (5); and Traitors and Spies (15). Most are universally acknowledged as infamous, criminal figures; in some cases, further light has been cast on the individuals to reveal that their evil reputations are not completely in accord with the facts.

## Essay Length and Format

Each essay ranges from 700 to 1,200 words (roughly 1 to 3 pages) and displays standard ready-reference top matter offering easy access to biographical information:

- The name of the individual is given as it is best known (monikers and epithets are not used here but appear in the "Also known as" line below).
- The individual's identity follows in the second line, including reign dates or terms of office where appropriate.
- The "Born" and "Died" lines list the most complete dates of birth and death available, followed by the most precise locations available, as well as an indication of when these are unknown, only probable, or only approximate; both contemporary and modern place-names (where different) are listed. A question mark (?)

is appended to a date or place if the information is considered likely to be the precise date or place but remains in question. A "c." denotes circa and indicates that historians have only enough information to place the date of birth or death in a more general period. When a range of dates is provided for birth or death, historians are relatively certain that it could not have occurred prior to or after the range.

- "Also known as" lists all known versions of the individual's name, including full names, birth names, aliases, monikers, and alternative spellings.
- "Cause of notoriety" (or, for criminals, "Major offenses") summarizes the reasons for the person's infamy.
- "Active" lists the date or range of years when the individual gained notoriety.
- "Locale" identifies the place or places where the individual was most active.
- "Sentence" appears where legal action led to a conviction and sentencing; the sentence and, where applicable, time served are listed here.

The body of each essay is divided into the following parts:

- "Early Life" provides facts about the individual's upbringing and the environment in which he or she was reared, as well as the pronunciation of his or her name. Where little is known about the individual's early life, historical context is provided.
- The "Career" section—e.g., "Criminal Career," "Political Career," "Military Career," or whatever most accurately describes the individual's activity—forms the heart of each essay, consisting of a straightforward account of the period during which the individual committed those acts that led to infamy.
- "Legal Action and Outcome" appears where applicable and summarizes the roles played by law enforcement and the criminal justice system (whether domestic or international).
- "Impact" assesses the historical impact and significance of the individual's actions: on law and law enforcement, criminal justice, public attitudes, social reform, history, even legend and the arts.
- "Further Reading," an annotated bibliography, lists approximately three to six books or articles that form a starting point for further research.
- "See also" cross-references other essays in the set covering personages who are related or may also be of interest (e.g., the essays on Clyde Barrow and Bonnie Parker are cross-referenced to each other).

## Special Features

All essays have annotated and up-to-date "Further Reading" sections for more in-depth study, and all essays list the name of the expert who contributed the essay. The set is illustrated with photographs, and 50 supplemental sidebars highlight important back stories or quote from primary sources.

The front matter to each volume contains a "Complete List of Contents" for readers' convenience, and at the end of Volume 2 we have provided three finding aids: a Chronological List of villains, a Category Index, and a Personages Index. Finally, a useful list of annotated Web Sites directs those studying America's "bad guys" to additional sources available on the Internet.

## Acknowledgments

Salem Press would like to extend its appreciation to all who have been involved in the development and production of this work. The essays were written and signed by sociologists, psychologists, criminologists, and historians, as well as independent scholars. Without their contributions, a project of this nature would not be possible. A full list of their names and affiliations appears in the front matter of this volume.

# List of Contributors

Patrick Adcock
*Henderson State University*

Charles Avinger
*Washtenaw Community College*

Thomas E. Baker
*University of Scranton*

Rachel Kate Bandy
*University of Colorado—Boulder*

Carl L. Bankston III
*Tulane University*

Frederic J. Baumgartner
*Virginia Polytechnic Institute & State University*

Alvin K. Benson
*Utah Valley State College*

Denise Paquette Boots
*University of Texas at Dallas*

Bernadette Lynn Bosky
*Independent Scholar*

Howard Bromberg
*Ave Maria School of Law*

Thomas W. Buchanan
*Ancilla Domini College*

Kevin G. Buckler
*Georgia Southern University*

Michael A. Buratovich
*Spring Arbor University*

Michael H. Burchett
*Limestone College*

David R. Champion
*Slippery Rock University*

Frederick B. Chary
*Indiana University Northwest*

Lindsay M. Christopher
*University of Denver*

S. E. Costanza
*Salem State College*

Mark R. Ellis
*University of Nebraska at Kearney*

Patricia E. Erickson
*Canisius College*

Thomas L. Erskine
*Salisbury University*

K. Thomas Finley
*SUNY—College at Brockport*

Gerald P. Fisher
*Georgia College and State University*

Dale L. Flesher
*University of Mississippi*

Jennifer C. Gibbs
*University of Maryland*

Sheldon Goldfarb
*University of British Columbia*

Scot M. Guenter
*San Jose State University*

Richard D. Hartley
*Texas A&M International University*

Peter B. Heller
*Manhattan College*

Patricia K. Hendrickson
*Tarleton State University*

Steve Hewitt
*University of Birmingham*

Carly M. Hilinski
*Indiana University of Pennsylvania*

Samuel B. Hoff
*Delaware State University*

Jerry W. Hollingsworth
*McMurry University*

Kimberley M. Holloway
*King College*

Gregory D. Horn
*Southwest Virginia Community College*

Nancy A. Horton
*University of Maryland Eastern Shore*

Charles C. Howard
*Tarleton State University*

Raymond Pierre Hylton
*Virginia Union University*

Cathy M. Jackson
*Norfolk State University*

Jenephyr James
*Indiana University of Pennsylvania*

Scott P. Johnson
*Frostburg State University*

Tracie L. Keesee
*Felician College*

Mara Kelly-Zukowski
*Felician College*

John C. Kilburn, Jr.
*Texas A&M International University*

Paul M. Klenowski
*Wheeling Jesuit University*

Gayla Koerting
*University of South Dakota*

Grove Koger
*Boise Public Library, Idaho*

David B. Kopel
*Independence Institute*

Karen F. Lahm
*Capital University*

Ann M. Legreid
*Central Missouri State University*

Margaret E. Leigey
*University of Delaware*

Thomas Tandy Lewis
*St. Cloud State University*

Ellen B. Lindsay
*Independent Scholar*

Anthony J. Luongo III
*Temple University*

Jennie MacDonald
*University of Colorado—Denver*

John L. McLean
*Missouri Valley College*

Laurence W. Mazzeno
*Alvernia College*

Randall L. Milstein
*Oregon State University*

Damon Mitchell
*Central Connecticut State University*

William V. Moore
*College of Charleston*

Douglas A. Orr
*Independent Scholar*

Robert J. Paradowski
*Rochester Institute of Technology*

Jim Pauff
*Tarleton State University*

Wayne J. Pitts
*University of Memphis*

Marguerite R. Plummer
*Louisiana State University in Shreveport*

Luke Powers
*Tennessee State University*

Maureen Puffer-Rothenberg
*Valdosta State University*

Steven J. Ramold
*Eastern Michigan University*

Cassandra L. Reyes
*Indiana University of Pennsylvania*

Betty Richardson
*Southern Illinois University, Edwardsville*

Janice G. Rienerth
*Appalachian State University*

James C. Roberts
*Independent Scholar*

Jean Owens Schaefer
*Independent Scholar*

Elizabeth D. Schafer
*Independent Scholar*

Rebecca Lovell Scott
*Northeastern University*

Brion Sever
*Monmouth University*

Manoj Sharma
*University of Cincinnati*

Ted Shields
*Charleston Southern University*

R. Baird Shuman
*University of Illinois at Urbana-Champaign*

Jules Simon
*University of Texas at El Paso*

Paul P. Sipiera
*William Rainey Harper College*

Glenn L. Swygart
*Tennessee Temple University*

Anh Tran
*Wichita State University*

Marcella Bush Trevino
*Barry University*

Sheryl L. Van Horne
*Rutgers University*

Sara Vidar
*Independent Scholar*

Linda Volonino
*Canisius College*

Mary C. Ware
*SUNY—College at Cortland*

Jack H. Westbrook
*Brookline Technologies*

Lisa A. Williams-Taylor
*CUNY Graduate Center*

Raymond Wilson
*Fort Hays State University*

Sharon Wilson
*Fort Hays State University*

# Key to Pronunciation

## Vowel Sounds

| *Symbol* | *Spelled (Pronounced)* |
|---|---|
| a | answer (AN-suhr), laugh (laf), sample (SAM-puhl), that (that) |
| ah | father (FAH-thur), hospital (HAHS-pih-tuhl) |
| aw | awful (AW-fuhl), caught (kawt) |
| ay | blaze (blayz), fade (fayd), waiter (WAYT-ur), weigh (way) |
| eh | bed (behd), head (hehd), said (sehd) |
| ee | believe (bee-LEEV), cedar (SEE-dur), leader (LEED-ur), liter (LEE-tur) |
| ew | boot (bewt), lose (lewz) |
| i | buy (bi), height (hit), lie (li), surprise (sur-PRIZ) |
| ih | bitter (BIH-tur), pill (pihl) |
| o | cotton (KO-tuhn), hot (hot) |
| oh | below (bee-LOH), coat (koht), note (noht), wholesome (HOHL-suhm) |
| oo | good (good), look (look) |
| ow | couch (kowch), how (how) |
| oy | boy (boy), coin (koyn) |
| uh | about (uh-BOWT), butter (BUH-tuhr), enough (ee-NUHF), other (UH-thur) |

## Consonant Sounds

| *Symbol* | *Spelled (Pronounced)* |
|---|---|
| ch | beach (beech), chimp (chihmp) |
| g | beg (behg), disguise (dihs-GIZ), get (geht) |
| j | digit (DIH-juht), edge (ehj), jet (jeht) |
| k | cat (kat), kitten (KIH-tuhn), hex (hehks) |
| s | cellar (SEHL-ur), save (sayv), scent (sehnt) |
| sh | champagne (sham-PAYN), issue (IH-shew), shop (shop) |
| ur | birth (burth), disturb (dihs-TURB), earth (urth), letter (LEH-tur) |
| y | useful (YEWS-fuhl), young (yuhng) |
| z | business (BIHZ-nehs), zest (zehst) |
| zh | vision (VIH-zhuhn) |

# Complete List of Contents

## Volume 1

## Volume 2

# American Villains

# Joe Adonis

## Mafia boss

**Born:** November 22, 1902; Montemarano, Italy
**Died:** November 26, 1972; Naples, Italy
**Also known as:** Giuseppe Antonio Doto (birth name); Joey A.; Joe Adone; Joe Arosa; James Arosa; Joe DeMio
**Major offenses:** Bootlegging, gambling, pimping, and murder
**Active:** 1920's-1950's
**Locale:** Primarily New York and New Jersey
**Sentence:** Deportation

### Early Life

Joe Adonis (ah-DAH-nihs) was born Giuseppe Antonio Doto in Montemarano, Italy, a small town near Naples. In 1915, at the age of thirteen, Doto illegally stowed away on an ocean liner headed for New York. Upon his arrival in the United States, Doto moved to Brooklyn, where he began a career of petty crime. He supported himself as a teenager by picking pockets and stealing all that he could.

It was during this time that Doto met another young street thug, Charles "Lucky" Luciano. The two quickly became loyal friends and began participating in petty crime rackets, including prostitution and organized gambling rings. Shortly after meeting Luciano in the early 1920's, Doto changed his name to Joe Adonis.

Adonis chose the moniker because of his extreme vanity. The name allowed Adonis to see himself as an irresistible Mediterranean god, which was the image he strove to project. Adonis was known for being sexually promiscuous and served time in jail on rape charges after a woman refused his advances.

### Criminal Career

By the late 1920's Adonis had acquired a strong reputation in the underground crime world and went to work as an enforcer for crime boss Frankie Yale. While employed by Yale, Adonis came into contact with key figures in organized crime, including Al Capone.

Luciano at this time was working for New York crime kingpin Joe Masseria. When Luciano organized a plot to murder Masseria, his loyal

*Joe Adonis*. (AP/Wide World Photos)

friend Adonis was one of the four gunmen (along with Bugsy Siegel, Vito Genovese, and Albert Anastasia) to carry out the job on April 15, 1931.

Adonis and Luciano went on to murder another underground crime lord, Salvatore Maranzano (Masseria's archrival). With two of the biggest New York Mafia bosses dead, Luciano created the National Crime Syndicate, which united the top Mafia gangs across the United States and placed Adonis on its board of directors. In his new position Adonis became extremely powerful, with politicians and members of the police force on his payroll. With his newfound power and influence, Adonis found himself ruling Broadway and midtown Manhattan but kept his headquarters in his Brooklyn restaurant, Joe's Italian Kitchen. Adonis continued to build his multimillion-dollar empire through illegal alcohol sales, prostitution, and cigarette sales. He bought several car dealerships across New Jersey, where his customers were coerced into buying ten-thousand-dollar insurance policies.

After World War II, Luciano was deported to Italy, never to set foot in the United States again. With Luciano out of the picture, Adonis took over the National Crime Syndicate, keeping a low profile and remaining unknown to the federal authorities. When his connections and control in underground crime became apparent and it was discovered that Adonis had never become a naturalized U.S. citizen, he agreed to be deported back to Italy in 1953 to avoid jail time. Adonis sailed home in luxury, with millions of dollars, to a villa awaiting him outside Naples.

In 1972 Italy began a crackdown on organized crime and set out to arrest all known members of the Mafia. Adonis was pulled from his villa on November 26, 1972, and taken to an undisclosed location to be questioned. It was during the excruciating interrogation that Adonis suffered a fatal heart attack. He received a small funeral attended by immediate family and was buried in Madonna Cemetery, Fort Lee, New Jersey.

### Legal Action and Outcome

In 1946, former mobster Abe Reles became a federal informant and told the government about Adonis and his power across the United States in underground crime. Realizing the mounting problem organized crime was presenting, the United States organized the Kefauver Committee, which sat from 1950 through 1951, composed of senators who were responsible for examining the underground crime epidemic. Adonis was brought before the committee and questioned extensively. Although he pleaded the Fifth Amendment to all questions and avoided jail time, he was suddenly closely monitored by the Federal Bureau of Investigation, culminating in his deportation in 1953.

### Impact

The growing difficulty presented by Joe Adonis and organized crime forced the U.S. government to take action. Through the Kefauver Committee, senators were able to explore the world of organized crime, uncover and interrogate its key criminals, and develop strategies to handle the existing dangers and prevent further issues from arising. As a result of the hearings, the government gained a deep understanding of the power and danger organized crime possessed, and Joe Adonis and many principal criminals were identified and monitored. The Kefauver Committee put Adonis in the spotlight, letting him know that his movements were watched and that actions against him and his activities were being taken.

Court hearings and the press placed Adonis, as well as other mob bosses and key Mafia figures, in the spotlight and also romanticized them in popular culture. They became recurring subjects in literature and films throughout the first half of the twentieth century, as did their slang and dress styles.

Adonis and the Mafia embodied the image of toughness during this time and were elevated to celebrity status.

**Further Reading**

Davis, John H. *Mafia Dynasty: The Rise and Fall of the Gambino Crime Family*. New York: HarperCollins, 1993. Davis provides a good foundation that traces and explains the beginnings of the Sicilian Mafia in New York.

Downey, Patrick. *Gangster City: The History of the New York Underworld, 1900-1935*. Fort Lee, N.J.: Barricade Books, 2004. A thorough and concise history of early Mafia bosses and kingpins. Offers the reader a well-researched chronology of the New York Mafia.

Reppetto, Thomas. *American Mafia: A History of Its Rise to Power*. New York: Henry Holt, 2004. Provides a clear time line, showing the mob's humble beginnings in the boroughs of New York to the national Kefauver Committee trials in the 1950's.

Turkus, Burton B., and Sid Feder. *Murder, Inc.: The Story of the "Syndicate."* Cambridge, Mass.: Da Capo Press, 2003. A comprehensive history of Mafia dealings and also a thoroughly researched book which explores, explains, and clears up myths about the mob.

*—Sara Vidar*

**See also:** Albert Anastasia; Vincent Coll; Joe Colombo; Carmine Galante; Carlo Gambino; Sam Giancana; Vincent Gigante; John Gotti; Sammy Gravano; Henry Hill; Richard Kuklinski; Meyer Lansky; Salvatore Maranzano; Carlos Marcello; Joseph Profaci.

## Aldrich Ames

### Spy and traitor

**Born:** June 16, 1941; River Falls, Wisconsin
**Also known as:** Aldrich Hazen Ames (full name); Rick Ames
**Major offenses:** Conspiracy to commit espionage and tax evasion
**Active:** April, 1985-February, 1994
**Locale:** United States, Europe, and Soviet Union
**Sentence:** Life in prison without possibility of parole

## Early Life

Aldrich Ames (AWL-drihch aymz) was born to Carleton Cecil and Rachel Aldrich Ames in River Falls, Wisconsin, the eldest of three children. His father was a college professor and his mother a high school English teacher, both in River Falls. His father began a career with the Central Intelligence Agency's (CIA's) directorate of operations in 1952, but because of alcohol abuse, his career with the agency was somewhat troubled. The younger Ames worked as a CIA records analyst, marking classified documents during the summer of 1957, and returned to the same job the following two summers. He graduated from McLean (Virginia) High School and entered the University of Chicago in 1959, taking classes in drama; he dropped out because of failing grades. Ames returned to the CIA as a clerk typist in 1962 and later took a job as a document analyst for the agency while attending George Washington University, from which he received a bachelor's degree in history in 1967.

## Espionage Career

Ames was accepted into the CIA's Career Trainee Program in 1967, where he was trained as an operations officer for the recruitment of foreign agents. He placed low in psychological evaluation for the job, but he finished his training with strong marks. His first overseas assignment was to Ankara, Turkey, which began in 1969. In the early 1970's, Ames received training in Russian language and was assigned to the Soviet-East European Division. From 1976 to 1981, he served as an agent in New York, and in 1982, he received his last promotion.

From April, 1985, to February, 1994, Ames led a double life as a mole for the KGB (the Soviet intelligence agency), providing it with an abundance of classified documents. He effectively shut down all CIA intelligence in the Soviet Union by revealing to the KGB the names of all Soviets employed as spies by the United States. In places such as Bogotá, Colombia, Caracas, Venezuela, Vienna, Austria, and Washington, D.C., Ames had numerous meetings with Soviet agents, sharing classified documents on sensitive security, defense, and foreign relations issues. The secrets included detailed information on double agent operations, security weaknesses, and the agency's mode of operation.

Ames would wrap classified documents in plastic bags in packets of five to seven pounds each and would carry them without suspicion from the agency. He became the highest paid spy in the world: His treasonous activities brought him $1.8 million in payoffs; an additional $900,000 was held for him in a Moscow bank. Ames lived a lavish lifestyle with luxury cars, expensive furniture, many charge cards, and a half-million-dollar home, yet these excesses did not raise suspicions within the CIA. After a long and often bungled investigation, in February, 1994, the fifty-two-year-old Ames was arrested at his home in Arlington, Virginia, and charged with espionage.

### Legal Action and Outcome

Ames was charged with conspiracy to commit espionage and tax evasion. He pleaded guilty to these charges on April 28, 1994. His wife, Maria del Rosario Casas Ames, was arrested later at their home on the same charges. Ames and his wife cooperated fully with authorities and arranged plea bargains by which they forfeited their assets to the U.S. government. About one-half million dollars of those assets were given to the Justice Department's Victims Assistance Fund.

Ames was sentenced to life in prison without the possibility of parole,

### The Ultimate Betrayal

*In 1999, George Washington University's National Security Archive published a declassified interview with Aldrich Ames. Asked if he had considered the effects of betraying the double agents of the Central Intelligence Agency (CIA), he replied:*

I knew quite well, when I gave the names of our agents in the Soviet Union, that I was exposing them to the full machinery of counterespionage and the law, and then prosecution, and capital punishment, certainly, in the case of KGB and GRU [Soviet military intelligence] officers who would be tried in a military court, and certainly others, that they were almost all at least potentially liable to capital punishment. There's simply no question about this. Now . . . I believed that the KGB with the support of the political leadership, would want to keep it very much under wraps, and I felt at the time that not only for the overriding reason, practical reason of protecting me, they would also find it useful to cover up the fact, the embarrassing fact of who so many of these people were, and that this would all have a somewhat dampening effect on the results of the compromise. But of course you know, given time and circumstances, obviously these folks I knew would have to answer for what they'd done.

*Later in the interview, Ames expressed surprise that the Soviets punished so many moles so swiftly. The disappearance of these agents eventually led to his own arrest.*

*Source:* National Security Archive, "Cold War, Episode 21: Spies" (March 14, 1999).

and Maria was given a sentence of sixty-three months. Based on interrogations and interviews after his arrest, it is clear that Ames's motive for spying changed markedly through the years, from a need to pay off modest debts to a desire to support a lavish lifestyle.

## Impact

The information provided by Aldrich Ames led to the compromise of approximately one hundred U.S. intelligence operations and the execution of ten U.S. sources. Ames arguably inflicted more harm on U.S. security than any single person in American history. He also engaged in flagrant personal and professional misconduct, including inattention to detail, alcohol abuse, financial excesses, administrative carelessness, and an extramarital affair with a foreign national. His egregious acts against the country went undetected for nine years; during his thirty-one years in the agency, he received no reprimands. In the long term, however, his actions contributed to a growing public mistrust and cynicism toward government agencies.

Ames committed espionage for money and ego, with no philosophical allegiance to the Soviet Union. Psychologists have characterized him as grandiose, impulsive, and interested in short-term financial gain. Numerous articles and books have been written on the case, and Ames's life was portrayed by Timothy Hutton in the 1998 television film *Aldrich Ames: Traitor Within.*

## Further Reading

Cherkashin, Victor. *Spy Handler: Memoir of a KGB Officer*. New York: Basic Books, 2005. A scholarly account of Cold War espionage by the retired KGB officer who recruited Ames for the Soviet Union.

Earley, Pete. *Confession of a Spy: The Real Story of Aldrich Ames*. New York: Putnam, 1997. Based on fifty hours of interviews with Ames and interviews with KGB handlers and the CIA agents who collected the evidence that ultimately led to Ames's arrest.

Richelson, Jeffrey T. *The U.S. Intelligence Community*. Boulder, Colo.: Westview Press, 1999. An overview of many dimensions of the intelligence community with numerous references to the Ames case.

*—Ann M. Legreid*

**See also:** Christopher John Boyce; Robert Philip Hanssen; Daulton Lee; Ethel Rosenberg; Julius Rosenberg.

## Albert Anastasia

### New York Mafia boss

**Born:** February 26, 1902; Tropea, Italy
**Died:** October 25, 1957; New York, New York
**Also known as:** Umberto Anastasio (birth name); Mad Hatter; High Executioner; Lord High Executioner
**Cause of notoriety:** Anastasia served as the homicide contract negotiator for the national crime syndicate.
**Active:** 1921-1957
**Locale:** New York, New York

### Early Life

Albert Anastasia (AL-burt ah-nah-STAHSH-yah) was born Umberto Anastasio in 1902. He and his brother Anthony ("Tough Tony") immigrated to the United States during World War I. By young adulthood, both brothers were employed on the New York docks, where Albert was arrested for murder in 1921. There were several witnesses to his crime, and Albert was convicted and sentenced to death. However, he won a new trial after spending eighteen months on death row in Sing Sing prison. During the new trial, four witnesses disappeared. Others reversed their statements. The trial could not continue, and Albert was free. In 1922, he changed his name from Anastasio to Anastasia. It is speculated that he anticipated a life of crime and did not want to embarrass his family. Tony kept the family name and continued to gain influence around the docks.

### Criminal Career

Anastasia began working as a bodyguard for Mafia boss Vincent Mangano during the 1920's. The Castellammarese War—a conflict between two Prohibition era crime bosses in New York, Joe Masseria and Salvatore Maranzano—raged from 1930 to 1931. In 1930, Charles "Lucky" Luciano approached Anastasia about overthrowing Masseria and Maranzano. Anastasia was enthusiastic and stated that he would "kill everybody" for the charismatic Luciano. Luciano successfully conspired with Meyer Lansky to gain the cooperation of many underbosses in overthrowing both Masseria and Maranzano. The coup left Luciano as the de facto "boss of bosses" in New York.

Luciano and Lansky then placed Anastasia, along with Louis Buchalter, in charge of a unit specially charged with carrying out syndicate-authorized murders. Crime historians have dubbed this unit Murder, Inc. In 1944 Buchalter was executed, and Anastasia became the singular head of Murder, Inc.

Anastasia achieved the title of "boss" in 1951, when Mangano disappeared. Both Anastasia and Frank Costello (who acted as syndicate boss during Luciano's exile) had reasons to want Mangano dead. Costello was facing a veiled threat from crime boss Vito Genovese. Mangano, never considered loyal to Luciano's upper echelon, could not provide Costello with "muscle." With Murder, Inc., at his disposal, Anastasia therefore seemed the logical replacement for Mangano.

Anastasia and Mangano had often squabbled about Anastasia's loyalty to Luciano, who in 1936 was sentenced to fifty years in prison for operating houses of prostitution. When an Allied troop ship caught fire during World War II, Luciano was tapped by the Navy to thwart pro-Nazi sabotage on the New York waterfront. Anastasia and his brother Tony were in a perfect position to "protect" the docks—and after the war, Luciano was pardoned.

Costello ensured that Anastasia, who named Carlo Gambino his underboss, was given the top seat in Mangano's former family. Unfortunately Anastasia (as Luciano had suspected) was better suited to killing than to acting as "godfather." Anastasia's lack of political savvy did little to thwart Genovese's plans to usurp Costello's leadership.

Genovese used an indirect approach, secretly undermining the authority of Costello. Genovese also gained a financial advantage by becoming one of the first Mafiosi to succeed in the narcotics market.

By 1957, Anastasia had lost favor with the syndicate. Some evidence suggests that Anastasia's psychopathic tendencies, which often disturbed other Mafia bosses, were the source of his undoing. Others have speculated that he was becoming too ambitious, attempting to interfere with Lansky's Cuban casino operations. On October 25, 1957, two assassins shot and killed Anastasia in the barbershop of a New York hotel.

### Legal Action and Outcome

In 1954, Anastasia was tried on charges of tax evasion after building a lavish home that, according to his tax statements, he could not afford. The government called Charles Ferri as a witness. Ferri was a plumber whom

*Albert Anastasia.*
(AP/Wide World Photos)

Anastasia had paid for work done on his home. Ferri's statement was damaging. The government intended to call next upon Vincent Macri, a former Anastasia bodyguard. After Macri was found dead, a mistrial was declared. In 1955, the government tried Anastasia again, with the intention of using Ferri as a key witness. However, when federal agents tried to locate Ferri, he could not be found. As the trial was finally about to begin, Anastasia pleaded guilty to tax evasion. The terms of his plea bargain were a sentence of one year in jail and a twenty-thousand-dollar fine. It was the first time since 1921 that Anastasia was imprisoned.

## Impact

Albert Anastasia was responsible for the prosperity of the New York crime syndicate after Prohibition. While he headed Murder, Inc., the syndicate asserted influence over underworld operations in several major cities. Anastasia's manipulation of waterfront operations ensured that Luciano, perhaps the most important figure in the syndicate, could maintain power.

Anastasia's failures as a Mafia don also bore a legacy. Genovese took Anastasia's murder to mean that he himself was now the top boss in New York. However, the ascension of Genovese to the chief position in the syndicate was convenient for Gambino. In 1959, Gambino helped federal agents collar Genovese in a narcotics bust. Genovese was convicted on weak evidence and spent the last years of his life in prison. His demise paved the way for Gambino, and the Gambino family emerged from the 1950's at the head of the syndicate. Gambino's territory was inherited by John Gotti in 1985. Gotti had always been fond of the Anastasia legend.

Anastasia's demise also lends credibility to the claim that the syndicate may have had some "code of honor" regarding murder. One famous anecdote involves Anastasia's 1952 execution of a clothing salesman. The man had helped police identify a bank robber and was then rewarded; his story appeared on national television. The bank robber was not affiliated with the syndicate in any regard, but Anastasia issued a curt order to his own men: "Hit that guy! I can't stand squealers!"

Anastasia's small funeral did not truly befit a don. His wife, Elsa, moved to Canada after his death. Tony lost most of his clout when his brother was killed. Federal agents tried to convince Tony to be an informant; however, he died of natural causes before he could pursue such a career.

**Further Reading**

Abadinsky, Howard. *Organized Crime*. 7th ed. New York: Thomas Dunne Books, 2005. An introductory text on the Mafia and organized crime.

Davis, John H. *Mafia Dynasty: The Rise and Fall of the Gambino Crime Family*. New York: Harper, 1994. Covers the history of the Gambino family.

Gosch, Martin A., and Richard Hammer. *The Last Testament of Lucky Luciano*. New York: Little, Brown, 1975. Luciano's account of Mafia activities in the United States.

Maas, Peter. *The Valachi Papers*. Rev. ed. New York: Pocket Books, 1986. Joseph Valachi's official testimony regarding the activities of the Mafia in the United States.

Raab, Selwyn. *The Five Families: The Rise, Decline, and Resurgence of America's Most Powerful Mafia Empires*. New York: Thomas Dunne Books, 2005. A comprehensive analysis of the Mafia families in New York City.

Turkus, Burton B., and Sid Feder. *Murder, Inc.: The Story of "the Syndicate."* New York: Da Capo Press, 2003. Covers the syndicate before, during, and after Anastasia's rule.

*—S. E. Costanza*

**See also:** Joe Adonis; Louis Buchalter; Paul Castellano; Vincent Coll; Joe Colombo; Carmine Galante; Carlo Gambino; Sam Giancana; Vincent Gigante; John Gotti; Sammy Gravano; Henry Hill; Richard Kuklinski; Meyer Lansky; Salvatore Maranzano; Carlos Marcello; Joe Masseria; Joseph Profaci; Dutch Schultz.

## Apache Kid

### Native American outlaw

**Born:** c. 1860; San Carlos Reservation, New Mexico Territory
**Died:** After 1894; place unknown
**Also known as:** Haskaybaynaynatyl (Apache for "Tall Man Who Dies Mysteriously"); Ski-be-nan-ted; the Kid
**Cause of notoriety:** A one-man crime wave in the 1880's and 1890's, the Apache Kid terrorized both the American Indian and Anglo-American communities in the Southwest near the Mexican border; crimes attributed to him include cattle rustling, kidnapping, rape, and murder.
**Active:** 1887-1894
**Locale:** San Carlos Reservation; New Mexico and Arizona Territories

#### Early Life

The Apache Kid (ah-PA-chee kihd) was born to the Pinal Apache band on the San Carlos Indian Reservation, located in the mountainous terrain of southern New Mexico. As a young man, he was known to the white settlers of nearby Globe, New Mexico, as simply the Apache Kid. He had assimilated enough into the Anglo-American community that famed U.S. Army scout Al Sieber recruited him into the corps of Native American Scouts, and the Kid participated in numerous military actions against renegade Apache bands, including that of Geronimo.

## Criminal Career

The Apache Kid's criminal career began in June, 1887: Under the influence of tiswin, a powerful Native American corn liquor, he murdered a fellow Apache in accordance with a tribal vendetta code. The Kid's attempt to turn himself in to San Carlos authorities, including Sieber, exploded into a shoot-out, which maimed the latter. When the Kid turned himself in a month later, he was court-martialed for the attempted murder of Sieber and sentenced to death, though a sympathetic General Nelson Miles commuted the death sentence to ten years' imprisonment. This sentence, and the verdict, were overturned in 1889, when civil authorities in Arizona prosecuted and convicted the Kid for the attempted murder of Sieber and sentenced him to seven years in the Yuma penitentiary. Ironically, he was never arrested or prosecuted for the original murder of his fellow Apache.

On the way to Yuma, the Kid escaped custody and went into hiding in the southwestern mountains. From the likable "Kid," he transformed into a despised outlaw capable of unbridled ruthlessness. In addition to rustling cattle, he was rumored to have supported himself on the outlaw trail by killing lone whites and American Indians. He was also alleged to have been a sexual predator who kidnapped, raped, and then murdered a series of Apache women. In the 1890's he was enough of a threat to both American Indian and Anglo-American communities that territorial authorities in Arizona offered the significant sum of five thousand dollars for his capture. However, few definite facts are known of his actual criminal career—even basic information such as whether he operated with a small band or alone. Unlike the renegade Apache Geronimo, the Apache Kid made no attempt to broaden his cause into a political conflict against U.S. oppression.

## Impact

Because he was never captured, the Apache Kid achieved mythic status. Although his criminal activities appear to have ceased in the mid-1890's, he became a romantic figure of the Old West in the following decades. Essentially forced into an outlaw existence, he was seen as a tragic victim, a man torn between two cultures—Apache and Anglo-American—who retreated from both into the vast spaces of the southwestern wilderness. According to one legend, the Kid retired from his life of crime to live into old age in the mountains of rural Mexico. A comic book that was published in the 1950's, titled *The Apache Kid*, was loosely based upon the Kid and featured an outlaw hero at odds with both the white and Indian communities.

**Further Reading**

Garza, Phyllis de la. *The Apache Kid*. Tucson, Ariz.: Westernlore Press, 1995. A thorough, dramatic retelling of the Kid's life, from a popular Western author.

Prassel, Frank Richard. *The Great American Outlaw: A Legacy of Fact and Fiction*. Norman: University of Oklahoma Press, 1993. Examines the social psychology of the enduring popularity of a number of Western "badmen," including the Apache Kid.

Thrapp, Dan. *Al Sieber: Chief of Scouts*. 1964. Reprint. Norman: University of Oklahoma Press, 1995. Classic biography of the Apache Kid's mentor-turned-antagonist. Provides rich background on the San Carlos Reservation and the U.S.-Apache Wars.

*—Luke Powers*

**See also:** Tom Bell; William H. Bonney; Curly Bill Brocius; Bob Dalton; Emmett Dalton; Bill Doolin; John Wesley Hardin; Doc Holliday; Jesse James; Tom Ketchum; Harry Longabaugh; Bill Longley; Johnny Ringo; Belle Starr; Henry Starr; Hank Vaughan; Cole Younger.

# Marshall Applewhite

## Cult leader

**Born:** May 17, 1931; Spur, Texas

**Died:** c. March 26, 1997; Rancho Santa Fe, California

**Also known as:** Marshall Herff Applewhite, Jr. (full name); Bo; Do; the Mouthpiece

**Cause of notoriety:** Applewhite, the leader of the Heaven's Gate cult, committed suicide along with thirty-eight of his followers.

**Active:** c. March 26, 1997

**Locale:** Western United States

### Early Life

Marshall Applewhite (A-puhl-wit) was the son of a Presbyterian minister in a small west Texas town. Intending to follow his father into the ministry, Applewhite entered a seminary after graduating from college in 1952. Soon he decided that his calling was music—his baritone voice had always won him praise—and he earned a master's degree from the University of Colorado. He was hired to direct choral groups at the University of Alabama. By that time he was married with two children, but in 1965, after he had a homosexual affair, his wife took the children and left. Shortly afterward, conflicts between Applewhite and university administration caused him to lose his job.

Applewhite moved to Houston, where he became the music director at St. Thomas University. He flourished there and even became engaged to a student. When he broke off the engagement, the student's father, a university trustee, used his influence to get Applewhite fired. Although Applewhite found work as choral director at a Houston theater, the loss of his job at St. Thomas and his ambivalence over his sexuality made him depressed. According to his account, it was while visiting a friend at a hospital in March, 1972, that he met Bonnie Nettles, who was working there as a nurse. Applewhite and Nettles would later recall that their meeting occurred on the propitious day of the spring equinox.

### Religious Career

Applewhite and Nettles immediately became inseparable. Although their relationship was reportedly platonic, Applewhite lost his job at the theater because he spent too much time with Nettles. She introduced him to theosophy, spiritualism, and channeling. The two founded the Christian Art Center in a Houston church, which taught astrology, theosophy, and mysticism. Only months later, lack of funds and rumors that they held séances in the church led to the center's closing. They both claimed to hear voices coming from unidentified flying objects (UFOs), persuading them that their destiny required them to leave behind their ordinary lives. Applewhite began to refer to himself as the "Mouthpiece" and Nettles as the "Battery."

They abruptly left Houston in 1973 and wandered about the western states. They eventually reached the Oregon coast, where after a month of meditation, their destiny was revealed to them: Like the two witnesses described in the biblical book of Revelation, they would be killed and resurrected; moreover, they believed they would be taken to Heaven in a spaceship. Others would be allowed to join them in their journey; those who wished to do so would have to undergo a metamorphosis, which required giving up human attachments and property and being celibate, as sex took energy away from the "Process," as they referred to the metamorphosis. The Process would be completed when they boarded the UFO. Meanwhile, their lack of money and hostility to convention led them to defraud motel keepers and credit card companies. Applewhite was arrested in August, 1974, for failing to return a rental car, and he spent four months in jail in St. Louis, where he was described as a model prisoner.

### Cult Leader

Once Applewhite was released from jail in early 1975, Nettles rejoined him. The two traveled to Los Angeles, where they won converts from a New Age group. They left the city within weeks, taking twenty-four followers with them. The believers were told that they could transform their human bodies into eternal, genderless, extraterrestrial bodies and that UFOs would soon pick them up. They traveled widely, speaking in public—mostly to college students—and soon they had some two hundred followers. Applewhite and Nettles, considering themselves the shepherds of their flock, began to call themselves Bo and Peep.

Peep announced that a UFO would pick them up in Colorado; when it failed to appear, many left the group. After being heckled at a meeting in

*Marshall Applewhite.* (AP/Wide World Photos)

### Still Crazy After All These Years

*In 2006, the Heaven's Gate Web site was still accessible, spreading its dangerous message and glorifying the tragic suicides that occurred in conjunction with the sighting of the Hale-Bopp comet in 1997:*

Whether Hale-Bopp has a "companion" or not is irrelevant from our perspective. However, its arrival is joyously very significant to us at "Heaven's Gate." The **joy** is that our Older Member in the Evolutionary Level Above Human (the "Kingdom of Heaven") has made it clear to us that Hale-Bopp's approach is the "marker" we've been waiting for—the time for the arrival of the spacecraft from the Level Above Human to take us home to "Their World"—in the literal Heavens. Our 22 years of classroom here on planet Earth is finally coming to conclusion—"graduation" from the Human Evolutionary Level. We are happily prepared to leave "this world" and go with Ti's crew. If you study the material on this website you will hopefully understand our joy and what our purpose here on Earth has been. You may even find your "boarding pass" to leave with us during this brief "window." We are so very thankful that we have been recipients of this opportunity to prepare for membership in Their Kingdom, and to experience Their boundless Caring and Nurturing.

Kansas in April, 1976, Applewhite and Nettles, who now called themselves Do and Ti after notes in the celestial harmony, became secretive and stopped trying to win converts. Little is known about their lives during the following years except that they dashed from place to place across the western states, expecting to board a UFO. When Nettles died of cancer in 1985, Applewhite declared that she had originally come from another planet to teach him the Process and that she had returned to the "level above human."

## Suicide

After remaining out of sight for seventeen years, Applewhite reappeared in 1993 with his followers, appearing on a video, advertising in magazines, and creating a Web site in order to win converts. The Web site was called

"Heaven's Gate," which became the popular name for the group. That year, eight male members, including Do, underwent castration in order to eliminate their sex drives. Do preached the message that weeds had taken over the earth, and the time had come for "spading." In 1996 the group rented a mansion in the San Diego suburb of Rancho Santa Fe, with money they had made by designing Web sites. By then Do was suffering from severe coronary arteriosclerosis.

When the comet Hale-Bopp came into view in 1997, rumors that a UFO had been sighted behind it led the Heaven's Gate members to conclude that Ti was coming to pick them up. Because it was necessary to leave their earthly vessels behind, Do and thirty-eight followers committed suicide in a meticulous fashion over a three-day period beginning on March 23, 1997.

### Impact

News of the mass suicide and the castration of several male members of the Heaven's Gate cult astounded the United States and reinforced the image of the mad cult leader who brainwashed his followers into blind obedience.

### Further Reading

Balch, Robert. "Bo and Peep: A Case Study of the Origins of Messianic Leadership." In *Millennialism and Charisma*, edited by Roy Wallis. Belfast: The Queen's Unversity, 1982. Balch and another sociologist joined Bo and Peep's group as observer-participants for two months in 1975; this article provides information on Applewhite's background and early beliefs, drawing on interviews and letters written before the events of 1997.

_______. "The Evolution of a New Age Cult: From Total Overcomers Anonymous to Death at Heaven's Gate." In *Sects, Cults, and Spiritual Communities*, edited by William Zellner. Westport, Conn.: Praeger, 1998. This article by a sociologist of charismatic leadership follows the story of Heaven's Gate from 1975 to the suicides of 1997.

Wessinger, Catherine. *How the Millennium Comes Violently: From Jonestown to Heaven's Gate*. New York: Seven Bridges Press, 2000. Contains a lengthy section on Heaven's Gate with details about Applewhite's life and includes valuable insights into the process of group suicide.

*—Frederic J. Baumgartner*

**See also:** Jim Jones; Charles Manson; Bonnie Nettles.

# Benedict Arnold

## Military general and traitor

**Born:** January 14, 1741; Norwich, Connecticut

**Died:** June 14, 1801; London, England

**Cause of notoriety:** In the United States, the name of Benedict Arnold, who sought to surrender West Point to the British during the American Revolutionary War, is now synonymous with treason.

**Active:** 1779-1780

**Locale:** West Point, New York

### Early Life

Benedict Arnold (BEHN-uh-dihkt AHR-nohld) was born on January 14, 1741, in Norwich, Connecticut. He was the son of Benedict Arnold, Sr., and Hannah Waterman King Arnold. He was one of six children, but only he and his sister Hannah survived into adulthood. Business setbacks led to financial struggles for the family, and young Benedict was forced to withdraw from school. He later served as an apprentice in the Norwich apothecary business of family cousins. He also briefly served in the Connecticut army during the French and Indian War (1754-1763). He moved to New Haven, Connecticut, in 1762 and became a druggist and bookseller there. He also acquired some property and became involved in the trading and shipping businesses. He married Margaret Mansfield on February 22, 1767; they had three sons before Margaret died in 1775.

### Military Career

Arnold achieved both fame and notoriety during the American Revolutionary War (1775-1783). He had become a captain in a Connecticut military company when he heard news of the battles at Lexington and Concord. The provincial Congress of Massachusetts commissioned him as a colonel, and the Massachusetts Committee of Safety approved his plan to capture Fort Ticonderoga on Lake Champlain. Arnold helped capture the fort as part of a larger force under the command of Ethan Allen and Allen's renowned Green Mountain Boys.

In 1775, Arnold and General Richard Montgomery led a two-pronged invasion of Canada. Arnold's men endured great hardships during their famous march through the wilderness to lay siege to Quebec. Montgomery

*Benedict Arnold.*
(Library of Congress)

captured Montreal and then joined Arnold to attack Quebec on December 30, 1775. During the fierce battle, Montgomery was killed and Arnold severely wounded in the leg. Arnold was promoted to the rank of brigadier general.

After the British drove the Americans from Canada, Arnold returned to New York to defend Lake Champlain. There he was involved in the Battle of Valcour Island. Despite Arnold's success in the naval battle, Congress passed over Arnold and promoted five brigadier generals with junior status to the rank of major general in February, 1777. Arnold finally received his promotion to major general later that year, after leading a successful attack on the British forces at Danbury, Connecticut. He was denied the restoration of his seniority, however, and he resigned in July, 1777, only to reconsider quickly.

Arnold fought in the New York wilderness under General Horatio Gates against British forces under the command of General John Burgoyne. Arnold's next major military accomplishment came in the Battle of Saratoga (September 19-October 7, 1777), the turning point of the Revolutionary War. Arnold had quarreled with Gates and had been ordered to the rear but valiantly fought without permission in the October 7 Battle of Bemis Heights. He suffered a severe wound in the same leg that he had injured earlier. The American victory helped cement a critical alliance with France.

The Continental Congress restored Arnold's military seniority in 1778 and gave him command of Philadelphia. It was there that the widower Arnold became engaged to his second wife, the teenage Margaret (Peggy) Shippen, daughter of Judge Edward Shippen. Arnold was in his mid-thirties. Money problems caused by a lavish lifestyle, quarrels with fellow commanders, and corruption charges led to Arnold's court-martial in 1780. He was exonerated of all but two minor corruption charges and received a mild reprimand from General George Washington; he soon resigned command of Philadelphia.

### The Text of Treachery

*On July 12, 1780, Benedict Arnold sent a letter, in cipher, to Major John André of the British Army:*

I wrote to Captain Beckwith on the 7th of June, that a French fleet and army were expected to act in conjunction with the American army. At the same time I gave Mr. Stansbury a manifesto intended to be published in Canada, and have from time to time communicated to him such intelligence as I thought interesting, which he assures me he has transmitted to you. I have received no answer from my Letter, or any verbal Message. I expect soon to command West Point and most seriously wish an interview with some intelligent officer in whom a mutual confidence could be placed. The necessity is evident to arrange and to cooperate. An officer might be taken Prisoner near that Post and permitted to return on parole, or some officer on Parole sent out to effect an exchange.

General Washington expects on the arrival of the French Troops to collect 30,000 Troops to act in conjunction; if not disappointed, New York is fixed on as the first Object, if his numbers are not sufficient for that Object Canada is the second; of which I can inform you in time, as well as of every other design. I have accepted the command at West Point As a Post in which I can render the most essential Services, and which will be in my disposal. The mass of the People are heartily tired of the War, and wish to be on their former footing. They are promised great events from this year's exertion. If disappointed you have only to persevere and the contest will soon be at an end. The present Struggles are like the pangs of a dying man, violent but of a short duration.

As Life and fortune are risked by serving His Majesty, it is Necessary that the latter shall be secured as well as the emoluments I give up, and a compensation for Services agreed on and a Sum advanced for that purpose, which I have mentioned in a letter which accompanies this, which Sir Henry [Clinton] will not, I believe, think unreasonable. I am Sir, your humble Servant.

*Source:* From the Clinton Collection of the Clements Library, University of Michigan, Ann Arbor.

**Treason**

Arnold's next actions would change him from a patriot to a traitor. In May of 1779, Arnold began a secret correspondence with British general Henry Clinton through the agency of several American Loyalists and, most notably, British major John André. Arnold sought and received command of the strategic American fortress at West Point in 1780, significant for its location on the Hudson River. He then negotiated its surrender to the British in exchange for a British military commission and a monetary settlement. Arnold's traitorous scheme was revealed when the Americans captured Major André in September, 1780.

André was executed as a spy, but Arnold was able to escape to the British and received a commission as a brigadier general, among other compensations. He led British troops in Connecticut and Virginia but never received a major command. He was never captured and did not face punishment for his traitorous actions. After a brief London stay, Arnold moved in 1787 to Saint John, New Brunswick, Canada, and began a shipping business. He settled in London, England, in 1791 and died there on June 14, 1801.

**Impact**

Benedict Arnold's actions, while demoralizing to the Americans and his friend and supporter George Washington, did not adversely affect the war's outcome. The capture of André prevented Arnold's plan from being carried out and kept West Point in American hands. The name Benedict Arnold would become synonymous with the word "traitor" in the United States and remained in use in modern-day English as a term for someone who has betrayed another.

**Further Reading**

Brandt, Clare. *The Man in the Mirror: A Life of Benedict Arnold.* New York: Random House, 1994. Brandt utilizes a variety of sources to outline Arnold's complete life and offers psychological insights into the possible causes of his actions.

Flexner, James Thomas. *The Traitor and the Spy: Benedict Arnold and John André.* 1975. Reprint. Syracuse, N.Y.: Syracuse University Press, 1991. This recounting of Arnold's defection and relationship with his chief accomplice André is considered a well-written and entertaining classic.

Martin, James Kirby. *Benedict Arnold, Revolutionary Hero: An American*

*Warrior Reconsidered.* New York: New York University Press, 2000. Outlines Arnold's significant contributions to the American Revolutionary War efforts that are often overlooked in light of his later treachery.

Sale, Richard T. *Traitors: The Worst Acts of Treason in American History, from Benedict Arnold to Robert Hanssen.* New York: Berkley, 2003. The section on Arnold offers a concise depiction of his treachery and places it within its historical context.

*—Marcella Bush Trevino*

**See also:** James Wilkinson.

## Joe Ball
**Serial killer**

**Born:** January 7, 1896; Elmendorf, Texas
**Died:** September 24, 1938; Elmendorf, Texas
**Also known as:** Joseph D. Ball (full name); Alligator Man; Butcher of Elmendorf; Bluebeard of Texas
**Cause of notoriety:** A bootlegger-turned-tavern owner, Ball murdered several of his girlfriends as well as barmaids, then shot himself when confronted by authorities.
**Active:** Summer, 1937-September, 1938
**Locale:** Elmendorf, Texas

### Early Life

Joseph D. Ball (bahl) was born on January 7, 1896, and was raised in the largely unsettled frontier of southern Texas by his parents, Frank Ball and Elizabeth Ball. Ball was the second of eight children and grew up in a comfortable and stable household. His father was a successful businessman who owned a general store in the small town of Elmendorf. Ball spent much of his childhood involved in outdoor activities such as fishing and target shooting. In 1917, he enlisted in the U.S. Army, serving on the front lines in Europe during World War I. In 1919, he received an honorable discharge and returned to Elmendorf.

## Criminal Career

After a brief stint working for his father's business, Ball began selling illegal whiskey to local customers. Ball's career as a bootlegger ended in 1933, when Prohibition ended after the Eighteenth Amendment. Shortly thereafter, he opened his own tavern, the Sociable Inn, just outside Elmendorf. Behind his tavern, Ball built a concrete pond, surrounded by a large wire fence and stocked with five alligators. As an attraction, Ball would entertain his intoxicated customers by feeding the reptiles live dogs, cats, and other animals. As another draw to his tavern, Ball would hire young, attractive barmaids and waitresses to work there.

Ball initiated romantic relationships with his women employees, often several at a time. In 1934 Ball met Minnie Gotthardt, and eventually she operated the tavern with him. Their relationship lasted three years, until Ball began courting a young waitress named Dolores Goodwin in 1937. That summer, Gotthardt disappeared. Ball began another relationship with a young barmaid named Hazel Brown. In September, 1937, Ball married Goodwin, but she disappeared the following April.

While local law enforcement was increasingly suspicious of Ball after the disappearances of several barmaids, his two girlfriends, and his wife, there was no real evidence to refute Ball's claims that the women "just moved on." In addition, Ball's intimidating personality and unusual business practices made local residents reluctant to challenge or cross him.

## Legal Action and Outcome

On September 23, 1938, Bexar County Deputy Sheriff John Gray was approached by a man who reported seeing a barrel covered in flies and smelling of human decomposition behind Ball's sister's barn. The next day, Deputy Sheriffs Gray and Klevenhagen went to the barn, but the barrel was gone. They questioned Ball, but he denied any wrongdoing. When they returned to the barn, Ball's sister confirmed the presence of the foul-smelling barrel. Deputies Gray and Klevenhagen returned to the Sociable Inn to transport Ball to San Antonio for interrogation. When confronted by the deputies, Ball opened the register and removed a .45-caliber revolver from the drawer. Ball turned the gun to his heart and shot himself dead.

With the magnitude of the crimes becoming clearer, Deputies Gray and Klevenhagen questioned Ball's handyman, Clifford Wheeler. Initially denying involvement, Wheeler then admitted to assisting Ball dispose of the bodies of two women. Minnie Gotthardt's body was found buried in sand near Corpus Christi, and Hazel Brown's dismembered body was found buried in a shallow grave near the San Antonio River. Wheeler claimed Ball killed Gotthardt because she was pregnant and that Ball had killed Brown because she wanted to end their relationship. Wheeler was incarcerated for two years after pleading guilty. When investigators searched Ball's property, they found a scrapbook with dozens of pictures of women. Many speculated that Ball might have killed at least twenty women, and the alligators disposed of the physical evidence. No human remains were found near the alligator pond to support that assertion.

### Impact

Joe Ball's criminal career was familiar in Texas folklore, but factual details of his life and crimes remained obscure until the twenty-first century. In 2002, newspaper editor Michael Hall published a detailed article in the July issue of *Texas Monthly* magazine. Ball's reputation also drew attention in Tobe Hooper's 1977 film *Eaten Alive*, inspired by Ball's crimes.

### Further Reading

Hall, Michael. "Two Barmaids, Five Alligators, and the Butcher of Elmendorf." *Texas Monthly* (July, 2002): 114-126. A comprehensive account of Ball's life in words, interviews, and photos. Also examines the legends and folklore surrounding Ball's serial murders.

Newton, Michael. *The Encyclopedia of Serial Killers*. New York: Checkmark Books, 2000. A brief, factual account of Ball's life and crimes.

*—Anthony J. Luongo III*

**See also:** David Berkowitz; Kenneth Bianchi; Ted Bundy; Angelo Buono, Jr.; Andrew Cunanan; Jeffrey Dahmer; Albert DeSalvo; Albert Fish; John Wayne Gacy; Ed Gein; Leonard Lake; Charles Ng; Dennis Rader; Richard Speck; Aileen Carol Wuornos.

# Velma Margie Barfield
**"Black widow" serial killer**

**Born:** October 29, 1932; Cumberland County, North Carolina
**Died:** November 2, 1984; Central Prison, Raleigh, North Carolina
**Also known as:** Margie Bullard (birth name); Death Row Granny
**Major offense:** First-degree murder
**Active:** 1969-1978
**Locale:** North Carolina
**Sentence:** Death by lethal injection

## Early Life
Velma Margie Barfield was born in rural North Carolina, the second child in a family of nine children. She claimed that her father beat and raped her and her sisters, although this claim was vehemently denied by her siblings. Velma dropped out of school at a young age, and by age nineteen she was married to Thomas Burke, with whom she had two children. Burke suffered severe head injuries in a car crash in 1966 and became unable to work. He became an alcoholic, and Velma began to take antidepressants and tranquilizers, to which she ultimately became addicted. Burke died in a house fire in 1969. Velma was remarried in 1970, to Jennings Barfield. Barfield was dead within six months of their marriage; physicians believed his death to have occurred from natural causes.

## Criminal Career
In 1974, Velma Barfield's mother, Lillie Bullard, died unexpectedly from what were believed to be natural causes. At the time of her death, Barfield had forged her mother's name on a one-thousand-dollar loan application. Barfield also served a short amount of time in a correctional facility for writing bad checks. After the death of her mother, Barfield, who was by now completely dependent on prescription drugs, took a job as a live-in maid for Dollie Edwards. During her employment with Edwards, Barfield met Edwards's nephew Stuart Taylor, with whom she began a romantic relationship which would last for two years. Her employment ended when Edwards died unexpectedly in 1977 from acute gastroenteritis.

Barfield then took a job with John Lee and his wife and began forging checks against the Lees' bank account. In June, 1977, John Lee died after suffering a severe stomach ailment for two months. Barfield began forging checks against Stuart Taylor's bank account. Taylor took ill around the time he became suspicious concerning his checking account activity. In February, 1978, Taylor died after suffering intense abdominal pains. The cause of his death was determined to be acute gastroenteritis. Taylor's relatives disagreed with the diagnosis and demanded a full autopsy. The autopsy showed that the actual cause of his death was arsenic poisoning, and Barfield was arrested. Once in custody, Barfield confessed to spiking Taylor's beer with arsenic. She then confessed to murdering her mother, whom she had poisoned with insecticide, as well as Dollie Edwards and John Lee.

### Legal Action and Outcome

Barfield was charged only with the death of Stuart Taylor. A jury found her guilty of first-degree murder and sentenced her to death. While in prison, Barfield came to be widely known as a deeply religious woman. She attempted to receive clemency from the governor of North Carolina but was denied and was executed by lethal injection on November 2, 1984, in Raleigh, North Carolina.

### Impact

Known as the Death Row Granny, Velma Margie Barfield became the first woman to be executed in the United States in more than twenty years and the first woman executed in the United States since the reinstatement of the death penalty in 1976. She was also the first woman to be executed by lethal injection.

### Further Reading

Barfield, Velma. *Woman on Death Row*. Nashville: Oliver Nelson Books, 1985. Barfield's autobiography.

Bledsoe, Jerry, and Velma Barfield. *Death Sentence: The True Story of Velma Barfield's Life, Crimes, and Execution*. New York: E. P. Dutton, 1998. Based mainly on anecdotes from Barfield's two children, Kim and Ronnie, this book details Barfield's childhood, her married years, her crimes, and her trial.

Kelleher, Michael D., and C. L. Kelleher. *Murder Most Rare*. New York: Dell, 1998. Provides examples and detailed biographical information for a variety of women serial killers, including Barfield.

Newton, Michael. *Bad Girls Do It: An Encyclopedia of Female Murderers*. Port Townsend, Wash.: Loompanics Unlimited, 1993. An encyclopedia of women serial killers, this book provides biographical sketches of female murderers throughout the world, including Barfield.

—*Carly M. Hilinski*

**See also:** Linda Burfield Hazzard; Marie Hilley; Karla Faye Tucker; Aileen Carol Wuornos.

# Ma Barker

## Gangland matriarch

**Born:** c. 1871; Ash Grove, near Springfield, Missouri
**Died:** January 16, 1935; Lake Weir, near Oklawaha, Florida
**Also known as:** Arizona Donnie Clark (birth name); Bloody Mama; Kate Barker; Arizona Donnie Barker
**Cause of notoriety:** Barker, as the matriarch of an outlaw gang, was implicated in kidnappings and robberies.
**Active:** 1925-1935
**Locale:** American West, Midwest, and South

### Early Life

Arizona Donnie Clark—to come down in legend as Ma Barker (BAHR-kuhr)—was born in Ash Grove, near Springfield, Missouri. She was raised in a religious family and believed in hard work and traditional values. She married George Barker at the age of twenty and had four boys: Herman, Lloyd, Arthur, and Fred. Her husband disappeared after the last son's birth and left her to raise the boys on her own. They lived in poverty, and the boys often got into trouble. She usually managed to get them out of jail by having emotional outbursts in police stations or with arresting officers.

### Criminal Career

Differing opinions exist on whether Ma Barker did, in fact, have a criminal career with her sons and another famous gangster, Alvin Karpis. Some allege that she was simply a mother, traveling and protecting her sons, who were criminals. Others have portrayed her as a mastermind of the sons' crimes. She has been credited with planning a number of bank robberies. Several kidnappings of major public figures were also attributed to the Barker-Karpis gang. In 1927, her son Herman was killed by a federal agent during a robbery in which he had killed a police officer. Federal Bureau of Investigation (FBI) head J. Edgar Hoover, in accounts after Ma's death, said that the death of her son turned her into an even more dangerous criminal.

In 1935, another son, Fred (called Freddie by his mother), was out on parole and living with his mother at a cottage on Lake Weir. Although Ma was never arrested or tried for a crime, she was considered dangerous by the FBI, and this fact was used as justification for her killing at the hands of FBI agents during a raid of the cottage. The FBI has extensive files on her and her sons, which later became available through the Freedom of Information Act.

### Impact

The life and death of Ma Barker gained much public attention and became the basis of numerous books and films. She was the main character portrayed in a 1970 film titled *Bloody Mama*, starring Shelley Winters. The 1996 film *Public Enemies* also included her life as part of its story. Much of the debate about her case stems from historical analysis of the actions of Hoover, who had described her as a dangerous criminal.

*Kate "Ma" Barker mugshot.* (Library of Congress)

**COP VS. ROBBER**

*To FBI chief J. Edgar Hoover, Ma Barker was a "veritable beast of prey":*

Ma Barker and her sons, and Alvin Karpis and his cronies, constituted the toughest gang of hoodlums the FBI ever has been called upon to eliminate. . . . Looking over the record of these criminals, I was repeatedly impressed by the cruelty of their depredations . . . murder of a policeman . . . murder of two policemen. . . . machine gun murder of an innocent citizen who got in the way during a bank robbery . . . kidnapping and extortion . . . train robbery . . . mail robbery . . . the protection of high police officials bought with tainted money . . . paroles bought.

*Source:* Ken Jones, *The FBI in Action* (New York: Signet, 1957).

Near Lake Weir, Florida, a reenactment of the final shoot-out is held annually to commemorate the biggest gun battle in FBI history (three to four thousand rounds were used). The event includes vintage cars, gunfights, and actors representing the Barkers and the FBI.

**FURTHER READING**

Gentry, Curt. *J. Edgar Hoover: The Man and the Secrets*. New York: W. W. Norton, 2001. This book is based on more than two hundred interviews and access to previously classified FBI documents. Despite lengthy footnotes and an extensive list of source materials, it is very readable. Since Hoover labeled Barker as a dangerous criminal, accounts of his life provide background on his pursuit of her and her sons.

Hamilton, Sue, and John Hamilton. *Public Enemy Number One: The Barkers*. Bloomington, Minn.: Abdo and Daughters, 1989. A book written for young adults, it summarizes the lives of Ma Barker and her sons.

Karpis, Alvin, with Robert Livesey. *On the Rock: The Prison Story of Alvin Karpis*. Toronto, Ont.: Beaufort Books, 1980. Karpis was associated with Barker's sons and took part in several of their major escapades. He was captured in 1936 and told his story while in captivity. A description of his association with the Barkers is included.

Maccabee, Paul. *John Dillinger Slept Here: A Crook's Tour of Crime and Corruption in St. Paul, 1920-1936*. St. Paul: Minnesota Historical Society Press, 1995. The Barkers were instrumental in two kidnappings in St. Paul: those of William Hamm, Jr., and Edward Bremer. Both of these crimes are chronicled in this definitive work on crime in St. Paul.

Winter, Robert. *Mean Men: The Sons of Ma Barker*. Danbury, Conn.: Routledge Books, 2000. Traces the escapades of Barker and her sons.

—*Mary C. Ware*

**See also:** Clyde Barrow; John Dillinger; Pretty Boy Floyd; Alvin Karpis; Machine Gun Kelly; Baby Face Nelson; Bonnie Parker.

## Clyde Barrow

### Robber, murderer, and gang leader

**Born:** March 24, 1909; near Telico, Texas

**Died:** May 23, 1934; near Gibsland, Bienville Parish, Louisiana

**Also known as:** Clyde Chestnut Barrow (full name); Clyde "Champion" Barrow

**Cause of notoriety:** Although the bank robberies Barrow and his gang committed were typically small in monetary yield, the brutal murders that often accompanied them placed Barrow and his partner Bonnie Parker among the most notorious "public enemies" of the Depression era.

**Active:** 1931-1934

**Locale:** Southern and midwestern United States

#### Early Life

Born to a poor family on a farm south of Dallas, Texas, Clyde Barrow reportedly began his criminal career at a young age, collaborating with his brother Ivan "Buck" Barrow on numerous burglaries, armed robberies, and other crimes. After his first two arrests in 1926, Barrow briefly held several legitimate jobs in addition to his ongoing criminal pursuits, barely escaping another arrest in a high-speed police chase that resulted in the apprehension and imprisonment of his brother. Shortly afterward, Barrow met Bonnie Parker, an unemployed waitress married to a convicted murderer serving a ninety-nine-year prison sentence.

**Criminal Career**

Barrow and Parker immediately forged a relationship, reportedly cohabitating as Barrow made another brief, unsuccessful attempt to earn a legitimate living. Convicted of burglary and auto theft in 1930, Barrow was sentenced to two years in prison, and after a brief escape was sent to the Texas State Prison at Eastham Farm. The harsh, brutal conditions at Eastham transformed Barrow into a seasoned criminal; it was there that he reportedly committed his first homicide. Pardoned by the Texas governor in 1932 after serving twenty months at Eastham, Barrow allegedly vowed that he would rather die than return to prison.

Following his release from prison, Barrow committed a series of robberies in Texas, often accompanied by Parker, who was arrested following a botched auto theft and served three months in prison. She returned to Barrow upon her release, and the couple resumed their criminal activity, along with a rotating gang of accomplices. Barrow was the undisputed leader of the gang, his reputation as a skilled driver augmented by a growing penchant for violent confrontations that often resulted in the deaths of resisting

*Bonnie Parker and Clyde Barrow.* (Library of Congress)

victims and pursuing law enforcement officers. Although the robberies Barrow and his gang committed were typically small in monetary terms, the brutal murders that often accompanied them rendered Barrow and Parker dangerous fugitives, placing them among the most notorious "public enemies" of the Great Depression era.

As the gang expanded the crime spree into several midwestern states, news media nationwide began to report sensationalized accounts of their exploits, which frequently portrayed Barrow and Parker, known to the public simply as "Bonnie and Clyde," as romantic antiheroes. Barrow and Parker actively exploited their public image: Parker submitted autobiographical poems to numerous newspapers, often with photographs showing the couple smoking cigars and brandishing firearms. Barrow is reputed to have sent a letter to Henry Ford praising a stolen Ford coupe, although the authenticity of the letter was never confirmed.

By mid-1933, the authorities were closing in on Barrow and his gang. After shoot-outs with police in Missouri and Iowa left Buck Barrow dead and Parker injured, members of the gang began to desert. Barrow and Parker remained on the run, alternating among several hiding places. In January of 1934, Barrow conducted a raid upon the Eastham prison farm, freeing several of his associates. The Texas Department of Corrections, embarrassed by the raid and exasperated by the failure of authorities to capture the Barrow gang, hired Frank Hamer, a former Texas Ranger with a reputation for engaging in shoot-outs with alleged criminals, to track down Barrow and Parker. On a tip from a former Barrow associate, Hamer and his assembled posse of Texas and Louisiana officers lay in wait for Barrow and Parker along a stretch of highway near Gibsland, Louisiana, on May 21, 1934. On the morning of May 23, Barrow and Parker, in a car, approached the decoy vehicle set by the posse and occupied by the father of the associate who tipped the authorities.

## Legal Action and Outcome

What happened afterward is the source of controversy. As the car came to a stop, the officers apparently opened fire without attempting to apprehend the couple or ordering them to surrender. One officer later admitted to having fired the first shot into Barrow's head at close range. The officers riddled the car and its occupants with bullets, firing more than 130 rounds.

Following the deaths of Barrow and Parker, Hamer publicly admitted that the posse had lain in wait for Barrow and Parker with the intent of ambushing them with deadly force. Newspapers continued to sensationalize the couple in death, publishing lurid accounts of the ambush and photographs of their bullet-riddled automobile. Barrow was buried in the Western Heights Cemetery in Dallas, Texas, next to his brother, Buck, but away from Parker, who was buried in another Dallas cemetery.

### Impact

The crimes and violent deaths of Clyde Barrow and his accomplices occurred during the final wave of the "public enemy" era, contemporaneous with the careers of other famous criminal gang leaders such as John Dillinger (1903-1934) and Kate "Ma" Barker (c. 1871-1935). Popular media trumpeted the killing of "Bonnie and Clyde" as a victory for law enforcement and evidence of the devastating and inevitable consequences of a life of crime. Yet the romantic legend of the couple survived, spawning a multitude of books, articles, feature films, and other popular culture references.

The criminal exploits of Barrow and other high-profile criminals of the Great Depression era prompted the U.S. government to consolidate its chief federal law enforcement agencies into the Federal Bureau of Investigation (FBI) in 1935, leading to an expansion of the role of the federal government in combating organized crime and inspiring the federalization of a number of crimes whose enforcement was previously the primary responsibility of the states.

### Further Reading

Barrow, Blanche, and John Neal Phillips. *My Life with Bonnie and Clyde*. Norman: University of Oklahoma Press, 2004. Memoir by the sister-in-law of Clyde Barrow includes accounts of her experiences with the Barrow gang and previously unpublished photographs from the author's personal collection.

Bruns, Roger. *The Bandit Kings from Jesse James to Pretty Boy Floyd*. New York: Crown, 1995. An examination of the outlaw as folk hero through case studies of prominent American criminals between 1850 and 1940.

Knight, James, and Jonathan Davis. *Bonnie and Clyde: A Twenty-first-Century Update*. Austin, Tex.: Eakin Press, 2003. A detailed biography of Bonnie Parker and Clyde Barrow, containing previously unpublished information and photographs.

Phillips, John Neal. "The Raid on Eastham." *American History* 35, no. 4 (October, 2000): 54. Recounts Barrow's orchestration of the prison raid that eventually led to his ambush by the Hamer posse.

—*Michael H. Burchett*

**See also:** Ma Barker; John Dillinger; Pretty Boy Floyd; Baby Face Nelson; Bonnie Parker.

# Sam Bass

## Highwayman

**Born:** July 21, 1851; near Mitchell, Indiana
**Died:** July 21, 1878; Round Rock, Texas
**Also known as:** Samuel Bass (full name)
**Cause of notoriety:** Bass was a frontier-era outlaw who robbed a Union Pacific train at Big Springs, Nebraska, and various stagecoaches.
**Active:** 1877-1878
**Locale:** Nebraska, Texas, and Dakota Territory

### Early Life

Samuel Bass (bas) was born the sixth of ten children to Daniel and Elizabeth (Sheeks) Bass on a farm near Mitchell, Indiana, on July 21, 1851. Tragically, Bass was orphaned before his thirteenth birthday and went to live with an uncle. Not much is known about Bass's early life, but periodic disagreements with his uncle probably enticed him to leave Indiana in 1869. At the age of eighteen, Bass left home, and after brief layovers in Missouri and Mississippi, he found his way to Denton, Texas. For several years, the young man worked as a freighter, laborer, and liveryman. After acquiring a fleet-footed horse in 1874, Bass focused all his energy on horse racing. His horse won race after race, and the animal gained legendary notoriety in North Texas as the Denton Mare. By 1876, Bass apparently became acquainted with a small-time thief named Joel Collins. At the same time, the goldfields in the Black Hills offered riches for those who could provide food, supplies, and materials to the mining communities. Bass and Collins headed north to Deadwood, Dakota Territory, with a herd of Texas longhorns. The pair reportedly cleared more than eight thousand dollars in the Black Hills mining camps but soon squandered their earnings on gambling and failed freighting and saloon operations. Down on their luck and low on finances, the pair eventually turned to the dangerous but lucrative field of highway robbery.

## Outlaw Career

Bass's outlaw career began in earnest in 1877, when he and Collins recruited a handful of men to rob stagecoaches in and around the Black Hills mining towns. The gang reportedly robbed seven stagecoaches but eventually came down the Sidney-Deadwood Trail to Nebraska. After losing money in the gaming houses of Sidney and Ogallala, Nebraska, the gang turned to train robbery. On the evening of September 18, 1877, Bass and five accomplices held up a Union Pacific passenger train near Big Springs, Nebraska, a small whistle-stop on the transcontinental line close to the Nebraska-Colorado border. The bandits made off with more than sixty thousand dollars but were quickly pursued by posses—including the United States Army—hoping to collect the sizable reward offered by the Union Pacific Railroad.

Within two weeks, pursuing posses killed Collins and several other accomplices. With the law hot on his trail, Bass returned to Texas, where he resumed his occupation as a stagecoach and train robber. After forming another gang, Bass and his fellow highwaymen held up stagecoaches and trains around the vicinity of Dallas. Bass's criminal exploits sparked one of the largest manhunts in Texas history, a chase that was followed enthusiastically by the Texas press. With each escape, the elusive Bass gained more notoriety. After eluding escape for more than four months, Bass was finally betrayed by Jim Murphy, a fellow gang member who turned informant. With information provided by Murphy, the Texas Rangers and local posses surprised the Bass gang in Round Rock, Texas, on July 19 as they prepared to rob a bank. In the ensuing gunfight, Bass was mortally wounded. He succumbed to his wounds on July 21, 1878, his twenty-seventh birthday.

## Impact

Sam Bass had a short and relatively unsuccessful criminal career. Other than his impressive haul during the Big Springs train robbery, Bass's earnings as a highwayman were insignificant. His outlaw career lasted barely more than a year, and it ended in a blazing gunfight with the Texas Rangers. Still, Bass's name and fame—particularly in Texas—reached legendary status. Shortly after his death, Bass, like Jesse James in Missouri, became immortalized as a Robin Hood-type figure who was forced into a life of crime because of the graft and malfeasance of those in power. Popular histories, songs, and Hollywood films have helped keep Bass's name and exploits alive. Less than a month after his death, for example, two books appeared that began building the Sam Bass myth, as did a song titled "The Ballad of Sam Bass," a tune sung by school-age children for more than a century. In 1949, the film *Calamity Jane and Sam Bass* portrayed Bass as a good-hearted cowboy who, through deceit, was forced into a life of crime in order to restore his good name. The Bass myth existed into the twenty-first century: Rumors of Bass gold, stashed in an undetected cave for more than one hundred years, abounded in north Texas and kept fortune seekers interested in sites where Bass was said to have visited. When entering Round Rock, Texas, from the north on Interstate 35, travelers see an exit sign pointing to "Sam Bass Road," a monument to a fallen cultural hero.

**Further Reading**

Gard, Wayne. *Sam Bass*. Boston: Houghton Mifflin, 1936. Written by a noted historian of the frontier American West, this book stood as the premier biography of Sam Bass for more than sixty years.

Hogg, Thomas E. *Authentic History of Sam Bass and His Gang*. 1878. Reprint. Bandera, Tex.: Frontier Times, 1926. The first biography of Sam Bass. Written and published within weeks of his death, this book began to mold Bass into a mythic Robin Hood figure.

Miller, Rick. *Sam Bass and Gang*. Austin, Tex.: State House Press, 1999. The definitive biography of Sam Bass. A thoroughly researched book that leaves few questions unanswered.

O'Neal, Bill. *Encyclopedia of Western Gunfighters*. Norman: University of Oklahoma Press, 1979. This valuable collection of 587 gunfighter biographies provides a biography of Bass along with short descriptions of his criminal exploits and three gunfights.

—*Mark R. Ellis*

**See also:** Apache Kid; Tom Bell; William H. Bonney; Curly Bill Brocius; Bob Dalton; Emmett Dalton; Bill Doolin; John Wesley Hardin; Doc Holliday; Jesse James; Tom Ketchum; Harry Longabaugh; Bill Longley; Johnny Ringo; Belle Starr; Hank Vaughan; Cole Younger.

# Byron De La Beckwith

## White supremacist and Ku Klux Klan leader

**Born:** November 9, 1920; Colusa, California
**Died:** January 21, 2001; Jackson, Mississippi
**Also known as:** Dee Lay
**Major offense:** Murder
**Active:** June 12, 1963
**Locale:** Jackson, Mississippi
**Sentence:** Life imprisonment

### Early Life

Byron De La Beckwith (BI-ruhn day lah BEHK-wihth) was born in Colusa, California, and moved to Mississippi with his widowed mother at the age of five. Upon entering adulthood, Beckwith joined the armed services and received the Purple Heart for his combat service during World War II. After returning to the United States, Beckwith became a fertilizer salesman in Mississippi.

Beckwith's early life in Mississippi and his return to the state after his military services appear to have shaped his attitudes about race and ethnicity rather substantially. Many residents of Mississippi and other southern states had clear inclinations toward preserving past racial separation policies. However, the United States was in the midst of a desegregation movement. The U.S. Supreme Court ruling in *Brown v. Board of Education* in 1954 had overruled the prior "separate but equal" doctrine of *Plessy v. Ferguson* (1896). These changes in society were viewed by Beckwith and many southerners as an attack on their way of life forced upon them by the federal government and civil rights advocates. Upon returning to Mississippi, Beckwith became a member and leader of the white supremacist group known as the Ku Klux Klan (KKK). The organization had a history of engaging in violence against African Americans. In the 1960's, this violence escalated in the form of lynchings, church bombings, and assaults against African Americans.

### Criminal Career

Beckwith gained his notoriety in the mid-1960's when he was tried twice for the assassination of Medgar Evers, a popular civil rights leader in Jackson, Mississippi. Myrlie Evers, Evers's wife, and her three young children were watching President John F. Kennedy's address to the nation on civil rights when a rifle shot rang out. Medgar Evers was shot in the back while standing in the driveway of his home. He managed to drag himself to the doorway of his home, where he was met by his frantic wife and children. He died less than one hour later.

**Legal Action and Outcome**

Beckwith was charged with the murder of Evers after his rifle was found at the scene of the crime and his fingerprints were found on the scope of the rifle. In addition, some witnesses came forward to make eyewitness identifications that placed Beckwith at the crime scene. Other witnesses reported seeing Beckwith's Plymouth Valiant in the vicinity of the Evers residence. Beckwith explained away the direct evidence against him by claiming that his rifle had been stolen. Moreover, Beckwith's attorney called two police officers from the town of Greenwood, Mississippi, to the witness stand; these two officers testified to seeing Beckwith there at a gas station. Greenwood is about eighty miles from Jackson, the scene of the crime; therefore, if the officer testimony was accurate, it would have been impossible for Beckwith to have committed the murder. On two different occasions, all-white male juries failed to convict Beckwith; instead, they returned hung verdicts, which led to mistrials.

During the civil rights era, it was traditionally very difficult to obtain a conviction in a Mississippi courtroom of a white offender charged with a crime against an African American victim. In many areas of Mississippi, the white-supremacist ideology was so entrenched that it frequently made its way into governmental offices, including local sheriff offices, police departments, and the courts. However, in one of Beckwith's trials, there was some indication that the powerful ideology of white supremacy had made its way all the way up to the governor's office. During the first trial, Mississippi governor Ross Barnett walked up to Beckwith and shook his hand in full view of the jury.

In the immediate aftermath of the trials, Beckwith remained in the public spotlight. In 1967, he ran for lieutenant governor of Mississippi, finishing fifth out of six candidates. In 1973, police stopped Beckwith in New Orleans, Louisiana, and found bombs inside his vehicle. He was convicted in state court of transporting explosives without a permit and was sentenced to five years in a Louisiana prison.

Beckwith was not held accountable for the murder of Evers until 1994. Myrlie Evers convinced Hinds County district attorney Bobby DeLaughter to bring Beckwith to court for a third trial in her husband's death. During his investigation, DeLaughter found several different witnesses to testify that Beckwith had, at various times, bragged both about his shooting death of Evers and about the fact that he had not been held accountable for the offense.

Beckwith had essentially believed that he would never be found guilty by a jury in Mississippi for killing an African American. He therefore apparently saw no harm in telling people about his involvement in the murder. During his third trial, Beckwith remained openly defiant and blatantly proud of his separatist views. He even wore a Confederate flag on his lapel during the trial. His incredible swagger would eventually lead to his downfall: After considering the new evidence, the jury—composed of eight blacks and four whites—convicted Beckwith of Evers's murder. Beckwith was sentenced to life imprisonment.

### Impact

The Byron De La Beckwith case was important for a variety of reasons. Most important, the case served as an important historical lens into the deep-seated racial biases and bigotry of the South that existed for most of the twentieth century. However, the case was also important because it served as a mechanism for change and clearly delineated a social shift toward white supremacist accountability for racist actions, even years after supremacist members committed their offenses.

Following Beckwith's conviction, several other cases of violent crimes committed against African Americans during the 1960's were reassessed and retried. In 1998, Sam Bowers was tried and convicted of the 1966 murder in Hattiesburg, Mississippi, of local National Association for the Advancement of Colored People (NAACP) president Vernon Dahmer. In 2000 and 2001, Thomas Blanton, Jr., and Bobby Frank Cherry were found guilty for their roles in the Birmingham church bombing that resulted in the deaths of four teenage African American girls in September, 1963.

### Further Reading

DeLaughter, Bobby. *Never Too Late: A Prosecutor's Story of Justice in the Medgar Evers Case*. New York: Simon & Schuster, 2001. Written by the prosecuting attorney who was instrumental in bringing Beckwith to trial for the third time in 1994, the book highlights the evidence against Beckwith and the difficulties and triumphs in bringing a thirty-year-old case to trial.

Morris, W. *Ghosts of Medgar Evers: A Tale of Race, Murder, Mississippi, and Hollywood.* New York: Random House, 1998. An account that traces the development of the 1994 trial against Beckwith, as well as the development of the 1996 *Ghosts of Mississippi* film that chronicled the case.

Wilkie, C. *Dixie: A Personal Odyssey Through Events That Shaped the Modern South.* New York: Simon & Schuster, 2001. Presents a historical look at some of the important race-related events of the 1960's and their influence on modern issues in the South.

*—Kevin G. Buckler*

**See also:** Matthew F. Hale; Robert Jay Mathews.

# Tom Bell

## Western outlaw and gang leader

**Born:** 1825; Rome, Tennessee

**Died:** October 4, 1856; near Nevada City, California

**Also known as:** Thomas J. Hodges (birth name); Outlaw Doc

**Cause of notoriety:** Bell and his outlaw gang are credited with the first attempted stagecoach holdup in California.

**Active:** October 8, 1851-October 4, 1856

**Locale:** Auburn, Calaveras, Nevada City, Sacramento, San Francisco, and Stockton, California

### Early Life

Thomas J. Hodges, also known as Tom Bell (behl), was born in 1825 just east of Nashville in Rome, Tennessee. Not much is known about his early life. At six feet, two inches tall, with long red hair and a striking beard, Bell was an imposing physical presence. Educated as a physician in Tennessee, Bell saw action in the Mexican-American War as an Army doctor. After his service in the military, he joined the gold rush to California, where he sought his fortune as a gambler.

## Outlaw Career

Before long, Bell's troubles with the law began. On October 8, 1851, he was sentenced to five years in state prison for grand larceny committed in Sacramento County. At the time, California's prison system was new, and Bell was only the twenty-fourth person sentenced to prison. Initially he was held in a ship just off the coast of San Francisco, but he was later housed at the newly constructed Angel Island Prison at San Quentin. On May 12, 1855, Bell escaped from custody along with several other convicts, including Bill Gristy (alias Bill White). Within months, Bell was the leader of a well-organized gang of more than thirty outlaws.

On August 12, 1856, Bell and his gang attempted a feat never before tried in California: robbing a stagecoach. They chose a Camptonville-Marysville stage carrying $100,000 worth of gold bullion. One passenger, the wife of a local barber, was killed, and two male passengers were wounded before Bell's gang was chased away by the stagecoach guards. A short time later, a Jewish peddler named Rosenthal was robbed and murdered by Bell and several members of his gang. The murder occurred not far from his Bell's suspected hideout. The robberies, and especially the death of the woman on the Marysville stage, led to a massive manhunt, led most notably by Bell's nemesis, Placer County sheriff John C. Boggs.

By late September, Gristy and many other suspected gang members had been captured. Sheriff Boggs and his deputies interrogated Gristy, who eventually shared information about Bell's hideout near the Mountaineer House, a hotel and tavern located about eight miles outside Auburn. Another suspect interrogated by Boggs, named Charley Hamilton, also reported that he knew Bell. Hamilton agreed to infiltrate the Bell gang and try to arrange the outlaw's capture. Simultaneously, Deputy Sheriff Bob Paul of Calaveras County posed as an outlaw and attempted to obtain evidence against Jack Phillips, the owner of the Mountaineer House and a suspected collaborator and fence for Bell's gang. Boggs had previously raided the Mountaineer House several times but had never been able to locate Bell.

## Legal Action and Outcome

On September 29, 1856, the hotelkeeper was arrested for harboring Bell, and the authorities began to close the net on the fugitive. Later that evening, Hamilton, the desperado who had gained Bell's trust, told Sheriff Boggs where Bell was camped. Sometime after midnight, while riding toward the suspected encampment, Boggs and his men intercepted Bell on the road, and a gunfight ensued. Outlaw Ned Conway was killed, but Bell and another outlaw known as Texas Jack escaped on foot, unharmed. Bell headed for another tavern and hotel about four miles away, known as the Pine Grove House, where he stole a horse and headed south toward the San Joaquin River. Four days later, on October 4, 1856, Bell was captured and lynched outside Nevada City by a posse from Stockton led by Judge George Belt.

### Impact

Following his prison break, Tom Bell, who has also been referred to as the "Outlaw Doc," became the most infamous fugitive to hit the California gold rush fields since Joaquín Murieta. He will be remembered primarily for attempting the first stagecoach holdup in California.

### Further Reading

Boessenecker, John. *Badge and Buckshot: Lawlessness in Old California*. Norman: University of Oklahoma Press, 1988. An authoritative narrative on lawlessness in the Old West. Provides a candid account of the sometimes ragged past of this important period in American history.

Drago, Sinclair. *Road Agents and Train Robbers: Half a Century of Western Banditry*. New York: Dodd, 1973. Does an excellent job of dispelling common misconceptions about criminal activities of well-known outlaws in the last half of the nineteenth century.

Secrest, William B. *California Desperadoes: Stories of Early California Outlaws in Their Own Words*. Clovis, Calif.: Word Dancer Press, 2000. The author has compiled an amazing collection of rare photographs and first-person accounts of authentic Old West desperadoes.

*—Wayne J. Pitts*

**See also:** Apache Kid; William H. Bonney; Curly Bill Brocius; Bob Dalton; Emmett Dalton; Bill Doolin; John Wesley Hardin; Doc Holliday; Jesse James; Tom Ketchum; Harry Longabaugh; Bill Longley; Johnny Ringo; Belle Starr; Henry Starr; Hank Vaughan; Cole Younger.

## Bambi Bembenek
### Murderer

**Born:** August 15, 1958; Milwaukee, Wisconsin
**Also known as:** Lawrencia Bembenek (full name); Laurie Bembenek (legal name after 1994)
**Major offenses:** Murder and escape from prison
**Active:** May, 1981
**Locale:** Milwaukee, Wisconsin
**Sentence:** Life in prison

### Early Life

Bambi Bembenek (BAM-bee behm-BEHN-ihk) grew up on the south side of Milwaukee, Wisconsin. She entered the Milwaukee Police Academy when she turned twenty-one but was dismissed in 1980 on suspicion of smoking marijuana. Following her dismissal, she filed a sex discrimination lawsuit against the department. Faced with large debts, she became a Playboy club waitress and aerobics instructor to pay her bills. She married police officer Elfred Schulz, Jr., after a brief courtship.

### Criminal Career

In May, 1981, four months after Bembenek married Schulz, his former wife, Christine, was shot to death in her home with Elfred's revolver. Bembenek was accused of the murder. She consistently denied any involvement in the crime and alleged that the police had focused their investigations on her to keep her from testifying in her sex discrimination suit.

### Legal Action and Outcome

In a trial widely described as sensational, Bembenek was convicted of first-degree murder and was sentenced to life in prison at Taycheedah Correctional Institute. While in prison, she initiated class-action suits, charging inhumane conditions. She assisted other inmates in researching their appeals and started a prison newspaper. She exercised for long hours every day and read extensively. Eventually, she won the right to be admitted to a college extension program and earned a bachelor's degree in humanities, graduating with honors.

After ten years in prison, Bembenek became romantically involved with

*Bambi Bembenek.*
(AP/Wide World Photos)

the brother of a fellow inmate. With his assistance, she escaped and fled to Canada, where she worked as a waitress for three months before a customer recognized her from the television show *America's Most Wanted* and notified police. She and her fiancé were arrested and returned to the United States, where he was sentenced for abetting her escape. She was placed in solitary confinement in a federal penitentiary.

Bembenek's lawyers appealed the case several times over the following years. The appeal filed after her escape from prison and recapture resulted in the vacating of her first-degree-murder life sentence because of evidence of sloppy police work at the time of the murder. Rather than face continued imprisonment, Bembenek decided not to fight for a new trial, instead pleading no contest to second-degree murder. In December, 1992, she was sentenced to twenty years in prison but was placed on parole, based on time already served.

The question of who murdered Christine Schulz may never be answered.

Bembenek passed all lie-detector tests relating to the killing, but Elfred Schulz remained convinced that Bembenek murdered his former wife. A case could be made against an acquaintance of theirs who was later convicted of armed robberies around the time of the murder and who bragged in prison of having killed Christine.

In 2002, Bembenek filed for DNA testing, but the results were equivocal. In 2003, she filed suit against Dr. Phil McGraw, alleging that the staff of his television program had imprisoned her in an apartment while awaiting results of their own DNA testing. She escaped from a window and shattered her leg, which later required amputation.

Thereafter, Bembenek disappeared from public view. Depressed and suffering from panic attacks, she admitted that she was an alcoholic and was returned to jail briefly for use of marijuana and cocaine. She contracted hepatitis C and moved to the Pacific Northwest, where she lived in poverty.

### Impact

Bambi Bembenek's case generated enormous publicity. She became a folk hero, with thousands of people following media accounts of the trials and her escape from prison and watching her appearances on celebrity television shows. The combination of her glamorous looks and the suggestions of a miscarriage of justice captured people's imagination and prompted sales of books, magazine articles, and two television movies that covered her story.

### Further Reading

Radish, Kris. *Run, Bambi, Run: The Beautiful Ex-Cop and Convicted Murderer Who Escaped to Freedom and Won America's Heart.* New York: Carol, 1992. A detailed account of the case against Bembenek and its numerous shortcomings.

Roddick, Bill. *After the Verdict: A History of the Lawrencia Bembenek Case*. Milwaukee, Wis.: Composition House, 1999. Questions the evidence against Bembenek.

*—Rebecca Lovell Scott*

**See also:** Antoinette Frank; Jean Harris; Sante Kimes; Pamela Ann Smart; Ruth Snyder; Harry Kendall Thaw; Carolyn Warmus.

# David Berg

## Cult leader

**Born:** February 18, 1919; Oakland, California
**Died:** November, 1994; Costa de Caparica, Portugal
**Also known as:** David Brandt Berg (full name); Moses David; Mo; King David; Father David; Dad; Grandpa
**Cause of notoriety:** Berg, as the leader of various pseudoreligious cults, engaged in pedophilia and sexual abuse of the cult's members.
**Active:** 1940's-1994
**Locale:** Worldwide

### Early Life

David Berg (buhrg) was born to Hjalmer Emmanuel Berg and the Reverend Virginia Lee Brandt. His mother was a Christian evangelist, and his father was a minister in the Christian and Missionary Alliance (CMA). Berg was the youngest of three children; two boys and one girl. He graduated from Monterey High School in Northern California in 1935 and continued his studies at the Elliott School of Business Administration. On July 22, 1944, Berg married Jane Miller in Glendale, California. The couple had four children: Linda, Paul Brandt, Jonathan Emanuel, and Faith.

By 1948, Berg had joined the CMA and was relocated to Valley Farms, Arizona, to begin his ministry. However, he was expelled from the church because of significant differences in his interpretation of the church's teachings and the true mission of the organization. He was also alleged to have engaged in sexual misconduct with a church employee. After his dismissal, Berg worked as an independent evangelist and later worked with the Reverend Fred Jordan's Soul Clinic in locations across the United States.

### Cult Career

In 1968, Berg and his children founded Teens for Christ in Huntington Beach, California. The group primarily preached to surfers and beachcombers, terrifying them with apocalyptic prophecies and urging them to renounce their lives of sin. It was during this period that Berg first adopted the alias Moses David and was affectionately referred to as "Mo" or "Dad" within the group. The group took on the name Children of God. Shortly after the group's founding, Berg separated from his first wife and married young follower Karen Zerby in August, 1969. Karen became known as Maria within the group, and Berg's first wife eventually left the movement.

The group quickly acquired followers by staging public demonstrations, stressing that America would soon experience God's wrath. The members would dress in sackcloth, smear their faces with ashes, and tie giant yokes around their necks. The group soon had an impressive following, and its momentum was growing. Berg saw himself as a prophet and relocated to England in 1971 in order to begin a worldwide mission. Berg also wanted to leave North America because of the growing anticult movements that began to surface in the early 1970's.

Berg encouraged an open sexual policy within the ministry, which was

### We are not a sect!

*In a letter dated 1972, David Berg discussed the nature of the Children of God:*

What church did the Children of God split off from? Is a new child a sect? No, he's a totally new birth!—An absolutely new creation!—Dropped out, yes, but a totally new creation! We are not a sect! We belonged to no religious denomination as a group. In order to be a sect, you must first be part of the whole to begin with. But we are not even a break with the Church System because we didn't break off from it, because we were never a part of it!

Every single sect or group that you can think of has been a split off or division of some former group. What religious body are we a split off from? They say we're separatists. We have separated ourselves from the churches. But most of us were never a part of any church. The word section itself means cut off. What church were we cut off of?—None! . . .

We are not Protestants or Catholics or Jews. We are not coming out of anything. . . . We were always the Children of God! He's just gathered us together. We are a new Nation, born in a day, this day, today! So we are God's seed & His Children & we were scattered abroad, but are now being gathered together by the Lord. We are no sect or cut-off of something else. We are His totally new creation!—Hallelujah!

referred to as the Law of Liberty and included the practice of having multiple sexual partners and swapping partners. In the 1970's, Children of God introduced "flirty fishing" (also called "hooking for Jesus"), a practice in which women would engage in sexual relationships with people to whom they were witnessing.

By the late 1970's, a paranoid Berg fired the managers of the Children of God and formed a new ministry, the Family of Love, and later, the Family. The Family promoted the same sexual freedoms but also focused on child rearing and children's sexuality. Berg's open stance regarding children and sex attracted pedophiles and other sex offenders to his organization. The Family's views on sex, especially involving minors, brought much criticism and investigations. Although Berg maintained that the Family's views on sexual relations with minors concerned teenagers and never young children, he was forced to change the movement's policies regarding the Law of Liberty, to end flirty fishing, and to denounce any type of sexual relationship with a minor.

## Legal Action and Outcome

In the late 1970's and early 1980's, former cult members and concerned relatives began producing evidence to foreign governments about sexual abuse and pedophilia occurring within the group. Investigations were launched, which resulted in several lawsuits in Australia, Argentina, France, Great Britain, and Spain. However, there was never enough evidence to convict Berg or any Family member criminally, and all cases were resolved in the Family's favor.

During this period, further and more troubling accusations against Berg surfaced. At least six women, including Berg's two daughters, his daughter-in-law, and his two granddaughters, alleged that Berg sexually molested them when they were children. As these women publicly accused Berg, others began to come forward in public interviews. With more accusations occurring and the anticult movement growing, Berg went into seclusion, moving frequently internationally with only the top members of the group knowing his location. As his health failed in the 1990's, Berg handed control of the organization over to his second wife, Karen "Maria" Zerby. Maria began drafting a new charter that addressed many of the complaints and concerns that the movement's critics voiced and granted its members new rights. In the twenty-first century, the Family continued to have more than nine thousand members across fifty countries.

## Impact

With families losing their children to David Berg's cult, concerned parents formed the Parents' Committee to Free Our Sons and Daughters from the Children of God, later called Free the Children of God, in the 1970's. The group launched the investigations that drew considerable press and resulted in widespread criticism of the group. As a result of the organization's efforts, the New York attorney general published an anti-Children of God broadside. The group was instrumental in paving the way for the Cult Awareness Network, which began in the 1980's.

## Further Reading

House, Wayne H. *Charts of Cults, Sects, and Religious Movements*. Grand Rapids, Mich.: Zondervan, 2000. A comprehensive resource listing the history and ideologies of cults and religious groups in an easy-to-read chart format.

Lewis, James R., and J. Gordon Melton, eds. *Sex, Slander, and Salvation: Investigating the Family/Children of God*. Stanford, Calif.: Center for Academic Publication, 1994. A thorough look into the history of the cult in its various incarnations, its members, and its leadership.

Pritchett, W. Douglas. *The Children of God, Family of Love: An Annotated Bibliography*. New York: Garland, 1985. Lists books and other sources about the Children of God and the Family movement.

Rhodes, Ron. *The Challenge of the Cults and New Religions*. Grand Rapids, Mich.: Zondervan, 2001. Rhodes examines cults and religious zealots, their doctrines, and their beliefs. The book reveals the way in which these groups stray from true Christianity and other organized religions.

Singer, Margaret Thaler. *Cults in Our Midst: The Continuing Fight Against Their Hidden Menace*. San Francisco: Jossey-Bass, 2003. An in-depth look at cult leaders and members. Singer reveals their techniques and warns of their dangers.

*—Sara Vidar*

**See also:** Marshall Applewhite; Jim Jones; Jeffrey Lundgren; Charles Manson; Bonnie Nettles.

# David Berkowitz

## Serial killer

**Born:** June 1, 1953; Brooklyn, New York
**Also known as:** Richard David Falco (birth name); David Falco Berkowitz (full name); Son of Sam; .44-Caliber Killer
**Major offense:** Murder
**Active:** 1976-1977
**Locale:** New York, New York
**Sentence:** 365 years in prison

### Early Life

David Berkowitz (DAY-vihd BUR-koh-wihtz) was born to Betty (Broder) Falco, as a result of her extramarital affair with Joseph Kleinman. Because Kleinman threatened to end the relationship, Falco gave up her son. Berkowitz was adopted by a middle-class Jewish couple, Nathan and Pearl Berkowitz. Reared in the Bronx, he had a relatively normal childhood. The only indicators of his future criminal behavior were his hyperactivity and his neighbors' characterization of him as a bully.

After his adopted mother died in 1967, Berkowitz began to exhibit marked changes, and his school performance was poor. Berkowitz lived with his adopted father until he remarried—his new wife did not relate well to David. The couple soon retired to Florida, leaving Berkowitz to drift. Berkowitz took a few classes at a community college and then spent three years in the Army. While in the Army, he contracted a venereal disease in Korea. He found his biological mother and sister, who were very welcoming, but Berkowitz ended contact with them soon afterward.

### Criminal Career

After he left the Army in 1974, Berkowitz committed almost fifteen hundred acts of arson, recording each one in a journal. Around Christmas of 1975, he stabbed two women, claiming that demons in his head had instructed him to do so. He began a murderous spree on July 29, 1976. Six murders were attributed to him, and he was also responsible for critically wounding seven people. The media christened him the .44-Caliber Killer, for the weapon he used. Berkowitz targeted young couples, usually in parked cars. After one double homicide, Berkowitz left a note, calling himself the "Son of Sam," and was known by that moniker after that.

*David Berkowitz.*
(AP/Wide World Photos)

Berkowitz's first shooting victims were Donna Lauria and Jody Valenti, two teenage women sitting in a parked car outside Lauria's apartment building in the Bronx. Lauria died, and Valenti survived a shot to her thigh. Three months later, Berkowitz attacked Carl Denaro, whom he shot in the head, and Rosemary Keenan in Queens. In November, he attacked Donna DeMasi and Joanne Lomino, teenagers who were walking home from a bus stop after a late-night movie. Both girls survived, but Lomino was rendered a paraplegic. Two months later, Berkowitz fatally shot Christine Freund. In March, 1977, he killed Virginia Voskerichian, a Barnard College student. In April, he shot and killed Valentina Suriani and her boyfriend Alexander Esau while they were sitting in a parked car. It was there that Berkowitz left the "Son of Sam" letter.

The recipient of much media attention, Berkowitz also wrote letters to local newspapers. In late June, he shot Judy Placido, wounding her in the arm, as she sat in a parked car with Sal Lupo. Two days before the anniversary of the first murder, Berkowitz struck again, killing Stacy Moskowitz and wounding her boyfriend Bobby Violante while they were parked in his father's car.

## Legal Action and Outcome

After Berkowitz killed his last two victims in Brooklyn, he drove away in his car—which had just been ticketed. The police investigated parking tickets in the area and were able to trace the murder to Berkowitz. He was arrested on August 10, 1977, outside his apartment in Yonkers, New York. There police found a collection of weapons in his trunk, apparently stored in anticipation of a suicide mission targeting a Long Island disco.

Berkowitz confessed right away. During interrogation, he revealed the origins of his nickname. He believed his neighbor, Sam, was a powerful demon who sent messages to his pet dog, a black Labrador retriever called Harvey. Berkowitz claimed to be following death orders from Sam's dog.

Although he was diagnosed with paranoid schizophrenia, Berkowitz was found competent to stand trial. He pleaded guilty and was sentenced on June 12, 1978, to 365 years' imprisonment. In prison, Berkowitz became a born-again Christian and also became a televangelist on public-access television. He requested the cancellation of his parole hearings, claiming that he did not want to be released from prison; the parole board denied his release in 2002 and 2004.

## Impact

The year David Berkowitz was arrested, the "Son of Sam" law was enacted by the New York State Legislature. Written in the wake of speculation about large sums offered Berkowitz to tell his story, the law held that the state of New York can confiscate any money earned by convicted criminals as a result of selling their criminal stories. The money went to a fund for crime victims. The law, however, was declared unconstitutional by the Supreme Court in *Simon & Schuster, Inc. vs. New York Crime Victims Board* (1991). "Son of Sam" also became the name or theme of several songs by popular bands. A film about Berkowitz's crimes directed by Spike Lee, *Summer of Sam*, was released in 1999.

## Further Reading

Fox, James Alan, and Jack Levin. *Extreme Killing: Understanding Serial and Mass Murder*. Thousand Oaks, Calif.: Sage, 2005. Explores the Son of Sam killings and other serial and mass murders through multiple theoretical approaches. Identifies factors related to such offenses.

Hickey, Eric W. *Serial Murderers and Their Victims*. Pacific Grove, Calif.:

Brooks/Cole, 1991. Takes a sociological approach to understanding serial murder, identifying its causes and correlates. Hickey applies criminological theories to gain insight into offenders, examining the lives of more than two hundred serial killers, including David Berkowitz.

Klausner, Lawrence D. *Son of Sam: Based on the Authorized Transcription of the Tapes, Official Documents, and Diaries of David Berkowitz*. New York: McGraw-Hill, 1981. Biography of Berkowitz recounts the Son of Sam crimes.

*—Jennifer C. Gibbs*

**See also:** Joe Ball; Kenneth Bianchi; Ted Bundy; Angelo Buono, Jr.; Andrew Cunanan; Jeffrey Dahmer; Albert DeSalvo; Albert Fish; John Wayne Gacy; Ed Gein; Leonard Lake; Charles Ng; Dennis Rader; Richard Speck; Aileen Carol Wuornos.

# Kenneth Bianchi

## Serial killer

**Born:** May 22, 1951; Rochester, New York
**Also known as:** Kenneth Alessio Bianchi (full name); Hillside Strangler
**Major offenses:** Kidnapping, rape, torture, strangulation, and murder
**Active:** October 16, 1977-October 22, 1979
**Locale:** Los Angeles, California; and Bellingham, Washington
**Sentence:** Life in prison without parole

### Early Life

Kenneth Bianchi (bee-AHN-kee) was adopted at a very young age. His birth mother was an alcoholic teenage prostitute, and his adoptive mother was controlling and manipulative. From an early age, Bianchi repeatedly wet the bed, had insomnia and problems with authority figures, displayed no emotion, and lacked impulse control. He engaged in frequent temper tantrums and theft both as a child and as an adult. Bianchi attended a community college and received training as a police officer and security guard, but he bounced from job to job. He also had a series of bad relationships with women. As a result of these failures, he moved to California in 1977, where he joined his cousin Angelo Buono, Jr. There, Bianchi was rejected for several law enforcement positions and began to hire out prostitutes with Buono. Eventually, Bianchi married and had a son.

## Criminal Career

Bianchi and Buono terrorized the city of Los Angeles for about four months during 1977 and 1978 with several murders; the bodies of the victims showed signs of rape and torture. Initially, their victims were mostly prostitutes: For Bianchi and Buono, the advantage of killing prostitutes was that no one would readily notice or care about the women's absence. The men would often rape the victims and then strangle them in some manner. They also tortured some of the victims with electrical burns, medical instruments, and asphyxiation. Bianchi and Buono then dumped the completely or partially nude victims' bodies on a hillside or in a heavily wooded area, thus earning the killers the nickname the Hillside Strangler.

Bianchi and Buono then moved from targeting prostitutes to victimizing young girls and middle-class women. In one particularly gruesome incident, they dumped two victims, both girls, in a rubbish dump. This change in targets made headlines in local newspapers and created panic among residents in Los Angeles. After this widespread publicity, the murders slowed a bit. Investigators later learned that during this time, Bianchi moved to Bellingham, Washington. Two murders then occurred in Bellingham in 1979; the bodies of the victims there showed similarities to those of the murdered women in Los Angeles, creating suspicion among authorities that they may have fallen to the same killer or killers. When police discovered that Bianchi had asked the two Bellingham women who were eventually murdered to house-sit for him, the police went to his residence, where they found jewelry belonging to some of the Los Angeles victims. Bianchi was then arrested. Police charged Bianchi with the murders of twelve victims who ranged from twelve to twenty-eight years old.

## Legal Action and Outcome

Bianchi pleaded guilty by reason of insanity to the crimes. His trial antics became almost as well known as the crimes themselves. He claimed that he had multiple personalities and that his evil personality, Steve Walker, killed several victims in Los Angeles and the two women in Washington. This alter ego of Bianchi also implicated Buono in the California killings. Moreover, Bianchi tried to convince psychiatrists that he had three other personalities. Several experts examined Bianchi, and they ultimately decided that Bianchi was faking his mental illness. Bianchi eventually admitted to faking his multiple personalities in order to avoid the death penalty. (Some researchers later came to believe that Bianchi in fact did suffer from multiple personality disorder.) He eventually agreed on a plea bargain and testified against his cousin Buono in 1981. As a result of this testimony, Bianchi was given a sentence of life without parole rather than the death penalty. He was moved to Walla Walla State Prison in Washington State to carry out his sentence.

### Impact

Bianchi's lengthy trial made headlines both for the gruesome crime details that emerged and for Bianchi's theatrics during his testimony. Bianchi's lies regarding multiple personality disorder forced criminal justice agents and experts to reexamine how mental illness is often used falsely as a defense tactic for offenders. Moreover, Bianchi's experience as an adopted child also shed light on experiences that can foster murderous tendencies in young people: As investigators were beginning to understand, isolation and feelings of abandonment during formative years, like those Bianchi had experienced, seemed to be a common factor in the histories of several serial killers who emerged during this period. The stories surrounding the Hillside Strangler outlived Bianchi's crime spree: The sheer brutality of the crimes provided ample fodder both for authors and for creators of television films.

### Further Reading

Fox, James A., and Jack Levin. *Overkill: Mass Murder and Serial Killing Exposed*. New York: Plenum Press, 1994. A comprehensive examination of how and why serial killers and mass murderers operate. The authors especially focus on the motives of these killers and how they picked their victims.

Hickey, Eric W. *Serial Murderers and Their Victims*. 1991. 4th ed. Belmont, Calif.: Thomson Higher Education, 2006. A thorough examination of all types of serial killers, including those who are male, female, or foreign or who work within a team. Also examines methods by which the killers are apprehended.

Schwartz, Ted. *The Hillside Strangler: A Murderer's Mind*. New York:

Vivisphere, 2001. An in-depth examination of Bianchi's life and crimes. The author suggests that Bianchi may have suffered from multiple personality disorder.

—*Karen F. Lahm*

**See also:** Joe Ball; David Berkowitz; Ted Bundy; Angelo Buono, Jr.; Andrew Cunanan; Albert DeSalvo; Albert Fish; John Wayne Gacy; Ed Gein; Leonard Lake; Charles Ng; Dennis Rader; Richard Speck; Aileen Carol Wuornos.

# Lou Blonger
## Swindler

**Born:** May 13, 1849; Swanton, Vermont
**Died:** April 20, 1924; Cañon City, Colorado
**Also known as:** Louis H. Belonger (birth name); the Fixer
**Major offenses:** Fraud and theft
**Active:** 1880's-1922
**Locale:** Denver, Colorado
**Sentence:** Seven to ten years in prison

### Early Life

Lou Blonger (BLAHN-guhr), who altered his surname's spelling, was the son of Simon Peter Belonger and Judith Kennedy Belonger. In 1853, Blonger moved from New England to Shullsburg, Wisconsin, with his family. Chores often disrupted his schooling. Blonger's mother died when he was ten. On May 10, 1864, Blonger enlisted as a musician for Company B of the 142d Illinois Regiment, injuring his left leg during a march.

After being discharged, Blonger accompanied his older brother, Samuel Blonger, to several Western states. They established the Blonger Brothers partnership, operating saloons and billiard halls wherever they lived. In Albuquerque, New Mexico, Blonger assisted his brother, who was the town marshal. He submitted a disability pension application in 1887, claiming his wartime injury prevented him from working, before moving to Denver and investing in nearby mines.

### Criminal Career

A skilled confidence man, Blonger began swindling people when he was a young man, stealing millions of dollars during his lifetime. He rigged gambling associated with his brother's racehorses, fixed elections, and cheated at poker. By the late 1890's, Blonger controlled most of Denver's politicians and law enforcement officials, who protected Blonger and his associates in exchange for money and favors. Blonger intimidated rival thieves unless they allied with him.

Blonger masterminded a scheme targeting tourists in Colorado, vacation areas along U.S. coasts, and Cuba. No longer directly scamming people, Blonger supervised approximately five hundred criminals who victimized wealthy tourists by befriending and convincing them to invest large amounts at Blonger's phony stock exchange. As the head swindler, Blonger received half of stolen monies.

### Legal Action and Outcome

Denver district attorney Philip Van Cise, who had refused Blonger's campaign contribution, vowed to gather irrefutable evidence to prove Blonger's swindling crimes. Law-abiding citizens gave Van Cise funds to allow him to investigate Blonger independently of law officers the suspect had influenced.

Van Cise hired detectives to put recording devices in Blonger's office chandelier, secured records concerning telegrams and phone calls he received, and arranged for janitors to save his trash. After collecting sufficient proof, including Blonger's notebook filled with contact information, Van Cise directed state rangers to arrest Blonger and his cohorts.

On August 24, 1922, rangers apprehended Blonger and thirty-three of his men, holding them in a local church because Van Cise distrusted jail workers, whom Blonger might have bribed. Blonger paid his twenty-five-thousand-dollar bond and was released.

The trial for Blonger and nineteen associates charged with crimes began on February 5, 1923. After six weeks of testimony, Blonger was convicted of being a conspirator to fraud on March 28, 1923. Refusing Blonger's request for a new trial, Judge George F. Dunklee sentenced him to a seven- to ten-year prison term on June 1, 1923. Because Blonger's health had weakened, he stayed in the Denver County jail until October 18, 1923, when he was transferred to the Cañon City, Colorado, penitentiary.

## Impact

Lou Blonger's criminal network affected people in the United States and internationally. Newspapers nationwide covered his trial, emphasizing Blonger's unique role as the mastermind of the largest gang of crooks in U.S. history at that time. Many of Blonger's supporters, including law enforcement personnel, were enraged by his conviction. Blonger became a popular character in local lore, which often romanticized his exploits and fabricated biographical information.

Denied both a pardon and parole, Blonger died within a year of being incarcerated. His will instructed his lawyers to continue demanding that the state supreme court contemplate an appeal to overturn Blonger's guilty verdict. Several victims, Van Cise, and the government successfully secured funds from Blonger's estate.

## Further Reading

Hyde, Stephen, and Geno Zanetti, eds. *Players: Con Men, Hustlers, Gamblers, and Scam Artists*. New York: Thunder's Mouth Press, 2002. Anthology contains several nonfiction essays examining the mind-set and strategies of swindlers.

Murphy, Jan. *Outlaw Tales of Colorado: True Stories of Colorado's Notorious Robbers, Rustlers, and Bandits*. Guilford, Conn.: The Globe Pequot Press, 2006. Includes a chapter featuring Blonger, detailing his confidence scheme involving a mock stock exchange and techniques his swindlers used.

Van Cise, Philip S. *Fighting the Underworld*. 1936. Reprint. New York: Greenwood Press, 1968. Written by the district attorney who prosecuted Blonger, with photos of people, sites, and evidence. Includes glossary and appendix of investigators, financial supporters, and Blonger's crooks.

*—Elizabeth D. Schafer*

**See also:** Apache Kid; Tom Bell; Curly Bill Brocius; Bob Dalton; Emmett Dalton; Bill Doolin; John Wesley Hardin; Doc Holliday; Jesse James; Tom Ketchum; Harry Longabaugh; Bill Longley; Johnny Ringo; Belle Starr; Henry Starr; Hank Vaughan; Cole Younger.

# William H. Bonney

## Western outlaw

**Born:** November 23, 1859; New York, New York
**Died:** July 14, 1881; Fort Sumner, New Mexico Territory
**Also known as:** Henry McCarty (birth name); Billy the Kid; Billy Antrim; Kid Antrim; Billy Bonney
**Major offenses:** Murder and cattle theft
**Active:** 1874-1881
**Locale:** New Mexico Territory
**Sentence:** Death; escaped prison while awaiting execution and was shot to death three months later

### Early Life

William H. Bonney (BAW-nee) was born Henry McCarty in 1859 to Irish immigrants in New York City's slums. Not much is known about his early childhood. Sources suggest that young Henry lived with his widowed mother, Catherine, and his younger brother, Joe, in Indianapolis, Indiana, during the Civil War. In 1870 the family, along with Catherine's future husband, William Antrim, relocated to Wichita, Kansas, where Catherine operated a laundry. Diagnosed with tuberculosis in 1871, Catherine again moved her family, eventually landing in Santa Fe, New Mexico, where she married Antrim on March 1, 1873. The Antrims settled in Silver City, a mining community in the southwestern part of the territory. Henry, now known as Henry Antrim, attended school and reportedly was an ordinary teenager. When his mother died in September, 1874, however, the future outlaw's life changed direction.

### Criminal Career

Now lacking parental guidance, Henry began associating with rough characters. Just a year after Catherine's death, he found himself facing theft charges after stealing a bundle of clothing from a Chinese laundry. Not wanting to stand trial, Henry escaped through the local jail's chimney and made his way into Arizona.

Now nicknamed "The Kid" because of his youth and diminutive size, Henry worked as a teamster and cowboy around Camp Grant. During his two years in Arizona, Henry honed his skills as a gunman and horseman.

While historians often describe the gunfighter as a cheerful and well-liked young man, nobody disagreed that he had a short and violent temper. That temper exploded on August 17, 1877, when seventeen-year-old Henry shot and killed Frank "Windy" Cahill, a much older and stronger man who had made a habit of verbally and physically abusing the teenager.

Now wanted for murder in Arizona, Henry escaped to New Mexico under the alias William "Billy" Bonney. Billy ended up in Lincoln County, New Mexico, where he worked as a cowboy for Englishman John Tunstall. In 1878, the county was dominated by the mercantile monopoly of Lawrence Murphy and James Dolan. Challenging the Murphy-Dolan alliance were Tunstall and a Scotsman named Alexander McSween, who sought to outbid their rivals for government contracts. Billy soon became involved in the Lincoln County War (1878-1879), in which Tunstall was killed by assassins from the Murphy-Dolan faction. During the war Billy rode with the "Regulators," a group of Tunstall employees who sought to avenge the

*William H. Bonney.* (Library of Congress)

### A Man More Sinned Against

"I don't blame you for writing of me as you have. You had to believe other stories, but then I don't know if any one would believe anything good of me anyway," Billy the Kid told a Las Vegas (New Mexico) *Gazette* reporter in 1880. The rumors, exaggerations, and lies about him had already spread. He knew the score. Still, the newspaper gave him a friendly description in 1881:

> He is about five feet eight or nine inches tall, slightly built and lithe, weighing about 140; a frank, open countenance, looking like a school boy, with the traditional silky fuzz on his upper lip; clear blue eyes, with a roguish snap about them; light hair and complexion. He is, in all, quite a handsome looking fellow, the only imperfection being two prominent front teeth slightly protruding like squirrel's teeth, and he has agreeable and winning ways.

In fact, far from the fiery-tempered sociopath that some accounts made him, Billy the Kid was widely liked, even by his foes in the Lincoln County War. He was said to be easygoing, cool under stress, and regularly cheerful. The historian- politician Miguel Antonio Otero, Jr. (1859-1944) wrote in his biography *The Real Billy the Kid* (Houston: Arte Público Press, 1998), "I have been told that Billy had an ungovernable temper; however, I never saw evidences of it. He was always in a pleasant humor when I saw him—laughing, sprightly, and good natured." As a young man, Otero was on the train that took Billy the Kid to jail. They talked at length. Otero admitted:

> I liked the Kid very much . . . and long before we reached Santa Fe, nothing would have pleased me more than to witness his escape. He had his share of good qualities and was very pleasant. He had a reputation for being considerate of the old, the young, and the poor; he was loyal to his friends and above all, loved his mother devotedly. He was unfortunate in starting life, and became a victim of circumstances. In looking back to my first meeting with Billy the Kid, my impressions were most favorable and I can honestly say that he was a man more sinned against than sinning.

death of their employer. For the following year, the two sides engaged in deadly retaliatory warfare. Billy's skills with a gun and his reckless bravado served the Tunstall-McSween faction well during the conflict. On March 9, 1878, the Regulators captured and killed Frank Baker and William Morton, both suspects in Tunstall's murder.

On April 1, 1878, Billy and several Regulators ambushed and killed Sheriff William Brady, an ally of the Murphy-Dolan faction. Just three days later, the Regulators battled Buckshot Roberts, a bounty hunter hired by the opposition, at Blazer's Saw Mill, about forty miles outside Lincoln. After a fierce battle, Dick Brewer, the leader of the Regulators, and Roberts lay dead or dying. The Lincoln County War climaxed in a five-day battle (July

15-19, 1878) in which McSween and several Regulators were also killed. On the final day of the battle, Billy led a gallant escape from a burning building under heavy gunfire.

## Legal Action and Outcome

In the years after the Lincoln County War, Billy teetered back and forth between ranching and rustling cattle. While the territorial governor pardoned most of the participants in the conflict, Billy was indicted for killing Sheriff Brady. He was arrested by the new sheriff, Pat Garrett, in December, 1880. After a questionable trial, the Kid was convicted of murder and sentenced to death. Just as he had several times before, Billy cheated his sentence before it could be carried out. On April 28, 1881, he killed two guards and escaped. The Kid's days were still numbered, as lawmen relentlessly hunted him. Finally, on July 14, 1881, Garrett tracked Billy to Fort Sumner, where he surprised the twenty-one-year-old outlaw under the cover of darkness. "¿Quién es? ¿Quién es? (Who is it?)" Billy asked as he heard someone enter the room where he slept. Without answering, Garrett fired two shots, killing Billy the Kid instantly.

## Impact

Within months of William H. Bonney's death, books and serialized stories began creating the Billy the Kid legend. During the twentieth century, Hollywood movies solidified his status as an American icon. Some described him as a swaggering, homicidal maniac. Others portrayed him as an American Robin Hood who became an outlaw to protect the innocent and the helpless. Somewhere in between these extremes is the historic Billy the Kid. He came of age in a rough frontier world where violence was commonplace. He killed when he thought necessary but not nearly as often as stories suggest. Legend credits Billy the Kid with twenty-one killings. History, however, can confirm only four killings by the Kid's own hand and five or six in which he participated as a member of the Regulators.

## Further Reading

Burns, Walter Noble. *The Saga of Billy the Kid*. New York: Grosset and Dunlap, 1926. A vivid and romanticized biography that helped create the image of Billy the Kid as an American Robin Hood.

O'Neal, Bill. *Encyclopedia of Western Gunfighters*. Norman: University of

Oklahoma Press, 1979. This valuable collection of 587 gunfighter biographies provides a biography of Billy the Kid along with short descriptions of his criminal exploits and gunfights.

Tuska, Jon. *Billy the Kid: His Life and Legend.* 1994. Reprint. Albuquerque: University of New Mexico Press, 1997. A thoroughly researched book that examines fallacies and inaccuracies in previous books, novels, and movies.

Utley, Robert. *Billy the Kid: A Short and Violent Life.* Lincoln: University of Nebraska Press, 1989. An authoritative and objective account of Billy the Kid, written by an eminent Western historian.

*—Mark R. Ellis*

**See also:** Apache Kid; Tom Bell; Curly Bill Brocius; Butch Cassidy; Bob Dalton; Emmett Dalton; Bill Doolin; John Wesley Hardin; Doc Holliday; Jesse James; Tom Ketchum; Harry Longabaugh; Bill Longley; Joaquín Murieta; Johnny Ringo; Belle Starr; Henry Starr; Hank Vaughan; Cole Younger.

# John Wilkes Booth

## Assassin of President Abraham Lincoln

**Born:** May 10, 1838; near Bel Air, Maryland

**Died:** April 26, 1865; near Bowling Green, Virginia

**Cause of notoriety:** Booth assassinated President Abraham Lincoln soon after the end of the Civil War.

**Active:** 1865

**Locale:** Washington, D.C.

### Early Life

John Wilkes Booth (jahn wihlks bewth) was one of ten children of the noted tragic actor Junius Brutus Booth. The younger Booth made his first theatrical appearance at seventeen and soon had established a solid reputation as an interpreter of many leading roles in the plays of William Shakespeare, particularly that of Romeo in *Romeo and Juliet* (c. 1595). Muscular, dark-haired, and handsome, Booth was perfect for the part.

Although he seldom prepared well for his roles, his innate ability and resplendent style carried him through his performances. Having mastered most of the major male roles in Shakespeare's plays, Booth toured the nation performing them. His good looks and outstanding talent made him irresistible to women.

## Criminal Career

When the Civil War erupted in 1861, most of Booth's family supported the Union. Booth, on the other hand, was violently pro-Confederate. He deplored Abraham Lincoln and, by 1864, had devised a scheme to kidnap the president and hold him hostage, to be ransomed only on the release of Confederate prisoners of war.

When this plot failed to materialize, Booth devised another scheme. As the Union victory in the Civil War appeared inevitable, he met with several conspirators at Mary Surratt's boardinghouse in Washington, D.C., and with them outlined his plan to assassinate the president, the vice president, and Lincoln's cabinet members. Booth, assuming the responsibility for killing Lincoln himself, wanted these assassinations to occur almost simultaneously.

On Good Friday, 1865, Booth learned from the manager of Ford's Theater, where he was well known and had often acted, that the president was expected to attend the evening performance of Tom Taylor's *Our American Cousin* (pr. 1865). The Lincolns were ambivalent about attending the play, but the president craved relaxation after an exhausting week. Mrs. Lincoln invited General and Mrs. Ulysses S. Grant to join them, but the Grants were about to leave town, so they declined their invitation.

Booth was determined to kill Lincoln that night. Early in the evening, he fortified himself with brandy at a bar near Ford's Theater. After the play began, he entered the theater and burst into the president's box, where he shot Lincoln, firing a single bullet from his derringer into the president's brain. An accomplice attacked Secretary of State William H. Seward at about the same time and almost killed him. Plans to assassinate Vice President Andrew Johnson went awry.

In the confusion following his shooting of Lincoln, Booth jumped onto the stage, but he became entangled in some drapery, causing him to land at an awkward angle and break his leg. Despite this injury, Booth limped from the theater, where David E. Herold joined him. The two rode to Maryland, stopping along the way to have Dr. Samuel Mudd set Booth's broken leg.

The fugitives hid out in Maryland for several days before making their way to Richard Garrett's farm near Bowling Green, Virginia. Meanwhile, Secretary of War Edwin M. Stanton launched a massive hunt to track down the fugitives. It was eleven days after the shooting and ten days after President Lincoln's death on April 15, 1865, that government agents tracked Booth to the farm where he was hiding.

With the farm surrounded, Herold, who had retreated into Garrett's tobacco barn with Booth, surrendered. Attempting to flush Booth from the barn, his pursuers set fire to the building. A shot rang out. It remains unclear whether Booth shot himself or Sergeant Boston Corbett fired the shot. At any rate, Booth, now dead, clearly could not be tried for Lincoln's assassination.

*John Wilkes Booth.*
(Library of Congress)

## Booth's Four Chances

John Wilkes Booth succeeded in assassinating President Lincoln after passing up three earlier opportunities, all which came to him because of his own soaring celebrity. He began acting in 1855. Five years later he was a star, his acting career flourishing. He was making $20,000 a year, and although based in Richmond, Virginia, he was in demand everywhere.

Booth was appearing as Duke Pescara in *The Apostate* when president-elect Lincoln attended a performance in New York while on his way to Washington, D.C. Booth, whose sympathies lay with the South, had not yet developed his deep loathing for Lincoln, so the president was only another audience member to him then. That changed once the Civil War started. Booth's hatred was swift and implacable. By the time that the president again saw him perform—on November 9, 1863—Booth could not disguise his feelings. This time the play was *The Marble Heart*, and the performance took place at Ford's Theater in Washington, D.C. Booth portrayed Raphael. A member of the president's party, Mary Clay, later recounted the evening:

> In the theater President and Mrs. Lincoln, Miss Sallie Clay and I, Mr. Nicolay and Mr. Hay, occupied the same box which the year after saw Mr. Lincoln slain by Booth. I do not recall the play, but Wilkes Booth played the part of the villain. The box was right on the stage, with a railing around it. Mr. Lincoln sat next to the rail, I next to Mrs. Lincoln, Miss Sallie Clay and the other gentlemen farther around. Twice Booth in uttering disagreeable threats in the play came very near and put his finger close to Mr. Lincoln's face; when he came a third time I was impressed by it, and said, "Mr. Lincoln, he looks as if he meant that for you." "Well," he said, "he does look pretty sharp at me, doesn't he?" At the same theater, the next April, Wilkes Booth shot our dear President.

Mary Clay misspoke the date by a year, and by then Booth had again come perilously close to Lincoln. He attended the second inaugural ball on March 4, 1865, with his fiancée, Lucy Hale. Afterward he said to a friend, "What an excellent chance I had to kill the President, if I had wished, on inauguration day!" Forty-one days later, he succeeded.

### Legal Action and Outcome

Although John Wilkes Booth's death placed him beyond the scope of the law, various conspirators were arrested and, in May, 1865, those most obviously involved were brought to trial. Many were given long prison sentences, and, on July 6, after a speedy trial that was a mockery of justice, four were sentenced to be hanged, including Herold and Surratt. The sentence was carried out the following day before swarms of spectators gathered at Washington's Old Arsenal to witness the executions.

## Impact

One impact of Lincoln's assassination, the first to befall an American president, was that presidential security was very much increased to prevent a recurrence of such a devastating event. A more historically important impact, however, was that Lincoln's death turned him into a martyr and greatly enhanced the nation's appreciation of him both as a man and as president. Scorned by many during his first term of office and reviled by many after his election to a second term, Lincoln assumed a hallowed position in American history. In most polls that measure the popularity of the American presidents, Lincoln's name leads the list.

## Further Reading

Clark, Champ. *The Assassination: Death of the President*. Alexandria, Va.: Time/Life, 1987. An accessible account of Lincoln's assassination written for general audiences.

Clarke, Asia Booth. *John Wilkes Booth: A Sister's Memoir*. Edited and with an introduction by Terry Alford. Jackson: University of Mississippi Press, 1996. Booth's sister provides details about her brother's early life and upbringing. Somewhat biased but nevertheless valuable, as is the penetrating introduction.

Goodrich, Thomas. *The Darkest Dawn: Lincoln, Booth, and the Great American Tragedy*. Bloomington: Indiana University Press, 2005. Part 2 focuses on the actual assassination and serves as an excellent presentation.

Hanchett, William. *The Lincoln Murder Conspiracy*. Urbana: University of Illinois Press, 1986. Hanchett reviews the varied threads of the conspiracy aimed at eliminating Lincoln, his vice president, and members of his cabinet.

Higham, Charles. *Murdering Mr. Lincoln: A New Detection of the Nineteenth Century's Most Famous Case*. Beverly Hills, Calif.: New Millennium Press, 2004. Detailed information about plans to assassinate Lincoln with special emphasis in chapter 8 on the actual assassination.

*—R. Baird Shuman*

**See also:** Leon Czolgosz; Charles Julius Guiteau; Lee Harvey Oswald; Lewis Powell.

# Lizzie Borden
## Accused murderer

**Born:** July 19, 1860; Fall River, Massachusetts
**Died:** June 1, 1927; Fall River, Massachusetts
**Also known as:** Lizzie Andrew Borden (full name); Lizbeth of Maplecroft; Lizbeth Andrews Borden
**Cause of notoriety:** Borden was tried and acquitted for the murders of her father and stepmother.
**Active:** 1892
**Locale:** Fall River, Massachusetts

### Early Life

Lizzie Andrew Borden (LIH-zee AN-droo BOHR-dehn) was born to Andrew J. Borden and his wife, Sarah Morse, on July 19, 1860, in Fall River, Massachusetts. Her father had hoped for a boy, accounting for Lizzie's unusual middle name. She had an older sister, Emma, with whom she remained close throughout much of her life. Sarah Borden died when Lizzie was a small child of about two or three years old. A few years afterward, Mr. Borden married Abby Durfee Gray, a woman in her late thirties.

Lizzie called her stepmother "Mother" for many years and then alternately called her Mrs. Borden. She remained distant from both of her parents after her father purchased property for Abby, despite his buying properties of equal value for Lizzie and Emma. This purchase, to which the rift is attributed, had seemingly indicated to both Lizzie and Emma that their father went to an extreme and expensive length to please his wife.

Lizzie had red hair and prominent pale eyes and liked to have her picture taken. In spite of the difficulties of her relationship with her father and stepmother in later years, Lizzie and her father were said to be very close.

Lizzie's father had begun his professional career as an undertaker in Fall River. He became a bank president and an astute businessman. At the time of his death, Mr. Borden was worth an estimated $250,000—a huge sum in 1892. Despite his acquired wealth, the family continued to live in the "unfashionable" part of Fall River. The children were reared in a home that was small, without running water or electricity and using food that was past its prime as a result of a lack of refrigeration. Such conditions are reported to have been against Lizzie's liking.

Like many women of her day, Lizzie had no formal career of which to speak. However, she busied herself with many social and religious-based organizations. She was an active member and secretary-treasurer for the Central Congregational Church, a member of the Ladies' Fruit and Flower Mission, a member of the Women's Christian Temperance Union, and a board member of the Good Samaritan Charity Hospital. She also taught Sunday school class for Chinese children.

### THE MURDERS

The Borden parents were both murdered at their home, killed by blows to the head with an ax. Lizzie was charged with the murders, which took place

### IF NOT LIZZIE, WHO?

More than a century following Lizzie Borden's murder acquittal, crime writers, Fall River residents, conspiracy buffs, and distinguished jurists continued to publish arguments for or against Borden's guilt. Some insist that she killed her father and stepmother to get control of the family wealth; others feel she did it while deranged in an epileptic fit. Those that think her to be innocent, if only partly, sometimes fix on other suspects.

- One theory has Lizzie's sister Emma as the murderer, with Lizzie's connivance. Again, the motive is envy over the portion of their father's estate dedicated to their stepmother in his will. Emma pretends to be out for the day and sneaks back for the murders. Lizzie allows herself to be arrested, and the sisters support each other in the cover-up.
- A second theory indicts Bridget, the Irish maid. Angered at having to wash windows on a blistering hot day, she quarrels with Mrs. Borden and later kills her. Later still, she kills Mr. Borden to prevent his reporting her earlier argument with his wife. A variation on this theory again has Lizzie as a co-conspirator who covers up the crime.
- An even stranger theory involves an illegitimate son of Mr. Borden, William. Mentally incapacitated and bitter at his father's treatment of him—and perhaps egged on by his half sisters—he does the killing. His sisters, their Uncle John Morse, the attending physician, and their lawyer all work together to protect William.
- From there, the speculations grow even more bizarre: Uncle Morse, the physician, and even a Chinese Sunday school student of Borden are all considered.
- The mystery endures into the twenty-first century. What most analysts of the case do agree upon, however, is that Borden's defense attorneys were far more skillful than the state's prosecutor. They made sure that two pieces of crucial evidence—Borden's conflicting testimony during the inquest and a report of her attempt to buy prussic acid (a poison) before the murders—were excluded from the trial. A friendly jury did not harm her chances either.

on August 4, 1892. At the time of the crime, her sister, Emma, was away visiting friends, and the family home was occupied by Lizzie, her parents, housekeeper Bridget Sullivan, and her biological mother's brother, John Morse, who was visiting from out of town.

Lizzie was suspected of having committed the murders for several reasons, including her conflicting answers at the inquest, her supposed lack of despair at her parents' deaths, her acknowledgment of the strain between her and her parents, and her attempted purchase of prussic acid. Others, such as members of the Fall River community, did not believe that a young woman from her background could have committed such a crime. Her sister and the church championed her innocence, while others testified against her.

### Legal Action and Outcome

An inquest, preliminary hearing, and trial were held. Lizzie never took the stand in her own defense. However, she was acquitted of all charges, and her acquittal was initially cheered by the townspeople. This reception was short-lived, however, and Lizzie was to face great isolation from her community. She purchased a new home, added an "s" to her middle name, and became known as Lizbeth of Maplecroft. She spent her years traveling to New York and Boston and befriending animals and people of the theater.

Lizzie died on June 1, 1927. She was followed in death, nine days later, by Emma. She and her sister were buried alongside their parents, stepmother, and baby sister, who had died shortly after birth. Much of Lizzie's money was left to the care of animals.

### Impact

Much, but not all, of what has been written about Lizzie Borden states that she indeed was guilty of ax murders that resulted from ten blows to her father and twenty to her stepmother—numbers that vary in the verse that children have subsequently sung about the case:

> Lizzie Borden took an ax
> And gave her mother forty whacks.
> When she saw what she had done
> She gave her father forty-one.

The controversy and mystery surrounding Lizzie and the Fall River murders continued to fascinate people into the twenty-first century, as evidenced by the continual writing of books, a Web site, and a museum, all of which introduce new generations to the case.

**Further Reading**

Avery, Donald R. "The Case of Lizzie Borden." In *The Press on Trial: Crimes and Trials as Media Events*, edited by Lloyd Chiasson, Jr. Westport, Conn.: Greenwood Press. 1997. The chapter provides the reader with a detailed look at the specifics of the Borden case, as well as the role such media outlets (primarily newspapers and reporters) played both in the case and in shaping the public's view of the crime.

Axelrod-Contrada, Joan. *The Lizzie Borden "Ax Murder" Trial: A Headline Court Case*. Berkeley Heights, N.J.: Enslow, 2000. Provides photographs of the main participants, transcript excerpts, and the known facts surrounding the murders. Also included are characterizations of the time period of the murders, along with a chronology of events.

Masterton, Willie L. *Lizzie Didn't Do It!* Boston: Brandon, 2000. The author provides newspaper headlines, photographs, character sketches, and the coroner's statement in his discussion of the Borden case. Uses modern-day forensic analyses, as well as the identification of the likely assailant, to determine that Lizzie Borden was innocent of the crimes.

*—Nancy A. Horton*

**See also:** Marie Hilley.

# Christopher John Boyce

## Spy and bank robber

**Born:** February 16, 1953; Santa Monica, California

**Also known as:** The Falcon; Jim Namcheck; Tony Lester

**Major offenses:** Espionage, escape from federal custody, and bank robbery

**Active:** 1970-1981

**Locale:** Mexico City, Mexico; California; Idaho; Montana; and Washington State

**Sentence:** Forty years' imprisonment for espionage; three years' imprisonment for prison escape; twenty-five years' imprisonment for bank robbery; served twenty-five years

## Early Life

Christopher John Boyce (BOYS) was one of nine children born to Charles and Noreen Boyce. He grew up in an upper-middle-class area of Southern California. Boyce was an altar boy at the Roman Catholic Church that he attended with his family in Palos Verde, California. During these early years, he developed an interest in peregrine falcons and a love of the outdoors (he was later nicknamed the Falcon).

Boyce dropped out of college. His father, a former Federal Bureau of Investigation (FBI) agent who was working in private security, helped him get a job at TRW, a defense-related American corporation. Boyce eventually was given a desk job that gave him access to the "vault," where, among other stored items, was information on satellite systems.

## Criminal Career

Boyce soon teamed up with his boyhood friend Daulton Lee. Lee had become involved in drugs—he used and sold marijuana and cocaine (leading to his nickname, the Snowman). Boyce and Lee developed a plan to become involved in espionage and international intrigue by selling information on American satellite systems to agents of the Soviet Union. Their plan included making contact with Soviet intelligence agents through the Soviet embassy in Mexico.

Boyce decided that being a spy would be an adventure and would enable him to act on his growing antigovernment ideals. It appeared that Lee was more motivated by the seventy-seven thousand dollars reportedly paid to the pair by the Soviets. Boyce later said that he had received only about twenty thousand dollars of the money that the Soviets paid his partner, and he denied that money was his motive.

## Legal Action and Outcome

In December, 1976, Lee was erroneously arrested in front of the Soviet embassy in Mexico City for the murder of a police officer. He was interrogated after a top-secret microfilm was found in his possession, and he confessed to being a Soviet spy. He also implicated Boyce, who was soon arrested.

*Christopher John Boyce.* (AP/Wide World Photos)

Boyce and Lee had separate jury trials for espionage. Their trials were held in front of the same judge in the federal district court in Los Angeles, California. Boyce testified on his own behalf, denying that he had any contact with the Soviets or their embassy in Mexico City. The jury apparently found Boyce unconvincing and came back with a guilty verdict after deliberating only a few hours. He was convicted of espionage on June 20, 1977, and sentenced to forty years in federal custody. Lee was also convicted in his jury trial. Both Lee and Boyce were sent to the U.S. penitentiary in Lompoc, California, to serve their sentences.

Boyce escaped from the penitentiary on January 21, 1980. He reportedly made a papier-mâché head to trick guards into thinking he was asleep in his cell. He hid for several hours in a small drainage hole inside the fence of the penitentiary. He then used a homemade ladder and pieces of tin to get through the fence.

After his escape, Boyce reportedly roamed the countryside for several days before finding a friend whom he knew from prison, who already had been released. His friend suggested that Boyce go up to Bonners Ferry, Idaho, and find a woman named Gloria White. According to the friend, White would help him.

Boyce located White in the Bonners Ferry area. White let Boyce stay at her cabin, and when Boyce expressed an interest in robbing banks, she taught him how to disguise himself using stage makeup. She also showed him that wearing baggy clothing and putting cotton in his mouth would make him look heavier and change his appearance.

During his nineteen months as a fugitive, Boyce robbed banks in Idaho, Washington State, and Montana. He became somewhat of a colorful local character when he purchased a mule and would often bring it with him when he came into Bonners Ferry. He also took flying lessons in Washington. It was reported that Boyce intended to fly to the Soviet Union via Alaska, where he believed he would receive a hero's welcome. Boyce eventually was arrested by U.S. marshals in Port Angeles, Washington, on August 21, 1981.

In late 1981, he pleaded guilty to the escape charge and received an additional three-year sentence. Then, in March, 1982, Boyce was tried and convicted of bank robberies in Idaho, Washington, and Montana. He was sentenced to twenty-five years' imprisonment, to be served at the end of his previous sentences for espionage and escape. White was also convicted for her role as a co-conspirator in the robberies. Boyce was released on parole on September 16, 2002.

## Impact

The satellite secrets sold by Christopher John Boyce and Daulton Lee to the Soviets greatly compromised U.S. intelligence-gathering capabilities and slowed the progress of U.S. and Soviet disarmament talks. In October, 1979, the FBI relinquished authority to investigate escapes to the U.S. Marshals Service. Boyce's escape in January, 1980, became the first high-profile fugitive case investigated by the marshals. The event helped establish the marshals' reputation as fugitive investigators.

Boyce and Lee's adventures became the basis for Robert Lindsey's best-selling 1979 book *The Falcon and the Snowman*, which was adapted to film in 1985 and starred Timothy Hutton and Sean Penn in the lead roles. Lindsey's book was followed by another in 1983, *The Flight of the Falcon.*

**Further Reading**

Lindsey, Robert. *The Falcon and the Snowman: A True Story of Friendship and Espionage*. New York: Simon & Schuster, 1979. A chronicle of the lives of Boyce and Lee up to and through the time of their trials and convictions for espionage.

_______. *The Flight of the Falcon*. New York: Simon & Schuster, 1983. An account of Boyce's escape from the penitentiary at Lompoc, his activities while a fugitive, and the massive manhunt leading to his arrest.

Serrano, Richard. "The Falcon and the Fallout." *The Los Angeles Times*, March 2, 2003. An account of Boyce's life at the time of his prison release.

*—Gerald P. Fisher*

**See also:** Aldrich Ames; Robert Philip Hanssen; Daulton Lee.

# Arthur Bremer

## Would-be assassin of Governor George Wallace

**Born:** August 21, 1950; Milwaukee, Wisconsin
**Also known as:** Arthur Herman Bremer (full name)
**Major offense:** Attempted murder of presidential candidate George Wallace, governor of Alabama
**Active:** May 15, 1972
**Locale:** Laurel, Maryland
**Sentence:** Sixty-three years in prison, later reduced to fifty-three years; served thirty-five years

**Early Life**

As a child, Arthur Bremer (BREH-mur) had little communication with his parents. Bremer's father was a Milwaukee truck driver who went to work, paid the bills, argued with his wife, and occasionally drank alcohol to relieve his frustrations. In short, Bremer grew up in an uncommunicative and conflict-ridden household. Bremer became emotionally withdrawn, filled with anxiety, and compliant in his behavior. At the age of eight or nine, he began fantasizing about committing suicide by lying down on railroad tracks near his home. During this same time period, Bremer began to find some peace by attending church and thought about becoming a priest. However, his family then moved away, and he never returned to church. After he failed the fifth grade, he thought of commiting suicide but never attempted such a thing. He graduated from high school in 1968, an average student. Although his high school years were fairly uneventful, during his senior year his parents did notice that Bremer changed his behavior dramatically. His passive compliance began to disappear, and he turned into a very aggressive and outspoken person, often irritated by his parents.

After high school, Bremer worked as a busboy at the Milwaukee Athletic Club and at an upscale restaurant. He also worked as a janitor at an elementary school for $2.70 per hour. Few coworkers remembered Bremer because he merely performed his menial tasks and rarely spoke to others. Bremer enrolled at the Milwaukee Technical College, where he took courses in psychology, photography, art, and writing in the fall, 1970, semester. He registered for spring courses but then dropped out and also moved out of his parents' house after a heated argument with his father. During this same time period, Bremer was demoted from busboy to kitchen worker because of his idiosyncratic habits such as mumbling to himself and whistling. After his demotion, Bremer filed a grievance with the Milwaukee Community Relations Commission.

While working at the elementary school, the twenty-one-year-old Bremer asked a fifteen-year-old student, Joan Pembrick, for a date. Pembrick would be the first and only love in his life. The two dated for roughly two months, but Pembrick quickly became frustrated with Bremer's immature behavior and offensive language.

### **Criminal Career**

After Pembrick's mother informed Bremer that her daughter wanted to end their relationship, Bremer became obsessed with suicidal and homicidal fantasies. He felt that his life was meaningless, and he became even more alienated from society. Wishing for fame and notoriety, Bremer developed a plan to assassinate President Richard M. Nixon while he was visiting Canada on March 1, 1972, but Bremer was unable to get close enough to the president in order to carry out the assassination.

Bremer then decided to murder Alabama governor and presidential candidate George Wallace, believing that he could get close enough to shoot Wallace, who did not have as many security guards as President Nixon. On

May 15, 1972, Bremer shot Wallace in Laurel, Maryland, after the presidential candidate delivered a speech before a crowd of roughly one thousand supporters. With a .38-caliber revolver, Bremer shot five times at Wallace, who survived the assassination attempt. However, one of the four bullets that hit Wallace lodged in the governor's spine, leaving him paralyzed for life.

### Legal Action and Outcome

A Maryland jury found Bremer guilty of attempted murder after a five-day trial in which evidence was presented from eight psychiatrists and two psychologists who had examined Bremer. The psychologists and psychiatrists divided on the issue of Bremer's sanity. Ultimately, the jury concluded, based upon Bremer's diary, that he knew what he was doing when he attempted to kill Wallace and also understood the consequences of his actions. In the end, Bremer's motive was that of a sociopath who wanted to commit a perverse act to harm society and gain publicity for himself. In short, he committed a premeditated act of violence simply because he felt like it.

Bremer was imprisoned at the Maryland Correctional Institute and was scheduled to be eligible for parole in 2015. He was released on November 9, 2007, after serving more than thirty-five years.

### Impact

The assassination attempt on Wallace caused conspiracy theorists to speculate that Arthur Bremer had ties to the Republican Party and to Nixon's reelection campaign. Nixon reportedly met with Federal Bureau of Investigation agent Mark Felt to discuss such concerns about the assassination attempt. Wallace was convinced that Nixon had ordered the assassination attempt and vowed revenge against Nixon by announcing that he would run for president in 1972 as a third-party candidate. Wallace, however, had to drop out of the race because of health problems related to the shooting.

Interestingly, Bremer's relationship with the fifteen-year-old Pembrick would later serve as inspiration for the Robert DeNiro character in the 1976 film *Taxi Driver*. DeNiro's character, a potential assassin named Travis Bickle, awkwardly tries to establish a relationship with an attractive young woman. Ironically, the Bickle character in *Taxi Driver* served as motivation for John Hinckley, Jr., to attempt the assassination of President Ronald Reagan in 1981.

### Further Reading

Bremer, Arthur H. *An Assassin's Diary*. New York: Harper's Magazine Press, 1973. Bremer's diary, in which he states that he was not opposed to George Wallace's politics but that his primary motive was to achieve fame and notoriety. He also states that, prior to his assassination attempt on Wallace, he had also stalked President Richard Nixon.

Clarke, James W. "Arthur Herman Bremer." Chapter 6 in *American Assassins: The Darker Side of Politics*. Rev. ed. Princeton, N.J.: Princeton University Press, 1990. Clarke develops a typology for analyzing sixteen political assassins in American history.

Healy, Thomas S. *The Two Deaths of George Wallace: The Question of Forgiveness*. Montgomery, Ala.: Black Belt Press, 1996. Explores the mind of Arthur Bremer by tracing his movements prior to the assassination attempt on George Wallace.

—*Scott P. Johnson*

**See also:** Samuel Joseph Byck; Lynette Fromme; John Hinckley, Jr.; Giuseppe Zangara.

## John R. Brinkley

**Medical fraudster**

**Born:** July 8, 1885; Jackson County, North Carolina

**Died:** May 26, 1942; San Antonio, Texas

**Also known as:** John Romulus Brinkley (full name); John Richard Brinkley; Goat Gland Doctor

**Cause of notoriety:** Brinkley claimed in his controversial "goat gland operation" to restore male virility. He was sued for malpractice and for libel and was indicted for mail fraud by the U.S. Postal Service.

**Active:** 1918-1942

**Locale:** Milford, Kansas; Villa Acuña, Mexico; and Del Rio, Texas

### Early Life

John R. Brinkley (BRIHN-klee) was the son of John Brinkley, an unlettered country doctor, and Candice Burnett. Orphaned at age ten, the young

Brinkley was raised by an aunt. He received his early education in Tuckaseigee, North Carolina, but never earned a diploma. In his mid-teens, he led a nomadic life and worked as a telegrapher. From 1907 through 1915 he received dubious credentials from schools of little repute, such as the Eclectic Medical University of Kansas City and the Bennett Medical College of Chicago.

### Medical Career

In spite of his questionable degrees, Brinkley was licensed to practice medicine in Arkansas and later established his practice in Milford, Kansas. He began performing his notorious "goat gland operation" in 1918, which involved implantation of Toggenberg goat glands in human men and which Brinkley claimed could restore male fertility as well as virility. Soon the $750 rejuvenation operation was in high demand, and Brinkley became wealthy.

In 1923 he created Kansas's first radio station and only the fourth commercial station in the United States. KFKB (which stood for Kansas's First, Kansas's Best) became a powerful radio station that broadcast and promoted ads for Brinkley's secret remedies. Brinkley also organized a network of pharmacies in his radio coverage area, known as the National Dr. Brinkley Pharmaceutical Association, and prescribed medicine by number which one could get only at the local affiliated pharmacy, which sent a portion of the profits to Brinkley.

In 1928 Dr. Morris Fishbein, secretary of the American Medical Association, lambasted Brinkley for diagnosing illnesses over the radio as well as promoting medicines on the air. As a result, the State Medical Board of Kansas revoked Brinkley's medical license in 1930. That year, the Federal Radio Commission would not renew his broadcasting license. Still widely popular, Brinkley next ran for governor, but none of his three campaigns—in 1930, 1932, and 1934—met with success.

In 1931 he received authority from Mexican officials to assemble the world's most powerful transmitter at Villa Acuña, Mexico. Under the call sign of XER, Brinkley used his new "border blaster" transmitter to reach listeners as far north as Canada. In 1933 he moved his entire medical staff and facilities across the border to the Roswell Hotel in Del Rio, Texas. The Mexican government issued a license for Brinkley to begin broadcasting from his 500-kilowatt transmitter under the new call letters XERA. The new

AM station, with its powerful antennas, could broadcast throughout the United States and Canada, and even as far as the Soviet Union. Brinkley's fabulously lucrative business supported his flashy lifestyle. Estimates are that he earned twelve million dollars between 1933 and 1938. In 1938 he moved his medical activities to Little Rock, Arkansas.

About the time Brinkley moved back to Arkansas, he lost a libel suit against Fishbein, fought numerous malpractice suits, battled the Internal Revenue Service over back taxes, and was indicted for mail fraud by the U.S. Postal Service. Soon, Brinkley's station was out of business, and in January, 1941, he filed for bankruptcy. When World War II began in Europe, Brinkley further provoked the U.S. government by allowing Nazi sympathizers to broadcast their propaganda. In 1941, XERA was expropriated by the Mexican government, and three days later Brinkley suffered a massive heart attack. On May 26, 1942, he died in San Antonio of heart failure. He was buried in Memphis, Tennessee.

## Impact

John R. Brinkley's role in exposing America's vulnerability to medical quackery cannot be understated, but he had an equally important impact on legislation to regulate radio broadcasting. Because of Brinkley's actions, in April of 1941 the Mexican government struck a deal with the United States to restrict cross-border links between U.S. radio studios and Mexican transmitters through the Communications Act of 1934, commonly known as the Brinkley Act, which led to the shutdown of XERA and placed limitations on the abuse of broadcasting.

## Further Reading

Juhnke, Eric S. *Quacks and Crusaders: The Fabulous Careers of John Brinkley, Norman Baker, and Harry Hoxsey*. Lawrence: University Press of Kansas, 2002. A major contribution to the understanding of medical quackery of yesteryear and today, this book examines the careers of Brinkley, Baker, and Hoxsey.

Lee, R. Alton. *The Bizarre Careers of John R. Brinkley*. Lexington: University Press of Kentucky, 2002. Perhaps the most complete account of Brinkley's life, delivered in academic yet humorous detail.

Young, James Harvey. *The Medical Messiahs: A Social History of Health Quackery in Twentieth-Century America*. 1966. Reprint. Princeton, N.J.:

Princeton University Press, 1992. Summarizes the development of patent medicines in America from the 1906 Pure Food and Drugs Act through the mid-1960's.

—*Wayne J. Pitts*

**See also:** Larry C. Ford; Linda Burfield Hazzard; Michael Swango.

# Curly Bill Brocius

## Western gunslinger and outlaw

**Born:** c. 1840; possibly in or near Crawfordsville, Indiana
**Died:** Probably March 24, 1882; probably near Iron Springs (now Mescal Springs), Arizona
**Also known as:** William Brocius Graham (birth name); William Brocius (full name); William Bresnaham; Curly Bill
**Cause of notoriety:** Brocius, as a member of the cattle-rustling and stagecoach-robbing Cowboys gang, associated with some of the best-known outlaws in the American West and was believed to be responsible for at least eight (and possibly thirty-two) murders.
**Active:** 1878-1882
**Locale:** Arizona, New Mexico, Texas, and Mexico

### Early Life

Evidence suggests that William "Curly Bill" Brocius (BRO-shyuhs) began life in the 1840's as William Graham, a struggling farmer in pre-Civil War Indiana. Graham was married with three children. Tired of being poor, Graham accepted five hundred dollars to perform military duty in place of a drafted wealthy man. When the Civil War ended in 1865, Graham did not return home but wandered the South. Returning to Indiana in 1869, Graham found that his wife had remarried and had had another child. Angry, Graham left Indiana.

Brocius has been described as somewhat heavyset, with dark skin, dark eyes, and thick, curly black hair. A portion of his left ear was missing, shot off by a Texas Ranger. In a separate incident, Brocius was shot in the left side of the neck, the bullet exiting his right cheek. No documented photographs of Brocius exist, though one photograph shows a man fitting his de-

### Bill Gets a Bullet

*On May 26, 1881, the* Arizona Weekly Star *reported a typical brawl involving Curly Bill and the Cowboys:*

A party of 8 or 9 cowboys, Curly Bill and his partner Jim Wallace among the number, were enjoying themselves in their usual manner, when deputy Sheriff Breakenridge of Tombstone, who was at Galeyville on business, happened along.

Wallace made some insulting remark to the deputy at the same time flourishing his revolver in an aggressive manner. Breakenridge did not pay much attention to this "break" of Wallace but quietly turned around and left the party. Shortly after this, Curly Bill, who it would seem had a friendly feeling for Breakenridge, insisted that Wallace should go and find him and apologize for the insult given. . . . By this time Curly Bill who had drank just enough to make him quarrelsome, was in one of his most dangerous moods and evidently desirous of increasing his record as a man killer. He commenced to abuse Wallace, who, by the way, had some pretensions himself as a desperado and bad man generally and finally said, "You d-d Lincoln county s-of a b—, I'll kill you anyhow." Wallace immediately went outside the door of the saloon, Curly Bill following close behind him. Just as the latter stepped outside, Wallace, who had meanwhile drawn his revolver, fired, the ball entering penetrating the left side of Curly Bill's neck and passing through, came out the right cheek, not breaking the jawbone. A scene of the wildest excitement ensued in the town. . . .

The wounded and apparently dying desperado was taken into an adjoining building, and a doctor summoned to dress his wounds. After examining the course of the bullet, the doctor pronounced the wound dangerous but not necessarily fatal, the chances for and against recovery being about equal. Wallace and Curly Bill have been Partners and fast friends for the past 4 or 6 months and so far is known, there was no cause for the quarrel, it being simply a drunken brawl.

scription with a bullet-wound scar to the right cheek. All life descriptions of Brocius share one common trait: Curly Bill was unburdened by a conscience.

## Criminal Career

Records of Brocius's criminal career first appear in the late 1870's, when he rode with cattle rustlers led by John Kinney, a central figure in the Lincoln County War. In 1878, Brocius, then using the alias William Bresnaham, helped rob an army wagon suspected of harboring cash. One soldier died in the attack, and after a shoot-out with Texas Rangers, Brocius was captured. He was charged with attempted robbery but not murder, and he was convicted and sentenced to five years in prison. He escaped and arrived in

Arizona in 1878 with a cattle herd bound for the San Carlos Apache Indian Reservation.

Upon his arrival in Tombstone, Brocius began his association with the outlaw gang that called itself the Cowboys, led by Newman "Old Man" Clanton. The Cowboys were a loose confederation whose principal occupation was stealing cattle and robbing stagecoaches, though members were free to pursue individual acts of criminal enterprise. The gang was protected by local law enforcement, notably Tombstone sheriff John Behan. Behan used Brocius as his "tax collector," and Curly Bill gained a reputation for shooting "taxpayers" who did not pay Behan's extortionary demands.

In 1881, during a drunken rampage in Tombstone, Brocius was asked to disarm by Marshal Fred White. While Brocius was surrendering his revolvers, one discharged and mortally wounded the marshal. Deputy Sheriff Wyatt Earp, arriving soon after, clubbed Brocius and arrested him. White gave a dying statement to witnesses that the shooting was accidental. Brocius was acquitted subsequently of a murder charge, with Earp testifying on his behalf regarding the accidental nature of White's death. Despite this, Brocius never forgave Earp for humiliating him with a pistol-whipping in front of Tombstone residents and his Cowboy associates.

Following Old Man Clanton's death in 1881, Curly Bill Brocius became the primary leader of the Cowboys. At that time the gang had more than four hundred members in Arizona, New Mexico, and old Mexico and had become the largest rustling operation in American history. In some instances, gang members rustled thousands of head of cattle at a time, and they did so with a total disregard to the international border with Mexico. This angered Mexican officials and President James Garfield, who ordered the gang be stopped at all costs.

In July, 1881, Brocius and Johnny Ringo rode to New Mexico for a revenge killing of two store owners who had killed two Cowboys during an attempted robbery. During this time, the men also led an attack on a cattle herd, killing six men. Brocius was out of Tombstone during the infamous gunfight at the O.K. Corral. Angered by the deaths of his comrades by the Earps and John "Doc" Holliday, Brocius masterminded the attack on Virgil Earp and the killing of Morgan Earp. These attacks began the legendary vendetta involving the Earps and the Cowboys.

The death of Curly Bill Brocius is linked to the legendary Earp vendetta ride. In March, 1882, after receiving information that Brocius and other

Cowboys were near Iron Springs, Arizona, Wyatt Earp, Holliday, and three other men rode to the area. The Earp posse was ambushed by the Cowboys; during the battle and at point-blank range, Curly Bill and Wyatt Earp faced each other, both discharging double shotgun blasts. Pellets from Brocius's gun tore through Earp's clothing. Earp's double blast took Brocius in the stomach, nearly tearing him in half.

## Impact

Despite the presidential order against the Cowboys, as well as his reputation as a killer and countless known criminal acts, Curly Bill Brocius's influence was such that he was never formally wanted for any crime in Arizona. The character of Brocius recurred in several well-known Hollywood films, including *Hour of the Gun* (1967), *Tombstone* (1993), and *Wyatt Earp* (1994).

## Further Reading

Breakenridge, William M. *Helldorado: Bringing the Law to the Mesquite*. New York: Houghton Mifflin, 1928. Memoirs of Sheriff Breakenridge and the only firsthand account of the Earp vendetta ride that does not come from an Earp family member.

Gatto, Steve. *Curly Bill: Tombstone's Most Famous Outlaw*. Lansing, Mich.: Protar House, 2003. A good biography of the life and times of Brocius.

Marks, Paula M. *And Die in the West: The Story of the O.K. Corral Gunfight*. Norman: University of Oklahoma Press, 1996. An in-depth look at the events leading up to and following the famous gunfight, including the Earp vendetta ride.

Turner, Alford E., ed. *The Earps Talk*. College Station, Pa.: Creative, 1980. A book of documented interviews with Wyatt Earp, Jesse James, and Virgil Earp.

Walters, Lorenzo D. *Tombstone's Yesterday: True Chronicles of Early Arizona*. Glorieta, N. Mex.: Rio Grande Press, 1928. Documented stories from Tombstone locals about the lawless days of the late nineteenth century.

*—Randall L. Milstein*

**See also:** Doc Holliday; Johnny Ringo.

# Louis Buchalter
## Gangster and murderer

**Born:** February 6, 1897; New York, New York
**Died:** March 4, 1944; Sing Sing Prison, Ossining, New York
**Also known as:** Louis Buckhouse (birth name); Lepke Buchalter; Judge Louis
**Major offenses:** Murder in the first degree and numerous gang-related crimes
**Active:** 1916-1939
**Locale:** New York, New York
**Sentence:** Death by electrocution

### Early Life

Louis Buchalter (BOOK-uhl-ter) was born in 1897 on New York City's lower East Side, home at that time to many Russian Jewish immigrants. His father ran a hardware store, and his siblings achieved success in life by honest means. Louis, known as Lepke, although quiet by nature, was drawn to street crime and rapidly made a name in the extortion rackets of New York's garment district.

### Criminal Career

By the era of the Great Depression in the 1930's, Buchalter's vicious tactics had allowed him to rise to boss of New York's labor and industrial rackets. He had also become prominent in both the national gang syndicates and in the newly powerful Jewish-Italian gangs of New York City, where he was associated with Lucky Luciano. Buchalter was involved in prostitution, hijacking, narcotics, and extortion—and soon a new form of criminal behavior: murder for hire. He headed the Brooklyn-based Murder, Inc., one of the most vicious organized gangs of murderers in urban history. Under contracts from other gangsters, the hit men of Murder, Inc. killed hundreds of citizens and rival criminals, the most famous being gangster Dutch Schultz in 1935. Buchalter is alleged to have committed scores of the murders himself.

### Legal Action and Outcome

Buchalter's first conviction was on a charge of theft in May, 1916. He was in and out of prison throughout the following two decades. Pursued by the police and the Federal Bureau of Investigation throughout the 1930's, Buchalter went into hiding in 1936. In 1939, he gave himself up and was sentenced to a fourteen-year term in Leavenworth Federal Penitentiary on a narcotics charge. In 1940, a Murder, Inc. hit man, Abe "Kid Twist" Reles, informed on Buchalter for four murders. Brought from Leavenworth for trial, Buchalter was quickly convicted of murder in the first degree and sentenced to death. After losing appeals all the way to the U.S. Supreme Court, Buchalter was executed in Sing Sing Prison's electric chair on March 4, 1944.

## Impact

The unassuming Louis Buchalter was a particularly vicious criminal, seizing control of New York City's lucrative labor and extortion rackets. His notoriety chiefly arises from two factors. First, Murder, Inc., which he headed, was an original entity in organized crime: a syndicate that carried out contract killings nationwide in an efficient and businesslike manner, using the most vicious methods, such as shotgun blasts, bludgeoning by lead pipes, assaults with ice picks, and stranglings. Second, Buchalter is commonly described as the only crime boss ever to be executed in the United States. His execution in 1944 brought about the quick end of Murder, Inc. and the Jewish gangs of New York City. While Buchalter was perhaps not outdone in brutality, he is the only syndicate chief to have paid the ultimate penalty.

## Further Reading

Cohen, Rich. *Tough Jews: Fathers, Sons, and Gangster Dreams in Jewish America*. New York: Simon & Schuster, 1998. Cohen presents a sociological and anecdotal account of the Jewish gangsters of pre-World War II New York and their lingering presence in the psyche of modern Jewish America.

Feder, Sid, and Burton Turkus. *Murder, Inc.: The Story of the Syndicate*. Cambridge, Mass.: Da Capo Press, 2003. Cowritten by the Brooklyn County assistant district attorney who prosecuted members of Murder, Inc., and helped send seven of them to the electric chair. An inside story of the rise and fall of the syndicate murderers.

Fox, Stephen. *Blood and Power: Organized Crime in Twentieth-Century America*. New York: William Morrow, 1993. Portrays organized crime in modern America and the interplay among corrupt politicians, Hollywood celebrities, and rival ethnic groups.

Kavieff, Paul. *The Life and Times of Lepke Buchalter: America's Most Ruthless Labor Racketeer*. Fort Lee, N.J.: Barricade Books, 2006. The first full-length biography of Buchalter also focuses on the New York City underworld.

*—Howard Bromberg*

**See also:** Joe Adonis; Albert Anastasia; Vincent Coll; Joe Colombo; Carlo Gambino; Sam Giancana; John Gotti; Sammy Gravano; Henry Hill; Richard Kuklinski; Meyer Lansky; Lucky Luciano; Salvatore Maranzano; Carlos Marcello; Dutch Schultz.

# Ted Bundy

## Serial killer

**Born:** November 24, 1946; Burlington, Vermont

**Died:** January 24, 1989; Florida State Prison, Starke, Florida

**Also known as:** Theodore Cowell (birth name); Theodore Robert Bundy (full name); Theodore Nelson

**Major offenses:** Murder, kidnapping, and attempted kidnapping

**Active:** 1974-1979

**Locale:** King County, Washington; Salt Lake City, Utah; Colorado; and Tallahassee, Florida

**Sentence:** Two death sentences and three ninety-year sentences

### Early Life

Theodore (Ted) Robert Bundy (BUHN-dee) was born Theodore Cowell to Eleanor Louise Cowell in a home for unwed mothers in 1946 in Vermont. He was raised for the first few years of life with his grandparents and his mother in Philadelphia, Pennsylvania, believing that his mother was his sister and his grandparents were his parents. Some believe that this early life influenced Bundy in later years and shaped his life course.

Ted and his mother moved to Tacoma, Washington, in 1950, and shortly thereafter Louise married and changed her son's name to Theodore Robert Bundy. Bundy stayed in Washington throughout his schooling and was a proficient student, graduating from high school and continuing on to college in Washington.

Bundy appeared in his early adulthood to have a bright future despite some problems in college, including a failed relationship with a girlfriend, Stephanie Brooks. He was an honor student and active in the political scene in Washington, particularly with the Republican Party, and worked at the Seattle Crisis Clinic. He was a man with many accomplishments and a seemingly ideal citizen.

## Criminal Career

Many believe Bundy's first murder occurred in 1974, when a young woman was taken from her basement apartment in Seattle; only bloodstains were left behind. A wave of abductions of young women around the King County area in Washington followed. Skeletal remains of the missing women were found later in the foothills of the Cascade Mountains. Bundy often rendered his victims unconscious and took them to remote locations, where he stran-

*Ted Bundy*. (AP/Wide World Photos)

**EVIL WEARS A SMILE**

*Ted Bundy was by all accounts affable, handsome, and extremely intelligent—fortunate in having come from a good family where he enjoyed a happy childhood. His disturbed personality and evil deeds were only magnified by those facts. In sentencing Bundy to death, Judge Edward Cowart expressed the incomprehensibility of a wasted life—and demonstrated how easy it was to be taken in by Bundy's charm:*

It is ordered that you be put to death by a current of electricity, that current be passed through your body until you are dead. Take care of yourself, young man. I say that to you sincerely; take care of yourself. It's a tragedy for this court to see such a total waste of humanity as I've experienced in this courtroom. You're a bright young man. You'd have made a good lawyer, and I'd have loved to have you practice in front of me, but you went the wrong way, partner. Take care of yourself. I don't have any animosity to you. I want you to know that. Take care of yourself.

gled them. All his victims were young females, most in their college years.

After Bundy moved to Utah in 1974, disappearances of young women also began there. In 1978, Bundy entered the Chi Omega sorority house in Florida and beat five girls, killing two by strangulation and biting one of the deceased on her left buttock; the teeth imprints eventually helped to convict Bundy. A month after the sorority attacks, Bundy abducted, assaulted, and killed a twelve-year-old girl, Kimberly Leach.

## LEGAL ACTION AND OUTCOME

Bundy was first arrested in Utah in 1975 for suspicion of burglary. He was then identified in a lineup for an attempted kidnapping that had occurred in 1974 and sentenced to one to fifteen years in prison on the charge. In 1977, he was extradited to Colorado to stand trial for a 1975 murder. In June, 1977, Bundy escaped from jail and was recaptured six days later. He escaped a second time in December, 1977, and fled to Tallahassee, Florida. He was arrested there in February, 1978, as he drove a stolen car.

After his arrest in Florida, Bundy was indicted on two counts of murder and three of attempted murder. He went on trial in June, 1979, and was found guilty. Then, in 1980, Bundy was found guilty of the Leach murder and received a death sentence for that crime.

Ultimately, Bundy was given two death sentences and three ninety-year sentences. He spent the next ten years on death row, using legal tactics to delay his execution. In January, 1989, the state of Florida executed Bundy for the death of Leach.

## Impact

Although not the first serial murderer in American history, Ted Bundy was one of the most intriguing because of his charm and ability to manipulate his victims and the legal system. Bundy enjoyed taunting the police and baiting the media, reveling in the attention. Scholars are still unsure of the exact number of Bundy's victims because of the fact that Bundy never fully confessed, although he had been connected to the deaths of at least thirty women. Even up until the last minute, Bundy tried to manipulate and con his way out of execution by offering to confess to his crimes; ultimately his ploy did not work.

## Further Reading

Michaud, Stephen, and Hugh Aynesworth. *Ted Bundy: Conversations with a Killer*. New York: Signet, 1989. The authors were able to interview Bundy preceding his execution in 1989; this is a transcription of those interviews.

Nelson, Polly. *Defending the Devil: My Story as Ted Bundy's Last Lawyer*. New York: Morrow, 1994. Nelson provides insight into the litigation surrounding Bundy's crimes.

Rule, Ann. *The Stranger Beside Me*. 4th ed. New York: W. W. Norton, 2000. Written by a woman who had been friends with Bundy, the book describes Bundy's life and criminal career. The fourth edition adds information about the impact Bundy had on society.

*—Jenephyr James*

**See also:** Joe Ball; David Berkowitz; Kenneth Bianchi; Angelo Buono, Jr.; Jeffrey Dahmer; Albert DeSalvo; John Wayne Gacy; Ed Gein; Leonard Lake; Charles Ng; Dennis Rader; Richard Speck; Aileen Carol Wuornos.

# Angelo Buono, Jr.
## Serial killer

**Born:** October 5, 1934; Rochester, New York
**Died:** September 21, 2002; Calipatria State Prison, Calipatria, California
**Also known as:** Hillside Strangler
**Major offense:** Murder
**Active:** October 17, 1977-February 16, 1978
**Locale:** Los Angeles, California
**Sentence:** Life in prison without the possibility of parole in nine separate sentences

### Early Life

Angelo Buono (BOH-noh) was born in Rochester, New York. After his parents' divorce, Buono, then five years of age, moved with his mother and sister to Glendale, California. In his youth, Buono developed a lifetime preoccupation with sexual violence against women and idolized the high-profile sex offender Caryl Chessman. Buono received poor grades in school and dropped out at the age of sixteen. As a juvenile, he was arrested several times for larceny and auto theft, sent to a reformatory school, escaped from the institution, and was later recaptured in December, 1951. In his early twenties, Buono became a husband and father. During his lifetime, he married four times and had eight children. Buono physically and sexually abused several of his wives and one of his female children. He was again arrested for larceny and auto theft in his thirties. In his forties, Buono, then separated from his latest wife, began an automobile upholstering business out of his home.

### Criminal Career

In 1976, Buono's cousin, Kenneth Bianchi, moved to Los Angeles. In order to supplement their incomes, Buono and Bianchi became pimps to several prostitutes. It was the anger resulting from the escape of two of the prostitutes employed by the cousins that led them to start killing women in the fall of 1977. The team would pose as police officers in order to lure victims back to Buono's residence. The victims were raped and tortured, and their nude bodies were then dumped on hillsides in the Los Angeles area. Their ten victims were young women ranging in age from twelve to twenty-eight, with such occupations as a prostitute, a student, and an aspiring actress and model. Police attention intensified after the bodies of two schoolgirls, the third and fourth victims, were discovered.

### Legal Action and Outcome

In 1978, Bianchi moved to Bellingham, Washington, and the next year, he was arrested for the murders of two local women. Bianchi claimed that he had dissociative identity disorder and implicated Buono in the Los Angeles murders. After admitting to fabricating his defense, Bianchi accepted a plea bargain that spared him the death penalty if he would testify against his cousin. Buono was arrested in October of 1979 for the murders of the young women in the Los Angeles area. In the early stages of the trial, the judge rejected a motion by the district attorney to dismiss the case against Buono based on lack of evidence. Thus two deputy attorneys general were appointed to prosecute the case.

Buono's defense team argued that Bianchi was the sole perpetrator of the murders; however, eyewitness testimony and circumstantial evidence directly implicated Buono in the murders. He was convicted of nine of the ten first-degree murder charges in October of 1983. The jury opted against a sentence of capital punishment, and Buono was sentenced to life imprisonment without the possibility of parole. He died in prison on September 21, 2002, at the age of sixty-seven, of a heart condition.

### Impact

With intense media reporting, the Hillside Strangler murders produced widespread fear in the Los Angeles area, especially among young women. The trial of Angelo Buono, Jr., moreover, was one of the longest in American history, beginning on November 16, 1981, and ending on November 18, 1983. Bianchi alone testified for approximately six months. Additionally, the judge and jury visited the different sites where the bodies were found, which is unusual in criminal trials.

### Further Reading

Boren, Roger W. "The Hillside Strangler Trial." *Loyola Law Review* 33, no. 2 (January, 2000): 705-725. California Court of Appeals justice Roger W. Boren details his experience as the prosecutor in the Buono trial.

O'Brien, Darcy. *Two of a Kind: The Hillside Stranglers*. New York: New American Library, 1985. Award-winning author O'Brien uses police reports, court transcripts, and interviews with witnesses to provide a detailed account of the murders and Buono's trial.

Schwartz, Ted. *The Hillside Strangler*. Sanger, Calif.: Quill Driver Books, 2001. Focusing mostly on Bianchi, *New York Times* best-selling author Schwartz provides a comprehensive narrative, based on interviews with Bianchi, his psychiatrists, and police officers assigned to the case, of the murders and police efforts to apprehend the Hillside Stranglers.

—*Margaret E. Leigey*

**See also:** Joe Ball; David Berkowitz; Kenneth Bianchi; Ted Bundy; Andrew Cunanan; Jeffrey Dahmer; Albert DeSalvo; Albert Fish; John Wayne Gacy; Ed Gein; Leonard Lake; Charles Ng; Dennis Rader; Richard Speck; Aileen Carol Wuornos.

# Richard Girnt Butler

## Official spokesperson for the Aryan Nations

**Born:** February 23, 1918; Bennett, Colorado
**Died:** September 8, 2004; Hayden, Idaho
**Also known as:** Richard Gernt Butler
**Cause of notoriety:** Butler was the voice of anti-Semitism for the neo-Nazi movement in North America.
**Active:** 1960's-2004
**Locale:** Idaho

### Early Life

Born in Bennett, Colorado, in 1918, Richard Girnt Butler (BUHT-luhr) moved during the Great Depression to Los Angeles, where he studied aeronautical engineering. During World War II, he served in the United States Army and was stationed in India. While the European community sought to eliminate Nazi aggression during the war, Butler became an admirer of Adolf Hitler and set out to learn more about the German leader's resolve to purge society of those races he claimed to be inferior. Butler returned to the United States believing that his own government many times acted contrary to the best interests of its Caucasian citizens.

It was at Lockheed in Southern California where Butler met William Potter Gale, a fellow veteran and leader of a local paramilitary group called the California Rangers. Gale introduced Butler to Christian Identity—a religious belief that claims God's chosen people are not Jewish but in fact are of European descent.

During the 1960's, Butler associated himself with the Christian Defense League, an anti-Semite organization. Its founder, Wesley Swift, mentored Butler and later appointed him to the position of director. Following Swift's death in 1971, Butler attempted to legitimize the Christian Identity faith by blending the Christian Defense League into a newly formed religious sect, the Church of Jesus Christ Christian. Soon thereafter, Butler moved this new ministry to a compound near Hayden Lake, Idaho, in an attempt to establish a homeland of racial purity—an Aryan nation.

### Militant Career

Butler's philosophy of racial solidarity flowed from a patchwork of diverse ideas. Combining religious bigotry with white nationalism, Butler transformed an otherwise heartless paramilitary organization into a passionate congregation focused upon preaching a message of racial purity in the hope of making the Pacific Northwest a homeland for the Caucasian race. While Butler's interpretation of Christian doctrine differed only slightly from the mainstream, his exaggerations of parables and prophecies were highly shocking to some. For example, Butler compared Hitler with Jesus Christ, suggesting that they were two of the greatest individuals who had ever lived.

Butler was well known for his friendship with Robert Jay Mathews and his support of the Order, a white separatist organization. During 1983 and 1984, the Order committed bombings, conducted armed robberies, and assassinated a Jewish radio personality from Denver. That same year, Mathews was killed during a confrontation with federal agents.

Although neatly hidden from the public eye, Butler's compound became host to white power advocates from all walks of life. In addition to hosting the annual World Congress of Aryan Nations, Butler promoted youth training camps and survivalist schools for the paramilitarily inclined. All of this, Butler claimed, would ready his people for the coming race war. It would be his associations with militant groups, however, that would ultimately contribute to the demise of the Aryan Nations in the Pacific Northwest. In 1998, armed members of Butler's security fired shots from inside the compound at a family repairing their car out on the roadway. Represented by the Southern Poverty Law Center, the family prevailed in a civil trial in which a Kootenai County jury found that Butler had been negligent in the training and supervision of the security detail. This action caused the Aryan Nations to claim bankruptcy and ultimately led to the loss of Butler's compound in Hayden Lake.

### Impact

The white supremacy movement might have remained fragmented were it not for the networking machine of Richard Butler's organization. For years his message to the Caucasian race came by way of newsletters, radio programs, demonstrations, pickets, and parades. Butler will best be remembered, however, for his ability to unite disparate racist factions under the umbrella of Christian Identity.

### Further Reading

Abanes, Richard. *American Militias*. Downers Grove, Ill.: Intervarsity Press, 1996. A fact-filled contemporary account of the militia phenomenon in the United States in the late twentieth century.

Ezekiel, Raphael S. *The Racist Mind*. New York: Penguin Books, 1995. Ezekiel interviews four different types of people belonging to the hate movement in the United States.

Landau, Elaine. *The White Power Movement: America's Racist Hate Groups*. Brookfield, Conn.: Millbrook Press, 1993. Offers a historical account of the white power movement and broadly examines the philosophical roots of racial hatred.

*—Douglas A. Orr*

**See also:** Matthew F. Hale; Robert Jay Mathews.

# Samuel Joseph Byck

## Attempted hijacker and assassin

**Born:** January 30, 1930; Philadelphia, Pennsylvania
**Died:** February 22, 1974; Baltimore, Maryland
**Also known as:** Sam Byck
**Cause of notoriety:** Byck attempted to hijack an airplane with the intention of crashing it into the White House and assassinating President Richard M. Nixon.
**Active:** November, 1968; February 22, 1974
**Locale:** Baltimore-Washington International Airport

### Early Life

Samuel Joseph Byck (bihk) was born in Philadelphia, the oldest of three brothers in a Jewish family. Byck viewed his father as a failure because of his financial difficulties, but he also saw his father as a kind person. After failing to complete high school and working odd jobs, he entered the army at age twenty-four. He left the army after two years with an honorable discharge.

In 1957, Byck married a woman within a month of his father's death, an act that his Jewish family felt was in bad taste. He tried to be a good husband and father to his four children but could not hold employment; this fact placed stress on his marriage. He failed in every job and business venture. His two brothers were financially successful, and he was jealous of them. Byck disowned his brothers, pretending that they had died by holding a Jewish ceremony to mourn their deaths.

### Criminal Career

In November, 1968, Byck was arrested for receiving stolen goods, but his case was thrown out of court in May, 1969. In 1969, Byck became angry at the federal government for rejecting his application for a twenty-thousand-dollar loan from the Small Business Administration to promote his business idea of selling at shopping centers the automobile tires from school buses. Byck was admitted to a psychiatric hospital for anxiety after his loan application was rejected; there, he was diagnosed as a manic-depressive (suffering from bipolar disorder).

Byck viewed his mental health problems as a product of his bad marriage and financial troubles, but he also viewed his personal problems as symptomatic of the political corruption of the Richard Nixon administration. He began to identify with the poor and minorities in society who were disadvantaged by the political system, and he perceived successful persons, such as his brothers, as "sell-outs."

Byck had been questioned by the Secret Service because he had suggested in conversations that someone should kill Nixon. The Secret Service, however, did not view him as a threat. He attended the inauguration of Nixon in 1973 and spoke with police officers and security personnel. On Christmas Day, 1973, Byck dressed up as Santa Claus and demonstrated outside the White House.

Byck and his wife eventually divorced, and he was allowed to see his children for only one hour per week. This was unbearable for him, so he began to plot the assassination of Nixon because he wanted his life to mean something. Byck became inspired by a man named Jimmy Essex, who killed six people by shooting from the top of a hotel in New Orleans. Byck devised a plan he called Operation Pandora's Box: He would hijack an airplane and crash it into the White House. Byck made tape recordings about his life frustrations and mailed the recordings to famous people such as composer Leonard Bernstein and physician Jonas Salk.

On February 22, 1974, Byck attempted to hijack Delta Flight 523 at the Baltimore-Washington International Airport. Byck shot and killed a police officer and then shot and killed one of the pilots before he was shot through a window of the plane by a police officer. As he lay wounded, Byck shot himself in the temple to end his own life.

## Impact

The Federal Aviation Administration published a document in 1987 on Samuel Byck's attempted hijacking to remind people about the potential dangers involved in civil aviation. In 2004, Byck gained notoriety when Sean Penn portrayed him in the film *The Assassination of Richard Nixon*. Byck also is portrayed in the Stephen Sondheim and John Weidman musical *Assassins*, which opened on Broadway in 2004. Finally, Byck gained some attention in the early twenty-first century when the 9/11 Commission mentioned his attempt to fly an airplane into the White House.

**Further Reading**

Clarke, James W. "Samuel Byck." In *American Assassins: The Darker Side of Politics*. Princeton, N.J.: Princeton University Press, 1982. In a book in which Clarke develops a typology for analyzing sixteen political assassins throughout American history, chapter 4 is devoted to Byck.

Sondheim, Stephen, and John Weidman. *Assassins*. 1991. Reprint. Bronxville, N.Y.: PS Classics, 2004. The script, lyrics, and musical score for a Broadway play based upon assassins and would-be assassins of presidents of the United States.

*—Scott P. Johnson*

**See also:** John Wilkes Booth; Arthur Bremer; Leon Czolgosz; Lynette Fromme; Charles Julius Guiteau; Richard Lawrence; Lee Harvey Oswald; Giuseppe Zangara.

# Al Capone

## Gangster

**Born:** January 17, 1899; Brooklyn, New York

**Died:** January 25, 1947; Palm Island, Florida

**Also known as:** Alphonse Gabriel Capone (full name); Scarface

**Major offenses:** Income tax evasion, contempt of court, and carrying concealed deadly weapons

**Active:** 1920's-1930's

**Locale:** Chicago, Philadelphia, and New York

**Sentence:** One year for carrying concealed deadly weapons and released nine months later for good behavior; eleven years in federal prison for income tax evasion, plus a fine of $50,000, $7,692 in court costs, and payment of $215,000 plus interest due on back taxes; concurrent six-months' imprisonment for contempt of court

### Early Life

Alphonse "Al" Capone (kah-POHN) was born January 17, 1899, in Brooklyn, New York, to Italian immigrants Gabriele and Teresina Raiola Capone. Alphonse soon joined two neighborhood gangs—the Forty Thieves Juniors and the Brooklyn Rippers. He quit school at age fourteen after fighting with a teacher. For a few years, he worked at odd jobs around Brooklyn and then joined the notorious Five Points Gang headed by Frankie Yale in Manhattan. He became bartender and bouncer in Yale's bar, the Harvard Inn. At Harvard Inn, Capone insulted the sister of Frank Gallucio, a thug who then slashed Capone's right cheek with a switchblade knife, leaving him scarred for life and earning him the nickname Scarface.

In 1918, Capone met an Irish girl, Mary (Mae) Coughlin, at a dance. On December 4, 1918, she gave birth to their son, Albert "Sonny" Francis Capone, and they were married on December 30, 1918, in Brooklyn. In 1919, they moved to Long Island in order to be close to Yale's business on "Rum Row." In New York, Capone was linked to two murders but was never tried. However, after Capone had a fight with a rival gang member, Yale sent him to Chicago to get a break from the New York scene. The Capone family moved to 7244 South Prairie Avenue in Chicago, where Capone launched his career as one of the most notorious gangsters in American history.

### Criminal Career

In Chicago, Capone worked for underworld boss Johnny Torrio, who quickly recognized Capone's talents for gang leadership. By 1922, Capone

*Al Capone*. (Library of Congress)

**JUST A BUSINESSMAN?**

*Al Capone once proudly said,*

I make my money by supplying a public demand. If I break the law, my customers, who number hundreds of the best people in Chicago, are as guilty as I am. The only difference is that I sell and they buy. Everybody calls me a racketeer. I call myself a businessman.

was Torrio's second in command and was soon made a full partner in Torrio's prostitution rackets, saloons, and gambling houses in Chicago. In 1925, after Torrio barely survived an assassination attempt, he turned the business over to Capone and left Chicago. Between 1925 and 1930, Capone expanded Chicago's vice industries into a multimillion-dollar business. He controlled distilleries and breweries, nightclubs, speakeasies, gambling houses, racetracks, and brothels; combined, these enterprises earned him $100 million a year.

By 1928, Capone's crime gang numbered more than one thousand experienced gunmen, and Capone could truthfully say he "owned" Chicago. At least half of the city's police force was on Capone's payroll. He bribed aldermen, state's attorneys, legislators, governors, Congress members, and mayors, including Chicago's own mayor, William "Big Bill" Thompson.

In 1928, Capone's Chicago headquarters included the Four Deuces on South Wabash and the Metropole and Lexington Hotels on South Michigan Avenue. He maintained suburban headquarters in Cicero and reputed hideouts in Indiana, Tennessee, and Arkansas. In 1928, Capone bought an estate in Palm Island, Florida, to which he retreated when his men carried out planned gangland killings. He was there on February 14, 1929, when his henchmen, led by John "Machine Gun" McGurn, ambushed Bugs Moran's gang on Chicago's North Side. In what became known as the St. Valentine's Day Massacre, Capone's gunmen slaughtered six Moran gang members and a friend in the S-M-C Cartage Company garage. Moran escaped the carnage because he was late to the meeting and never entered the building. Though Capone's connection was obvious, no person was ever prosecuted for the crime. The massacre did, however, end Moran's control of the North Side; his gang vanished, leaving Chicago open to Capone's takeover.

Moreover, the incident brought Capone's criminal activities under scrutiny at the Federal Bureau of Investigation (FBI) and eventually led to his conviction for income tax evasion in 1931.

### Legal Action and Outcome

When Capone resisted a federal grand jury subpoena to appear in court on March 12, 1929, on the grounds that he was too ill to attend, the FBI obtained evidence to the contrary, and Capone was ordered to appear on March 20. He completed his testimony on March 27 and was arrested for contempt of court; he was released on a $5,000 bond. On May 17, 1929, Capone was arrested in Philadelphia for carrying a concealed deadly weapon and sentenced to one year in prison. He was released nine months later for good behavior, on March 17, 1930.

Meanwhile, the U.S. Treasury Department had filed charges of tax evasion against Capone. On June 16, 1931, Capone pleaded guilty to tax evasion, bragging to the press that he had a deal to serve two and a half years in prison. The federal judge rejected the deal, and Capone changed his plea to not guilty. Tried and convicted on October 18, 1931, Capone was sentenced November 24, 1931, to eleven years in prison, fined $50,000 and $7,692 in court costs, and ordered to pay $215,000 plus interest due on back taxes; the six-month contempt of court sentence ran concurrently. He was released November 16, 1939, having paid all fines and taxes and having served seven and a half years in the federal penitentiary at Atlanta and Alcatraz.

Capone was unable to return either to Chicago or to gangland politics. A victim of syphilitic paresis, his mentality had deteriorated in prison to that of a twelve-year-old person. He retired to Palm Island, Florida, and lived in seclusion until his death from stroke and pneumonia on January 25, 1947.

### Impact

During Prohibition and the Great Depression era, the historical and social conditions for immigrants were such that many turned to organized crime as a source of jobs and income. Al Capone's career as a powerful crime boss during this period remains a popular subject of literature and film. He became a mythic figure as public enemy number one and was romanticized in magazines, books, films, and television.

**Further Reading**

Bergreen, Laurence. *Capone: The Man and the Era*. New York: Simon & Schuster, 1994. Describes the rise of Capone to crime syndicate leadership during the 1920's and 1930's.

Kobler, John. *Capone: The Life and World of Al Capone*. New York: Da Capo Press, 1992. A biography of Capone as a famous crime boss and unrecognized philanthropist.

Ruth, David E. *Inventing the Public Enemy: The Gangster in American Culture, 1918-1934*. Chicago: University of Chicago Press, 1996. Provides a commentary on the cultural impact of organized crime.

*—Marguerite R. Plummer*

**See also:** Bugs Moran; Dion O'Banion; Hymie Weiss.

## Butch Cassidy

### Bank robber and horse rustler

**Born:** April 13, 1866; Beaver, Utah

**Died:** Possibly November 7, 1908; possibly San Vicente, Bolivia

**Also known as:** Robert LeRoy Parker (birth name); George Parker; George Cassidy; Lowe Maxwell; James Ryan; Robin Hood of the West

**Cause of notoriety:** Cassidy and his Wild Bunch Gang were responsible for countless robberies and thefts, becoming folk legends in the process.

**Active:** 1894-1896

**Locale:** American West and Southwest, Argentina, and Bolivia

**Early Life**

Robert LeRoy Parker, who would later come to be known as Butch Cassidy (CAS-ih-dee), was born in Beaver, Utah, on April 13, 1866. Known as Roy as a child, Cassidy was the oldest of thirteen children born to Mormon pioneers from England. During his childhood, the Parkers spent much of their time in Circleville, Utah, as homesteaders. As a teenager, Roy worked on ranches throughout western Utah. It was while working on such ranches that he came under the tutelage of an unscrupulous rancher named Mike

*Butch Cassidy.*

Cassidy; Roy would later adopt Cassidy's last name. Originally taking the name George Cassidy, Roy would later be labeled with the nickname "Butch" as a result of his work with local Utah butcher Charlie Crouse. It has been largely speculated that Roy assumed a new identity to avoid bringing shame to his family name.

Roy's first run-in with the law came at a young age, when he let himself into a closed shop in order to steal a pair of pants (legend has it that he left an "IOU" note, promising to return and pay the merchant). Cassidy began his more consistent criminal activity as a cattle rustler. He disliked the manner in which larger ranchers would drive small-time ranchers out of business and began his criminal career rustling from the larger ranches. As his actions were initially designed to hurt the substantial landowners and help the small ones, he was labeled the Robin Hood of the West. Cassidy was convicted for horse theft on July 4, 1894. He received a two-year sentence in the prison at Laramie, Wyoming, and was released on January 6, 1896.

Cassidy robbed his first bank in June, 1889, when he and three partners held up the San Miguel Valley Bank in Telluride, Colorado. While fleeing with their twenty-thousand-dollar bounty, Cassidy and his gang were among the first to make use of the Outlaw Trail, a long, dangerous route running through Mexico, Utah, Wyoming, and Montana. The trail linked together a series of hideouts, including the infamous Robbers Roost in Utah and Wyoming's Hole-in-the-Wall.

After his time in prison between 1894 and 1896, Cassidy returned to the rustler's life along the Arizona-Utah border. At this time, he began to assemble what would become his most renowned gang, the Wild Bunch—a group of seasoned cowboys, robbers, and rustlers. Membership often

## BUTCH CASSIDY DIES AGAIN . . . AND AGAIN

Nothing could elevate a nineteenth century desperado's reputation and turn him into a folk hero more readily than a spectacular or mysterious death. Butch Cassidy had both. In fact, he seems to have died frequently and on three continents.

Historians Daniel Buck and Anne Meadows looked into the many reports of Cassidy's death. In their 2006 Internet article "Butch and Sundance: Still Dead?" they report that the rumors had become laughable even before the two outlaws left for South America. A turn-of-the-century article in the *Vernal Express* (Utah), for instance, jokes,

> Butch Cassidy is receiving as much unsolicited notoriety as a New York Tammany leader. He has been reported killed a dozen times in the last five years, and yet every time a notorious train or bank robbery occurs, Butch comes to life and is credited with being the leader of the gang. He certainly must have more lives than a whole family of cats.

According to Buck and Meadows, Cassidy was first reported dead in 1898, when he was 32, and last in 1978, when he was 112. In between, under various aliases, he was reported to have died on numerous dates and in numerous places, including in Chile in 1904, 1906, 1908, 1909, 1911, 1912, 1913, and 1935; Bolivia in 1908 and 1909; Utah in 1913 and 1955; on an island off Mexico's coast in 1932; Arizona and Georgia in 1936; and Washington, California, and Oregon in 1937. There were also rumors of his dying in Denver, Colorado, in the late 1930's; a small Nevada mining town in the early 1940's; and in Ireland at an unknown date. The Sundance Kid, while not dying quite so often, had a similar series of fates.

Buck and Meadows explain, "Their 1908 deaths in Bolivia did not become common—albeit controversial—knowledge until decades later." Thus, in addition to innocent misidentifications, rumors and hoaxes had free rein.

changed and rarely exceeded ten people, but the gang's more prominent members included Flat Nose George Curry, Harvey "Kid Curry" Logan, Bill Carver, Elzy Lay, and Harry "Sundance Kid" Longabaugh.

On August 13, 1896, the Wild Bunch made off with seven thousand dollars from a bank in Montpelier, Idaho. Cassidy and his gang then robbed the Pleasant Valley Coal Company payroll of eight thousand dollars. Known for intricate planning, the gang would set up checkpoints with new horses to replace their tired horses after a heist. Thus, law enforcement officers would be chasing fresh horses on their own tired horses.

Following the coal company holdup, the gang began bringing in larger sums of money in robberies throughout South Dakota, New Mexico, Nevada, and Wyoming, including an estimated seventy thousand dollars from a train robbery near Folsom, New Mexico. However, by this time, the Wild Bunch had an array of law enforcement officers on their trail wherever they traveled. Operatives of the Pinkerton National Detective Agency were specifically tracking Cassidy, known to be the leader of the gang.

In 1900, the gang is said to have asked Utah governor Heber Wells for amnesty in exchange for mending their criminal ways. When this idea failed, the band disbanded under the heat of law enforcement pursuit, and the members went in separate directions. After the gang disbanded in 1902, Cassidy traveled to England and then met up with Longabaugh (the Sundance Kid) and his girlfriend, Etta Place, in Fort Worth, Texas. The three then traveled to Argentina.

After farming for a time, Cassidy and Sundance went back to robbing payrolls and trains in Argentina and Bolivia until they were supposedly killed by soldiers in San Vicente, Bolivia, on November 7, 1908. However, the exact circumstances of their deaths remain unknown. In one account, two polite American bandits robbed a coal-mine payroll in early November, 1908, and hid in San Vicente, where they celebrated their success. Three days later, they were surrounded by Bolivian soldiers and killed in a gunfight. The bandits were buried in unmarked graves and assumed to be Cassidy and Sundance. Another legend has it that Cassidy put Sundance out of his misery after he was seriously wounded and then turned the gun on himself. Yet another legend has it that it was not Cassidy and Sundance whom soldiers killed but two other bandits. This legend concludes with Cassidy traveling to Europe, later returning to the United States as William Phillips and marrying a woman named Gertrude Livesay. The Phillips family is said to have lived a law-abiding life in Arizona and then in Washington. William Phillips, after nearing bankruptcy and returning to Utah and Wyoming to look for some buried caches from the Wild Bunch days, was diagnosed with cancer and died on July 20, 1937.

## Impact

Butch Cassidy's legend has had more influence on American perceptions of the Old West than perhaps any other. Known as the Robin Hood of the West, Cassidy, for right or wrong, became known as a gentleman criminal. His image was that of the working-class hero standing up for the little guy against larger ranchers. As a holdup man and bank robber, Cassidy was known to be polite and as gentle as possible. This mode of operation, along with what has been viewed as his general good nature, has made Cassidy the Old West's quinessential "good guy" criminal. His legend was solidified in film in 1969 with the release of *Butch Cassidy and the Sundance Kid*, starring Paul Newman as Cassidy and Robert Redford as Sundance.

## Further Reading

Kelly, Charles. *The Outlaw Tail: A History of Butch Cassidy and His Wild Bunch*. Omaha: University of Nebraska Press, 1996. Kelly weaves together the lives of Cassidy and his contemporaries. The historical analysis includes depictions of both the famous Hole-in-the-Wall and Robbers Roost hideouts.

Meadows, Anne. *Digging up Butch and Sundance*. Lincoln, Nebr.: Bison Books, 2003. After finding out that Butch and Sundance had lived for several years in their beloved Patagonia, the author and her husband set out to trace the final days of the pair. The couple unearthed documents, followed leads, and analyzed DNA evidence in an attempt to trace the demise of the two outlaws. Eventually, they traced their deaths to San Vicente, Bolivia, in 1908. This, for many, has become the accepted location in which Cassidy and Sundance Kid were finally shot and killed.

Patterson, Richardson. *Butch Cassidy: A Biography*. Omaha: University of Nebraska Press, 1998. Devoted to the life and times of Cassidy.

*—Ted Shields*

**See also:** Harry Longabaugh.

# Paul Castellano

## Mafia boss

**Born:** June 20, 1915; Brooklyn, New York
**Died:** December 16, 1985; New York, New York
**Also known as:** Constantino Paul Castellano (full name); Big Paul; PC; Big Pauly
**Cause of notoriety:** As head of the Gambino family, Castellano oversaw labor racketeering and the corruption of businesses and public officials.
**Active:** 1934-1985
**Locale:** New York

### Early Life

Paul Castellano (kahs-tehl-LAN-oh) was born in Brooklyn in 1915 to Sicilian immigrants. His father was a butcher who sold Italian lottery tickets in their neighborhood. Paul dropped out of school by the eighth grade and began selling lottery tickets and helping his father in the butcher shop. In 1934 the nineteen-year-old Castellano spent three months in jail in Connecticut for armed robbery. In 1937 he married Nina Manno, who was the sister-in-law of Carlo Gambino, a rising Mafia member in the crime "family" of Albert Anastasia. Gambino was married to Castellano's sister Katharine. As Gambino rose within the New York Mafia, Castellano would assume greater and greater criminal responsibilities. In October, 1957, Anastasia was murdered in a barber's chair in New York, and Gambino became boss of what became known as the Gambino family.

### Criminal Career

Gambino appeared to be a slight and unassuming man at first sight. He had a fearsome reputation, however, as an underworld figure. During the time of his brother-in-law's leadership, Castellano's fortunes grew. His principal assets were his diplomatic ability in the underworld and his success in corrupting legitimate businesses. Castellano's main interest was the meat business. He and his sons controlled meat distribution concerns and had influence with labor unions. Castellano would force supermarket chains to carry certain brands, and he would "encourage" butcher shops and other outlets to stock his brand and not others. Gam-

**PROMISES, PROMISES**

There are certain promises you make that are more sacred than anything that happens in a court of law, I don't care how many Bibles you put your hand on. Some of the promises, it's true, you make too young, before you really have an understanding of what they mean. But once you've made those first promises, other promises are called for. And the thing is you can't deny the new ones without betraying the old ones. The promises get bigger, there are more people to be hurt and disappointed if you don't live up to them. Then, at some point, your called upon to make a promise to a dying man.

—*Paul Castellano*

bino, as he was dying in 1976, anointed Castellano as his successor.

Castellano became head of the Gambino family in 1976. The group was already divided between street criminals, such as John Gotti, and businessmen, such as Castellano. As Castellano gained both prominence and wealth, he abandoned the Brooklyn and Queens neighborhoods in which he had spent his younger days for a fashionable mansion on Staten Island. He also forbade the members of his family from becoming involved in the narcotics trade. Over the next several years, tensions between the two factions became more pronounced as Castellano became more isolated. Castellano's organization was heavily involved in labor racketeering and the corruption of businesses and public officials. The group's street crew, headed by Aniello Dellacroce (and later John Gotti), carried on traditional criminal activities such as hijacking, loan-sharking, and bookmaking.

### LEGAL ACTION AND OUTCOME

In 1983 the Federal Bureau of Investigation (FBI) planted an electronic listening device in Castellano's home. The bug revealed many of the inner workings of the Gambino family as well as sordid details of Castellano's personal life. Over the next two years, the FBI gathered evidence against Castellano and several other members of the Gambino family. Finally, a joint federal task force arrested Castellano and several other members of organized crime's ruling body, "The Commission." On February 25, 1985, FBI agents arrested many, if not all, of the major organized crime figures in New York, including Castellano.

Castellano never went to trial for his many alleged crimes. On December 16, 1985, while arriving for dinner at a favorite restaurant, he and his bodyguard were ambushed and killed by unidentified men. Many blamed the murder on Gotti, the leader of the street crew for the Gambinos and representative of the new guard of Mafia leaders.

## Impact

The impact of Castellano's death was greater than that of his life. Paul Castellano represented the last link to the older, more traditional Mafia. His death signaled an end to that tradition and ushered in the era of Gotti, the dapper don. Gotti was a high-profile street thug whose many trials and acquittals were widely covered by the New York media. However, the criminal organization that Gotti inherited was a shell of its former self. The impact of FBI investigations and federal prosecutions destroyed much of the effectiveness of the older criminal organization, and new criminal groups became more powerful over the prevailing years.

## Further Reading

Cummings, John, and Ernest Volkman. *Gombata: The Improbable Rise and Fall of John Gotti and His Gang*. New York: Avon Books, 1990. Chronicles the career of John Gotti, who assumed control of the Gambino family after Castellano's death. Shows the deep differences in style and personality between Castellano and Gotti.

Maas, Peter. *The Valachi Papers*. New York: Putnam, 1968. Firsthand account of a small-time Mafia member gives some interesting views of the early period of Mafia organization from the 1930's to the 1950's.

O'Brien, Joseph, and Andris Kurins. *Boss of Bosses: The FBI and Paul Castellano*. New York: Dell, 1991. This book by two FBI agents is a blow-by-blow account of the FBI's attack on the Gambino family. Examines both technical and ethical aspects of the case.

*—Charles C. Howard*

**See also:** Joe Adonis; Albert Anastasia; Louis Buchalter; Vincent Coll; Joe Colombo; Carmine Galante; Carlo Gambino; Sam Giancana; Vincent Gigante; John Gotti; Sammy Gravano; Henry Hill; Richard Kuklinski; Meyer Lansky; Salvatore Maranzano; Carlos Marcello; Joseph Profaci; Arnold Rothstein; Dutch Schultz.

# Whittaker Chambers

## Spy and informer

**Born:** April 1, 1901; Philadelphia, Pennsylvania

**Died:** July 9, 1961; Westminster, Maryland

**Also known as:** Jay Vivian Chambers (full name); David Whittaker Chambers (alias); David Breen (alias); Lloyd Cantwell (alias); Karl or Carl (alias); Bob (alias); Harold Phillips (alias); Arthur Dwyer (alias); Charles Adams (alias); Charles Whittaker (alias); George Crosley (alias); John Kelly (literary pseudonym)

**Cause of notoriety:** Chambers, a onetime Communist spy, became notorious less for his own espionage than for making accusations of espionage against Alger Hiss.

**Active:** 1932-1950

**Locale:** Baltimore; Washington, D.C.; New York City; and Westminster, Maryland

### Early Life

Despite the best efforts of his mother, the upbringing of Whittaker Chambers (WIHT-uh-kur CHAYM-burz) in Lynbrook on New York's Long Island was anything but respectable or conventional. His mother was an unsuccessful actress, and his father was an artist who at one point abandoned the family to live with a male lover. Chambers's grandmother frightened the family by brandishing scissors and knives and claiming that people were trying to kill her, and his only brother committed suicide.

In high school Chambers kept to himself but was teased and called derisive names like Girlie and Stinky. He had bad teeth because his mother would not pay for dentist visits, and he got in trouble at his graduation ceremonies by predicting that one of his classmates would end up as a prostitute. He began to feel like an outcast and briefly ran off to Baltimore and New Orleans before enrolling at Columbia University in 1920.

At Columbia he got in trouble for a political satire about Jesus that he published in *The Morningside*, the student literary annual. He left the university as a result and in 1923 traveled to Europe, where he was attracted by Communist political protests.

On his return he began reading political literature, including a pamphlet by Vladimir Ilich Lenin, and he joined the Communist Party in 1925, working for its newspaper, *The Daily Worker*. He supplemented his income with translation work, making the first English translation of the famous animal story *Bambi* (1928). After a split in the Communist Party in 1929, Chambers was forced to leave but returned to its good graces in 1931 through a series of short stories he submitted to the Communist literary journal, *The New Masses*.

## Espionage Career

Chambers became editor of *The New Masses* and then, in 1932, was recruited for special underground work, which consisted of espionage for the Soviet Union. For the following six years Chambers worked as a courier, transmitting government documents to agents of the GRU, the Soviet military intelligence department.

In 1938, in the wake of purges in the Soviet Union and among its agents abroad, Chambers escaped from the Communist underground and went into hiding for a year until he was able to surface with a job writing for the book section of *Time* magazine. Now a committed anti-Communist, Chambers wrote extensively about the dangers of Communism and the Soviet Union, alienating some of his fellow journalists, who thought him biased and extreme.

Concerned about the Nazi-Soviet pact of August, 1939, Chambers reported to the U.S. State Department on some of his past espionage activities, but no action was taken then or in the early 1940's after he was interviewed by the Federal Bureau of Investigation.

After World War II, however, the House Committee on Un-American Activities (HUAC) became interested in Soviet espionage and subpoenaed Chambers, who accused several individuals of having been secret members of the Communist Party. One of these individuals was Alger Hiss.

**Sick Society**

At issue in the Hiss Case was the question whether this sick society, which we call Western civilization, could in its extremity still cast up a man whose faith in it was so great that he would voluntarily abandon those things which men hold good, including life, to defend it.

—*Whittaker Chambers*

### The Hiss Case

After a distinguished career at the State Department, Hiss had just become president of the Carnegie Endowment for International Peace. He denied being a Communist and sued Chambers for slander. Chambers then added to his allegations, saying Hiss had been not only a Communist but also a spy. Led by Congressman Richard Nixon, the HUAC continued hearings on these matters; a grand jury began investigating them as well, leading to two charges of perjury against Hiss.

To support his accusations, Chambers produced various documents, including the so-called Pumpkin Papers, microfilm of stolen government documents that he had hidden in a pumpkin on his farm in Maryland. The documents included materials typed on what appeared to be Hiss's typewriter and notes made in his handwriting and seemed to indicate that a Communist spy ring had been active in Washington. After a mistrial, a second trial found Hiss guilty of perjury in January, 1950.

### Impact

The Hiss-Chambers case divided the United States. Many on the left saw the conviction of Hiss as a frame-up intended as part of an attack on liberals and Democrats. Conservatives saw it as an important blow against Soviet espionage. Whittaker Chambers himself saw his actions as part of the worldwide struggle against Communism on behalf of Christianity, to which he had become converted.

Whether or not Hiss was guilty—and by the end of the twentieth century most commentators were convinced that he was—the effect of Chambers's charges against him was to provide support for Senator Joseph McCarthy's attacks on supposed Communists in the 1950's, which cost many innocent people their jobs. Chambers himself was involved in one such incident which ruined the career of the diplomat Edmund Clubb.

Chambers had reservations about McCarthy's attacks, but he expressed them only privately, and he himself, in such writings as *Witness* (1952), tended to lump liberals together with Communists, thus contributing to the McCarthyist mind-set.

President Ronald Reagan posthumously awarded a Medal of Freedom to Chambers in 1984 and praised him for aiding the struggle against Communism. Perhaps in some distant way Chambers contributed to the fall of the Soviet Union. In the short term, his charges against Hiss fanned the flames of Cold War hysteria.

**Further Reading**

Chambers, Whittaker. *Witness*. New York: Random House, 1952. Chambers's autobiography, describing the lure of Communism, his life as a spy, and his upbringing.

Roazen, Paul. "The Strange Case of Alger Hiss and Whittaker Chambers." *Queen's Quarterly* (December, 1999): 518-533. Discusses the split among intellectuals over the Hiss-Chambers case.

Swan, Patrick, ed. *Alger Hiss, Whittaker Chambers, and the Schism in the American Soul*. Wilmington, Del.: ISI Books, 2003. Collection of articles written between 1950 and 2001 by various writers analyzing the Hiss-Chambers case.

Tanenhaus, Sam. *Whittaker Chambers: A Biography*. New York: Random House, 1997. Full-scale biography, tracing Chambers's life from childhood through his Communist and post-Communist periods, with emphasis on the Hiss hearings and trials.

Weinstein, Allen. *Perjury: The Hiss-Chambers Case*. 2d ed. New York: Random House, 1997. Provides biographical information on Hiss and Chambers and massive detail on the Hiss hearings and trials.

*—Sheldon Goldfarb*

**See also:** Joseph McCarthy.

# Mark David Chapman

## Murderer

**Born:** May 10, 1955; Fort Worth, Texas
**Major offense:** Second-degree murder in the death of John Lennon
**Active:** December 8, 1980
**Locale:** Central Park West, New York City, New York
**Sentence:** Twenty years to life imprisonment

### Early Life

The formative years of Mark David Chapman (CHAP-muhn) in Decatur, Georgia, were troubled by an oversolicitous mother and an emotionally detached, abusive father. Early in life he imagined he was the ruler or hero of a city of "little people" whom he either had to save or had to destroy because of their waywardness. He became addicted to drugs and obsessed with the pop music group the Beatles but at sixteen rejected his past and turned to evangelical Christianity. His disillusionment with the Beatles increased both with the claim by musician John Lennon that the Beatles were more popular than Jesus and with the 1971 release of Lennon's *Imagine* album, which called forth an idealist vision of a world beyond religious sectarianism, capitalist consumerism, and international war. Chapman psychologically identified with Holden Caulfield, the antisocial protagonist of J. D. Salinger's *The Catcher in the Rye* (1951), who ran away to New York to sort out his life.

Before Chapman made his own way to New York City, he worked for the Young Men's Christian Association (YMCA) in Georgia, Russia, and Beirut, Lebanon. He then attended Dekalb Community College in Clarkson, Georgia, and fell in love with Jessica Blankenship. He followed her to the conservative Christian Covenant College in Tennessee but left as a result of a mental breakdown.

### Criminal Career

In the 1970's, Chapman worked as an armed security guard but became dissatisfied with life and flew to Hawaii, where he twice attempted suicide. In 1979, he traveled to Asia and married Gloria Abe, a Japanese American travel agent who had arranged his trip and who reminded him of Yoko Ono, Lennon's wife. The couple returned to Hawaii, where he again became ob-

**CHAPMAN & LENNON**

I feel that I see John Lennon now as not a celebrity. I did then. I saw him as a cardboard cutout on an album cover.

*—Mark David Chapman*

sessed with Caulfield and began debating with his "little people" whether to kill Lennon.

On October 30, 1980, he flew to New York to kill Lennon, convinced that Lennon was a phony for rejecting Christianity and a hypocrite for singing about an ideal world without borders and war and people without greed or money. Unable to buy bullets in New York, Chapman left to buy them in Georgia and returned on November 10. However, Abe convinced him to return home, where his demons were temporarily quelled.

Chapman returned to New York City on December 6; two days later he staked out Lennon in front of Lennon's residence, the Dakota. That afternoon, he had Lennon autograph *Double Fantasy*, the recently released album by Lennon and Ono, before the couple departed for their recording studio. When they returned at 10:50 P.M., Chapman, with *The Catcher in the Rye* in his pocket, shot Lennon with four hollow-point cartridges. Lennon died shortly thereafter.

### LEGAL ACTION AND OUTCOME

Chapman was charged with second-degree murder. The threat of public lynching was so great that he was transferred from Bellevue Hospital, where he had been taken for a psychiatric examination, to Rikers Island jail. After dozens of tests, six psychiatrists were prepared to testify that Chapman was psychotic; three were prepared to testify that his delusions fell short of the legal definition of psychosis. Chapman rejected the advice of his lawyer and the defense psychiatrists and pleaded guilty, saying that was what God wanted. On June 22, 1981, his plea that he intentionally caused the death of Lennon was accepted, and he was sentenced to twenty years to life in Attica State Prison. Despite being a model prisoner, he was denied parole in 2000, 2002, and 2004.

### Impact

For many Americans, the assassination of Lennon signaled the end of an era. Mark David Chapman murdered a highly visible icon for peace activism and the counterculture that dominated the United States and Europe from the mid-1960's through the mid-1970's. The Chapman case brought to light the relatively new phenomenon of abnormal psychology associated with crimes against celebrities and highlighted the ongoing problematic way that psychopathic individuals are treated in the American justice system. Lennon is still mourned by friends and fans, and Chapman has refused any treatment for his illness while in prison.

### Further Reading

Bresler, Fenton. *Who Killed John Lennon?* New York: St. Martin's Press, 1989. A speculative account claiming that Chapman was programmed by the Central Intelligence Agency (CIA) through drugs and hypnosis to assassinate Lennon for political reasons.

Hamilton, Sue. *The Killing of a Rock Star: John Lennon (Days of Tragedy).* Edited by John Hamilton. Minneapolis: Abdo & Daughters, 1989. Brief children's version of Lennon's biography and Chapman's role in killing him.

Jones, Jack. *Let Me Take You Down: Inside the Mind of Mark David Chapman, the Man Who Shot John Lennon.* New York: Villard Books, 1992. Based on personal interviews, the book gives a thorough account of Chapman and the mental conditions that led him to murder Lennon.

—*Jules Simon*

**See also:** John Hinckley, Jr.; Yolanda Saldívar.

# Benjamin Church
## Colonist and spy

**Born:** August 24, 1734; Newport, Rhode Island
**Died:** January, 1778; at sea
**Also known as:** Benjamin Church, Jr. (full name)
**Major offense:** Criminal correspondence with the enemy British
**Active:** 1774-1775
**Locale:** Massachusetts
**Sentence:** Life in prison; later commuted to voluntary exile

### Early Life

Benjamin Church was the son of Benjamin Church, Sr., a merchant of Boston, and was the grandson of another Benjamin Church, who was a colonel in the colonial forces during King Philip's (Metacom's) War in 1675. The young Church attended Boston Latin School and graduated from Harvard College in 1754. He studied medicine under Dr. Joseph Pynchon and continued his studies in London. While there, he married Hannah Hill. Upon his return to Boston, he soon built a fine reputation as a physician and surgeon.

### Treasonous Career

In addition to his medical practice, Church was a published poet, philosopher, orator, and newspaper editor. He was a member of both the Provincial Congress of Massachusetts and of the Sons of Liberty, together with John and Samuel Adams, Joseph Warren, Paul Revere, John Hancock, and others. Church was rather extravagant in his personal life, having built an elegant country house in Raynham near Boston in 1768 and also maintaining a mistress. Apparently this lifestyle was supported with periodic payments by the British for his spying activities. On the other hand, Church was the first physician on the scene following the Boston Massacre and was also a participant in the Boston Tea Party.

Apparently, it was upon Church's information that the British marched to seize colonial supplies at Concord, which resulted in the Battle of Lexington and Concord (1775). Later Church was named the first surgeon general of the Continental Army. During a trip to occupied Philadelphia, supposedly to obtain needed medicines for the army, Church met with British general Thomas Gage. A communication in cipher from Church to

Gage—forwarded by Church's mistress to Major Kane of the British army in Boston—was intercepted, was deciphered, and led to Church's arrest and court-martial. It was later deduced that Church had begun spying for and communicating with the British perhaps as early as 1774.

Curiously, Church also had connections with two other notorious individuals. When Benedict Arnold offered in 1775 to capture Ticonderoga, it was Church who endorsed the plan and secured for Arnold a commission as colonel to carry it out. Also, Charles Lee was one of those serving on the examining board for Church's court-martial.

### Legal Action and Outcome

At his 1775 court-martial, Church was sentenced to life imprisonment "and debarred from the use of pen, ink, and paper." He was subsequently confined to jail at Norwich, Connecticut. While there, he became seriously ill and as a consequence was allowed on May 13, 1776, to return on parole to Massachusetts. His subsequent petition for voluntary exile to the West Indies was approved, but the vessel on which he departed in 1778 was lost at sea and never heard from again.

### Impact

Benjamin Church goes down in history along with those, such as Benedict Arnold and Charles Lee, who will be remembered by Americans as traitors to the revolutionary cause. Had Church's treachery not been discovered early, he might have had a substantial impact on the outcome of the War for Independence, because of his outstanding reputation and involvement with leading American politicians. As a result of the disclosure of his treachery and his subsequent early demise, however, he had little contemporary impact and has virtually disappeared from popular history.

### Further Reading

French, Allen. *General Gage's Informers*. 1932. Reprint. Westport, Conn.: Greenwood Press, 1968. The primary study that shaped twentieth century assessments of Church, based on Paul Revere's reminiscences of Church's treasonous activities, Church's performance as director of the Continental Army hospital, and the patriots' response to the captured letter. French concludes, after having discovered several letters from Church to Gage, that Church was truly a traitor.

Kiracofe, David. "Dr. Benjamin Church and the Dilemma of Treason in Revolutionary Massachusetts." *New England Quarterly* 70, no. 3 (1997): 443-462. Analyzes Church's behavior in light of the lack of treason laws in his day, his background (he was from a prominent Massachusetts family), his status as a Whig, and the pained reactions of his colleagues. Concludes nevertheless that he was guilty of treason.

Norwood, William Frederick. "The Enigma of Dr. Benjamin Church: A High-Level Scandal in the American Colonial Army Medical Service." *Medical Arts and Sciences* 10, no. 2 (1956): 71-93. A substantial analysis of why Church undertook his treasonous activities.

Walker, Jeffrey B. *Devil Undone: The Life and Poetry of Benjamin Church, 1734-1778*. New York: Arno Press, 1982. Looks beyond the treason to assess Church's entire career and varied talents.

*—Jack H. Westbrook*

**See also:** Benedict Arnold.

# Vincent Coll

## Gangster

**Born:** July 20, 1908; Rosses, County Donegal, Ireland
**Died:** February 8, 1932; New York, New York
**Also known as:** Mad Dog Coll; Mad Mick
**Cause of notoriety:** "Mad Dog Coll" was a Mafioso bootlegger, loan shark, enforcer, kidnapper, and hit man whose attempt to establish his own empire ultimately failed with his death at the age of twenty-three.
**Active:** 1920-1932
**Locale:** Greater New York City area

### Early Life

The infamous gangster Vincent Coll (kohl) was born in the Rosses of County Donegal, Ireland, on July 20, 1908. At the age of one, Vincent immigrated with his family to the United States and settled in the Bronx, New York. Vincent experienced much heartache and personal tragedy from an early age. Before he turned twelve, his father deserted the family, and soon thereafter five of Vincent's siblings, along with this mother, died from a combination of disease and poverty. His only remaining friend was his older brother, Peter, who became Vincent's partner in crime throughout the late 1920's and early 1930's.

Vincent and his brother embarked on a rash of minor criminal acts throughout the Hell's Kitchen section of New York. As a consequence, Vincent was consigned to a Catholic boys' reformatory. After serving his time there, he and Peter decided to enlist to become Mafia enforcers and rumrunners for the infamous Jewish gangster Dutch Schultz, a decision that sparked the formidable yet short career of Coll.

### Criminal Career

Vincent and Peter excelled at their job of inflicting pain and suffering—and in some cases death—on any threat to Schultz and his enterprise. In 1931, after a few years of apprenticeship, Coll asked Schultz for a percentage of the illegal alcohol profits, but Schultz turned down the request. His denial enraged Coll, causing him to break away from his mentor to form his own criminal operation. He recruited Peter and some other low-ranking Schultz enforcers to assist him in establishing his criminal gang, which would attempt to operate in both the Bronx and Harlem.

In order to establish himself as a mobster, Coll and his crew chose to send a strong message to Schultz and other mobsters: that they were now legitimate and deserved respect in the crime underworld. With this aim, Coll assassinated two of Schultz's top-ranking lieutenants. In retaliation, Schultz had Coll's brother, Peter, shot the following day. Peter's death sent Vincent into an insatiable rage and ignited a war between Coll and Schultz. More than twenty men from both gangs were killed during this gang war.

However, it was Coll's murder plot in Spanish Harlem that made him one of the most notorious gangsters of all time and gave him his nickname of Mad Dog. During a failed assassination attempt on two of Schultz's officers, Coll opened fire on a crowd of innocent citizens that included five children. When the gunfire ceased, adults and children lay severely injured, including a five-year-old boy who ultimately died from the gunshot wounds. Coll was later acquitted of the boy's murder and continued his illicit operations.

Lacking sophistication in business, Coll had to find a way to finance his war against Schultz. He turned to kidnapping famous celebrities with mob connections as well as rival mobsters and their crews; he also offered murder for hire. Coll was recruited and paid by famous mob boss Salvatore Maranzano to kill rival boss Lucky Luciano and his crew. Ironically, Luciano discovered the plot and had Maranzano killed. In the end, Coll was paid twenty-five thousand dollars without having to lift a finger.

On February 8, 1932, at the age of twenty-three, Coll was gunned down in broad daylight while standing in a telephone booth. He was demanding a ransom from reputed mobster Owney Madden at the time. Coll's body was literally torn in half by bullets fired by Schultz's hit men.

## Impact

Vincent Coll was one of the most violent mobsters of the Prohibition era and the quintessential Irish immigrant mobster who survived tragedy and poverty only to find an ultimately destructive way of survival. His brutal crimes and misdeeds gave him the reputation as one of the most prolific hit men and racketeers in the history of organized crime. His early death made him a symbol of the violent and wasteful lifestyle of mid-twentieth century crime families. Two films, both titled *Mad Dog Coll*, have fictionalized Coll's life. One released in 1961 starred John Davis Chandler as Coll, and one released in 1993 starred Christopher Bradley in the title role.

## Further Reading

Delap, Breandán. *Mad Dog Coll: An Irish Gangster*. Dublin: Mercier Press, 1999. An unbiased account of Coll's life, from his tragic upbringing to his trademark violent behavior, which ultimately landed him on the Federal Bureau of Investigation's most wanted list.

Reppetto, Thomas. *American Mafia*. New York: Holt, 2004. A chronicle of the Mafia's rise to power in the United States from 1890 to 1951. Includes an excellent bibliography.

Sifakis, Carl. *The Mafia Encyclopedia*. 2d ed. New York: Facts On File, 1999. Comprehensive overview of organized crime personalities, power clashes, hangouts, hideaways, and rackets.

*—Paul M. Klenowski*

**See also:** Joe Adonis; Albert Anastasia; Paul Castellano; Joe Colombo; Carmine Galante; Carlo Gambino; Sam Giancana; Vincent Gigante; John Gotti; Sammy Gravano; Henry Hill; Richard Kuklinski; Meyer Lansky; Lucky Luciano; Salvatore Maranzano; Carlos Marcello; Joe Masseria; Joseph Profaci; Arnold Rothstein; Dutch Schultz.

# Frank Collin

## Founder of the National Socialist Party of America

**Born:** November 3, 1944; Chicago, Illinois
**Also known as:** Frank Joseph Collin (full name); Frank Joseph
**Cause of notoriety:** Collin proposed a march by neo-Nazis in a Jewish suburb of Chicago and saw the Supreme Court uphold his group's right to march.
**Active:** 1960's-1980
**Locale:** Illinois

### Early Life

Frank Collin (CAWL-ihn) was born in Chicago. His father, Max Cohn, was a furniture store owner and a German-born Jew who spent time in Germany's Dachau concentration camp. Max Collin became a naturalized American citizen in 1946, changing his name from Cohn to Collin.

Frank Collin attended Southern Illinois University from 1962 to 1964, where he claimed a fellow student introduced him to the National Socialist Party. Collin left Southern Illinois University in June, 1964, and enrolled at Hiram Scott College in Scotts Bluff, Nebraska. In 1967 he returned to Southern Illinois University. Between 1967 and 1969 he became increasingly involved with National Socialism. Eventually he dropped out of college to devote all his time to the Nazi Party.

### Political Career

Collin joined George Lincoln Rockwell's American Nazi Party in the 1960's. Later he became the Midwest coordinator for its successor, the National Socialist White Peoples Party (NSWPP). In 1970 Collin was expelled from the NSWPP after it was revealed that his father was Jewish. Collin then formed the National Socialist Party of America (NSPA) and set up headquarters in Chicago. Its membership was less than one hundred and consisted primarily of young men and adolescents. Its activities generally consisted of marches and rallies, which attracted attention and frequently ended in clashes between party members and opponents.

In 1975, Collin ran for alderman in Chicago and received 16 percent of the vote. In October, 1976, he received national publicity when he announced plans to hold a rally in Skokie, Illinois, a predominately Jewish suburb of Chicago. The Skokie Park District Board of Commissioners responded by passing an ordinance requiring prospective marchers to obtain a permit at least thirty days in advance of the parade date and to post an insurance bond equal to $350,000. In June, 1977, Collin requested a permit for the National Socialist Party of America to march in front of Skokie Village Hall. In response, the Village Board passed three ordinances. The first required a $350,000 indemnity bond to be posted in advance of any march. The second prohibited the distribution of printed material that promoted hatred of groups of people. The third prohibited demonstrations by individuals wearing military-style uniforms. The Village of Skokie then denied the NSPA the right to march in military-style uniforms.

Collin challenged these actions in court with the assistance of the American Civil Liberties Union. In January, 1978, the Illinois Supreme Court upheld the First Amendment right of the Nazis to march and declared that the

*Frank Collin.* (©Chip Berlet/Courtesy, PRA)

swastika was symbolic of political speech. The Federal District Court of the Northern District of Illinois, the U.S. Court of Appeals for the Seventh Circuit, and the U.S. Supreme Court refused to prohibit the march. On May 25, 1978, the Village of Skokie issued a permit allowing the NSPA to demonstrate in front of the Village Hall. Collin, however, canceled the march. In its place, he and about twenty-five followers held a rally in Marquette Park in Chicago on July 9, 1978. While Collin and the NSPA never marched in Skokie, he received national publicity for his movement. In addition, a made-for-television film titled *Skokie* was aired in 1981.

In 1980 Collin was convicted of sexually molesting adolescent boys at his party headquarters. For these crimes he served three years at Pontiac State Prison. Following his release from prison, Collin changed his name to Frank Joseph and established himself as an author, editor, and neo-pagan. He wrote several books, including *The Destruction of Atlantis* (1987). He also wrote articles for *Fate* magazine and served as editor of *The Ancient American*.

### Impact

Frank Collin's neo-Nazi organization had almost no support from or appeal to Americans. However, he is remembered because of his attempt to march in Skokie and the First Amendment issues his effort raised.

### Further Reading

George, John, and Laird Wilcox. *American Extremists*. Amherst, N.Y.: Prometheus Books, 1996. Examines a number of American extremist groups, including the National Socialist Party of America and other neo-Nazi groups.

Strum, Philippa. *When the Nazis Came to Skokie: Freedom for Speech We Hate*. Lawrence: University of Kansas Press, 1999. A detailed analysis of the First Amendment issues related to the proposed march through Skokie.

—*William V. Moore*

**See also:** Richard Girnt Butler; Matthew F. Hale; Robert Jay Mathews; Tom Metzger; J. B. Stoner.

# Joe Colombo
## Mafia boss

**Born:** June 16, 1923; Brooklyn, New York
**Died:** May 22 or 23, 1978; Newburgh, New York
**Also known as:** Joseph Anthony Colombo, Sr. (full name)
**Cause of notoriety:** A hit man for the Profaci crime family, Colombo later became boss of the family and renamed it after himself. He ran gambling operations, extortion and loan-sharking rackets, and other criminal enterprises. He also organized a civil rights league supposedly created to protect the rights of Italian Americans.
**Active:** 1945-1971
**Locale:** New York, New York

### Early Life

Joe Colombo (koh-LUHM-boh) was born in Brooklyn, New York, in 1923. His parents were Anthony "Nino" and Catherine Colombo. Nino was a Brazilian immigrant born to Italian parents. He became a small-time extortionist and all-around minor hood. In 1938 or 1939, the elder Colombo was found murdered in his car, alongside his presumed mistress Christina Oliveri, the wife of a Profaci soldier. The two had been strangled with a cord.

While little is known of Joe's early life, he attended New Utrecht High School and served in the U.S. Coast Guard from 1942 to 1945. He was discharged after being diagnosed with a nervous disorder. After his military service, Colombo worked as an associate for the Profaci crime family. He ran dice games, worked as an enforcer on the docks, and eventually took over the Mafia-operated gambling enterprises in Brooklyn and Long Island.

### Criminal Career

Joe, along with the Gallo brothers ("Crazy Joe" and Larry) and two others, formed a five-man hit squad for Profaci. In the early 1960's, Joseph Bonanno of the Bonnano crime family contacted Joe Magliocco (who later became boss of the Profaci family and an ally of Bonanno) to carry out the assassination of several key Mafia figures, including Carlo Gambino and Stefano Magaddino of Buffalo, New York. Magliocco, in turn, gave the contract to his top enforcer, Joe Colombo.

Colombo, however, presumably out of an instinct for self-preservation, decided to go to each target of Bonanno's victim list and warn him of the plan. Bonanno was subsequently kidnapped by his cousin Magaddino, and Colombo took control of the Profaci family as a reward for thwarting the mass murder, renaming the family after himself.

Colombo's leadership was marked by internal strife. He called unwanted attention to the Mafia by picketing offices of the Federal Bureau of Investigation (FBI) for its 1970 arrest of his son, Joe Jr. He alienated the Gallo brothers because of his greed, skimming heavily from the soldiers' operations. Colombo further displeased his fellow mobsters by forming the Italian American Civil Rights League, an organization supposedly dedicated to celebrating Italian heritage and, ironically, to combat the gangster stereotype of Italian Americans.

Colombo's penchant for creating public spectacles culminated at a "Unity Day" rally on June 28, 1971. As the crowd formed for the rally, an African American man with press credentials shot Colombo in the head three times. The shooter, named Jerome Johnson, was then immediately killed by an unidentified man who managed to escape. Observers believe that Joe Gallo set up the murder because of Gallo's known alliance with African American criminals and "Crazy Joe's" hatred of Colombo. Colombo did not die that day, but he remained in a vegetative state until his death in 1978.

## Impact

Joe Colombo's 1960's-style social activism and public persona anticipated the flashiness and popular appeal of John Gotti in the 1980's but in his own time stirred consternation among law enforcement agencies and his fellow mobsters alike. Nevertheless, Colombo appealed to many honest Italian Americans, fifty thousand of whom attended the first Unity Day rally and proclaimed Colombo "man of the year." Similarly, Colombo's son Christopher achieved a celebrity status, starring in a 2005 HBO "reality"-style special that profiled the Mafia scion as he served a modified house-arrest while facing charges for racketeering, loan-sharking, and extortion. Such mob figures who attempt to develop a positive (or at least public) image may speak to the romanticism that, for some, still clings to certain aspects of mob life.

**Further Reading**

Capeci, Jerry. *Jerry Capeci's Gang Land*. New York: Alpha Books, 2003. A compilation of journalist and Mafia expert Capeci's columns in the *New York Daily News* covering organized crime activity in New York City from 1989 through 1995.

Raab, Selwyn. *The Five Families: The Rise, Decline, and Resurgence of America's Most Powerful Mafia Empires*. New York: Thomas Dunne Books, 2005. Recounts the history of the New York crime families; spotlights major figures and events of organized crime in New York.

Talese, Gay. *Honor Thy Father*. New York: World, 1971. Biographical sketch of Joe Bonanno's reign, from the Castellammarese War until the infamous Banana Wars.

—*David R. Champion*

**See also:** Joe Adonis; Albert Anastasia; Paul Castellano; Vincent Coll; Carmine Galante; Carlo Gambino; Sam Giancana; Vincent Gigante; John Gotti; Sammy Gravano; Henry Hill; Richard Kuklinski; Meyer Lansky; Salvatore Maranzano; Carlos Marcello; Joe Masseria; Joseph Profaci; Arnold Rothstein; Dutch Schultz.

# D. B. Cooper

## Skyjacker

**Born:** Mid-1920's; place unknown

**Died:** Possibly November 24, 1971; Southwest Washington

**Also known as:** Dan Cooper

**Cause of notoriety:** Cooper carried a bomb on board a passenger airliner; upon his threat to detonate it he was given money, with which he escaped midair, never to be caught.

**Active:** November 24, 1971

**Locale:** Oregon and Washington State

### Early Life

Because D. B. Cooper (KEW-puhr) was never caught or positively identified, information on his early life or why he committed his crime is not available.

*Artist sketches of D. B. Cooper.* (AP/Wide World Photos)

**Criminal Career**

On November 24, 1971, a man identifying himself as Dan Cooper entered the Portland International Airport in Oregon. Witnesses would later describe him as slender, about forty-five years of age, of medium height, and dressed in a dark suit with a pearl tiepin. He purchased a ticket for Northwest-Orient Airlines flight 305 to Seattle, scheduled to leave at 4:35 P.M. Shortly after takeoff, Cooper summoned flight attendant Florence Schaffner and handed her a note that said he had a bomb in his briefcase. Cooper's demands for $200,000 in cash and four parachutes equipped with manual ripcords were forwarded to authorities by the pilot, Captain William Scott.

When the plane landed at Seattle-Tacoma International Airport, Cooper released the passengers in exchange for the parachutes and money, which amounted to twenty-one pounds of twenty-dollar bills. Cooper kept the crew as hostages. He then ordered Scott to fly the plane to Mexico City but not to exceed 10,000 feet in altitude or 150 knots airspeed. The plane could not reach Mexico City, so Cooper agreed to Scott's request to refuel in Reno, Nevada. Shadowed by three U.S. Air Force aircraft, Scott turned the plane toward Reno. At 8:24 P.M., over the wilderness of Washington and Oregon, Cooper let down the plane's aft stairway and parachuted into the night. The tailing Air Force pilots did not observe Cooper's parachute escape. When the plane landed in Reno, Cooper, two of the parachutes, and the money were gone.

In the following days, the Federal Bureau of Investigation (FBI) conducted an extensive ground search for Cooper. In the process, the skyjacker's name became irrevocably changed. Questioning suspects with similar names, the FBI interviewed someone named D. B. Cooper. He had no connection to the crime, but in the subsequent news reporting "Dan" Cooper became known as "D. B." Cooper. Despite an intense eighteen-day manhunt and months of follow-up searches, authorities failed to locate either the skyjacker or the money. Although Cooper left fingerprints behind, the FBI could not find a match.

## Deathbed Confession

"I'm Dan Cooper," said Duane Weber to his wife as he lay dying in a Florida hospital in 1995. Jo had been married to the antiques dealer for seventeen years, yet she had no idea what he was talking about. Duane had always been secretive about his past. "Oh, let it die with me," he told her, apparently annoyed at her puzzlement.

A year later, Jo learned from a library book that "Dan Cooper" was the name used by an airline hijacker in 1971; he was better known as D. B. Cooper. The book also gave the hijacker's description: mid-forties, six feet tall, 170 pounds, black hair, and a chain-smoking bourbon drinker. In 1971, Jo remembered, Weber had been black-haired, an inch taller than six feet, 185 pounds, and a chain-smoking bourbon drinker. Moreover, the match between the composite sketch of the hijacker made by the Federal Bureau of Investigation (FBI) and a photo of her husband was striking. What she really found strange, however, was a pencil notation in the book. It appeared to be in her husband's handwriting, and it named the Washington town where the placard from the rear ramp of the Northwest-Orient Airlines jet had landed.

Then Jo recalled certain items and incidents from Duane's life that seemed to relate to the Cooper hijacking: a white bag the couple owned that matched the description of the canvas bag in which the $200,000 ransom was stowed; a mysterious Northwest ticket stub for a Seattle-Portland flight that her husband disclaimed as unimportant but later disappeared; and another of Duane's deathbed comments, this one referring to a bucket in which he had buried $173,000. Above all, Jo particularly recalled a 1979 vacation to Washington State. They stopped by the Columbia River not far from Portland, and her husband continued to the river edge by himself. Was he searching for something? In the same area, a boy found nearly $5,800 of the ransom money four months later.

All that was uncovered that might relate the case to Duane was considered circumstantial evidence, and the FBI remained skeptical. The FBI did compare Duane's fingerprints with the sixty-six unidentified fingerprints taken from the hijacked plane. There was no match; however, the FBI was unclear that any of the prints came from "Dan Cooper" in the first place. While the former lead agent in the case was intrigued, the FBI dropped the Weber investigation in 1998 for lack of solid evidence; nonetheless, Duane remained among the most likely of several candidate Coopers.

*Source:* Cooper quoted in *U.S. News and World Report*, July 24, 2000.

In subsequent years, the FBI investigated many leads, but all proved fruitless. In 1979, fifty-eight hundred dollars of the ransom money was unearthed near the Columbia River, suggesting that Cooper made it to the ground intact. Whether he lived has remained under speculation. Cooper parachuted wearing the clothes that he wore onto the aircraft, so investigators doubted he survived the frigid descent or the wilderness conditions when he landed. Moreover, no more ransom money has resurfaced, suggesting that Cooper did not live to spend the money. Some researchers, however, believe that he survived, suggesting that Cooper carried additional clothing with him in his briefcase. Supporting this theory, Cooper left behind his tie and its distinctive pearl tiepin, implying that he changed his attire before escaping.

Four months after Cooper's crime, a nearly identical skyjacking occurred in California. An FBI investigation led to Richard McCoy, a former Green Beret. In McCoy's home, police found money from the California skyjacking. McCoy received a forty-five-year prison sentence, but he escaped and later died in a shoot-out with police in 1974. The similarity of the skyjackings convinced many investigators that McCoy was D. B. Cooper.

## Impact

D. B. Cooper's audacious act set off a wave of copycat crimes, most of which failed miserably. Cooper's exploits did demonstrate, however, the woeful state of U.S. airport security, which increased dramatically afterward. Perpetuating Cooper's fame, a device that became known as the Cooper vane was subsequently added to all Boeing 727-model craft to prevent the rear door from opening while in flight.

## Further Reading

Calame, Russell, and Bernie Rhodes. *D. B. Cooper: The Real McCoy*. Salt Lake City: University of Utah Press, 1991. Trying to put the Cooper case to rest, Calame, an FBI agent, claims that convicted skyjacker Richard McCoy was D. B. Cooper.

Himmelsbach, Ralph P., and Thomas K. Worcester. *Norjak: The Investigation of D. B. Cooper*. West Linn, Oreg.: Norjak Project, 1986. Written by the FBI agent in charge of the Cooper investigation, this book discredits many of the Cooper theories.

Tosaw, Richard T. *D. B. Cooper: Dead or Alive?* Ceres, Calif.: Torsaw, 1984. Written by another FBI investigator, the book postulates that Cooper drowned in the Columbia River, which explains the found money and the fact that his body and parachutes were never recovered.

—*Steven J. Ramold*

**See also:** Samuel Joseph Byck; Theodore Kaczynski.

## Frank Costello
### Mafia kingpin

**Born:** January 26, 1891; Lauropoli, Calabria, Italy
**Died:** February 18, 1973; New York, New York
**Also known as:** Francesco Castiglia (birth name); Prime Minister of the Mob
**Major offenses:** Contempt of Congress and tax evasion
**Active:** 1920's-1973
**Locale:** United States, mainly New York, New York
**Sentence:** Eighteen months' imprisonment for contempt of Congress, of which he served fourteen months; five years' imprisonment for tax evasion, of which he served forty-two months

#### Early Life
Frank Costello (caws-TEHL-oh) was born Francesco Castiglia in Italy, and at the age of four years, he sailed to the United States, carried by his mother in a large cooking pot. He despised his father's acceptance of poverty in their East Harlem ghetto, so he left school in the fifth grade and turned to various street crimes: purse-snatching, petty theft, and rifling vending machines. One day, in the balcony of a film theater, he met Lucky Luciano; both boys were kicked out of the theater for throwing trash at the audience below.

#### Criminal Career
In 1914, Costello, a Roman Catholic, met and married a Jewish girl, Loretta Geigerman. A year later, he was sentenced to one year in prison for carrying a concealed weapon. Thereafter, he resolved to work with persuasion rather

than with weapons and used his skill at meeting the right people to work in his favor. His circle of close acquaintances included Owney Madden, a beer baron who became a celebrity gangster, and Arnold Rothstein, a businessman who reputedly fixed the 1919 World Series. Costello also worked with other known mobsters, including Meyer Lansky, Bugsy Siegel, Vito Genovese, Vincent Alo, Joseph Doto (better known as Joe Adonis), and William Vincent Dwyer, who was later elected mayor of New York.

During Prohibition, Costello, working in partnership with Lansky under Luciano's leadership, made a fortune in bootlegging with such daring tactics as using seaplanes to keep hijackers away from his boats filled with alcohol. However, he was soon arrested and charged with organizing a multimillion-dollar liquor ring and bribing the coastguard to let liquor into the country. The jury in this case was hung, and Costello went free on January 20, 1927.

After Prohibition, Costello focused on slot machines. When Mayor Fiorello La Guardia attempted to prosecute Costello's operation, Costello moved it to New Orleans, where it found tacit protection from Senator Huey Long, the former governor of Louisiana. Costello poured his profits into joint ventures with friends in order to build swanky nightclubs and casinos in New York and Florida, as well as regional vice centers around the country. Later, along with Luciano and Lansky, Costello invested heavily in Siegel's dream to build the casino capital of the world in Las Vegas, Nevada, where gambling was legal.

Costello inherited valuable connections with Democratic politicians in New York from Rothstein, who was killed in 1928. Because Costello's Mafia niche was his skill with political influence, his friends counted on him to protect their illegal activities by bribing police, politicians, and judges. He accompanied Jimmy Hines, Manhattan's Democratic party boss, to the Democratic National Convention, where he helped Franklin D. Roosevelt win the presidential nomination in 1932.

Costello wielded enormous political influence during the 1930's and 1940's. Legend has it that, during this period, no judge reached the bench in New York without Costello's approval. In 1940, Costello used his political influence to arrange a payoff to police in exchange for silencing a witness who had turned into an informer. Abe "Kid Twist" Reles began telling authorities what he knew about forty-nine mob killings. However, while in police custody, Reles mysteriously fell to his death from a hotel window.

In 1934, after mob leader Luciano was jailed and left Genovese in charge as his underboss, Genovese fled to avoid prosecution for the murder of mobster Ferdinand Boccia. Captured by Army officers in Italy, Genovese was returned to the United States after World War II. However, before trial, the key witness against him was poisoned in his prison cell, and Genovese was released on June 11, 1946. Costello had served as "caretaker" while Genovese was away, but Genovese began to resume power upon his return, a move contested by Costello. The power struggle between the men had repercussions more than a decade later, when Genovese's bodyguard, Vincent Gigante, shot Costello at point-blank range on May 2, 1957. The bullet grazed Costello's skull but did not kill him. True to the Mafia code, Costello refused to identify his assailant in court.

## Legal Action and Outcome

During the 1950's, Costello was in and out of courtrooms and jails. He was subpoenaed to appear before the Kefauver Committee investigations into organized crime in March, 1951. However, his reluctance to answer questions before the Senate committee led both to his conviction of contempt of the Senate and to a sentence of eighteen months in prison; he served fourteen months. In April, 1954, Costello was convicted of evading federal tax on $51,095 income. He served forty-two months of a five-year sentence.

Costello faced more trouble in 1957 after police, investigating the attempt on Costello's life by Gigante, found a note in Costello's coat pocket that proved the mob was behind the buildup of Las Vegas. Costello was sent to prison for fifteen days for contempt of court for refusing to answer questions about the murder attempt.

Lengthy legal maneuvers to deport Costello came to a surprising end in February, 1961, when the United States Supreme Court overturned his deportation order. The high council of the American Mafia then allowed Costello to take most of his money into retirement with his wife on Long Island.

## Impact

With his dapper dress, dignified bearing, and diplomatic aplomb, Frank Costello brought to organized crime more than a veneer of civility. To a degree, he was able to suppress violence and prevent Las Vegas and New York from becoming violent cities, as Chicago had become. Known as the Prime

Minister of the Mob, he was a peacemaker who reconciled opposing factions, adjudicated disputes, and brought about significant results.

Costello was, foremost, a bridge between the underworld and the political powers of his era. Despite his penchant for crime, he was a practical man who took a long-range view of what needed to be accomplished. He saw that both bootlegging and gambling supplied public demands, which were soon to be declared legal and operated as government monopolies.

At a time when the Mafia was abandoning its old ways and reorganizing itself according to principles of business management, Costello perfected the art of political corruption. A man with old-fashioned moral values, he understood the benefits and detractions of bribery. He shunned drug dealing and ordered his associates not to engage in it. Because he hated fascism, he supported Roosevelt and other politicians who waged war against Adolf Hitler and Benito Mussolini. Likewise, because he hated bigotry, he supported politicians who respected diversity and who put equality on the national agenda.

**Further Reading**

Katz, Leonard. *Uncle Frank: The Biography of Frank Costello*. New York: Drake, 1973. A sympathetic portrait drawn principally from published accounts and interviews with people who knew Costello. Photographs and index are included.

Raab, Selwyn. *The Five Families: The Rise, Decline, and Resurgence of America's Most Powerful Mafia Empires*. New York: Thomas Dunne Books, 2005. Definitive history of the rise and fall of New York's most powerful mobs, written by a *New York Times* reporter.

Reppetto, Thomas. *American Mafia*. New York: Holt, 2004. A chronicle of the Mafia's rise to power in the United States from 1890 to 1951. Includes an excellent bibliography.

*—John L. McLean*

**See also:** Joe Adonis; Vito Genovese; Meyer Lansky; Lucky Luciano; Arnold Rothstein; Bugsy Siegel.

# Andrew Cunanan

## Serial killer

**Born:** August 31, 1969; Rancho Bernardo, California

**Died:** July 23, 1997; Miami, Florida

**Also known as:** Andrew Phillip Cunanan (full name); Andrew De Silva; Lieutenant Commander Cummings

**Cause of notoriety:** Cunanan engaged in a killing spree that left five people dead, including well-known fashion designer Gianni Versace. He committed suicide before he could be arrested.

**Active:** April 25-July 23, 1997

**Locale:** San Diego, California; Minneapolis and Rush City, Minnesota; Chicago, Illinois; Pennsville, New Jersey; and Miami, Florida

### Early Life

Growing up in San Diego, California, Andrew Phillip Cunanan (coo-NAN-an) attended the upper-class Bishop's School, graduating in 1987. A cross-country runner and good student, he obscured his middle-class background from his classmates, most of whom were from upper-class families. In the school yearbook, students named Andrew "the most likely to be remembered." A year after Cunanan finished high school, his father, Modesto, who had been in the United States Navy and was a stockbroker, returned to his native Philippines, presumably to escape investigation about questionable business dealings. Cunanan followed Modesto to the Philippines but soon returned, dismayed by the squalid conditions in which his father lived. Modesto also had a violent streak, which might have had an impact on Cunanan's decision.

Cunanan then distanced himself from his family, using assumed names and passing himself off as a Hollywood film official or prosperous antique merchant. He frequented gay bars and had numerous gay contacts. He was also not above bartering sexual favors for money.

Cunanan was physically attractive and glib, projecting a self-assurance that masked his intrinsic phoniness. He was extravagant, usually picking up the check when he was out with people for meals or drinks. People considered him a rich, if somewhat improvident, acquaintance. He financed his generosity by taking money from the older men whom he allowed to seduce him. He also sold illicit drugs to raise money in order to maintain his deceit.

## Criminal Career

As the acquired immunodeficiency syndrome (AIDS) epidemic erupted, Cunanan feared that he was HIV-positive, although a postmortem test revealed otherwise. Some people theorized that it was Cunanan's fear of the disease that sparked his murderous spree of five people and his eventual suicide.

Cunanan left San Diego on April 25, 1997, going first to Minneapolis, where, on April 29, he bludgeoned twenty-eight-year-old Jeffrey Trail to death. Trail was a friend of David Madson, who had recently moved to Minnesota. On May 3, Madson's body was found on the shore of East Rush Lake, north of Minneapolis. He was shot three times. The following day, the body of real estate developer Lee Miglin was found in Chicago; Miglin's throat was cut, his Lexus was missing, and Madson's car was found near the Miglin house. The Lexus was discovered on May 9 near the office of William Reese, a cemetery caretaker, who was then found shot to death in his office. Reese's Chevrolet pickup truck was missing.

More than two months passed before Cunanan's next murder, which was that of fashion designer Gianni Versace at the gates of his Miami mansion on July 15. Reese's Chevrolet truck, bearing stolen license plates, was found in a nearby garage. On July 23, Cunanan, who had hidden on an unoccupied houseboat after the Versace murder, was found dead in an upper bedroom of the boat; he had shot himself in the mouth and had died instantly.

## Impact

Andrew Cunanan's crimes made national headlines, especially after the murder of Versace, both as authorities tried to locate Cunanan and as news broke of Cunanan's subsequent suicide. Cunanan left behind many clues to his identity and his whereabouts at crime scenes, including a pawn ticket with his thumbprint on it. Investigators later learned that the pawnbroker had turned it over to the police, who then failed to pursue the lead. Following the events surrounding the killing spree, law enforcement authorities became more vigilant in checking details that might connect crimes under investigation to other crimes.

## Further Reading

Clarkson, Wensley. *Death at Every Stop*. New York: St. Martin's Press, 1997. Accurate account of Cunanan's murderous rampage that began in California and ended in Florida.

Crowley, Harry. "Homocidal Homosexual." *The Advocate*, September 2, 1998, 27-31. Focuses on the media coverage of Versace's murder and the search for his killer.

Indiana, Gary. *Three Month Fever: The Andrew Cunanan Story*. New York: HarperCollins, 1999. A thorough analysis of Cunanan's killing spree.

Orth, Maureen. *Vulgar Favors: Andrew Cunanan, Gianni Versace, and the Largest Failed Manhunt in U.S. History*. New York: Delacorte, 1999. Orth packs considerable detail into this book's lengthy discussion and gives an excellent summary of the gruesome events surrounding Cunanan's crime spree.

Thomas, Evan. "End of the Road." *Newsweek* 130, no. 5 (August 4, 1997): 22-28. Comprehensive account of Cunanan's murderous spree before his suicide.

*—R. Baird Shuman*

**See also:** Joe Ball; David Berkowitz; Kenneth Bianchi; Ted Bundy; Angelo Buono, Jr.; Albert DeSalvo; Albert Fish; John Wayne Gacy; Ed Gein; Leonard Lake; Charles Ng; Dennis Rader; Richard Speck; Charles Starkweather; Aileen Carol Wuornos.

# Leon Czolgosz

## Assassin of President William McKinley

**Born:** 1873; Detroit, Michigan
**Died:** October 29, 1901; Auburn Prison, Auburn, New York
**Also known as:** Leon Frank Czolgosz (full name); Fred C. Nieman
**Major offense:** Murder of President William McKinley
**Active:** September 6, 1901
**Locale:** Buffalo, New York
**Sentence:** Convicted of first-degree murder; executed by electrocution

### Early Life

Leon Frank Czolgosz (CHEWL-gawsh) was born into brutal poverty with parents who were Polish immigrants. His mother died when Czolgosz was twelve while she was giving birth to a child. At the age of fourteen, Czolgosz began working in the steel and glass factories of Cleveland and

*Leon Czolgosz.* (Library of Congress)

Pittsburgh. Because he was earning only four dollars a day, Czolgosz joined a union and went on strike, but this resulted in his being fired. Czolgosz and his family usually had little money left for housing and medical care. As a young man, he had only one girlfriend, who broke up with him; after this relationship, he was too shy to talk to women. Czolgosz was always fairly quiet and withdrawn. He was also known to sleep a great deal, and he refused to eat food prepared by his stepmother because he feared that she might poison him.

Czolgosz was influenced by the Haymarket Square bombing in 1886—a labor rally in Chicago during which a bomb exploded, killing eleven persons. Anarchists were arrested for the crime, although there was little evidence against them. Czolgosz was angry that five anarchists were executed for the bombing and saw this as an injustice against the labor movement. He also rejected religion, believing that God had abandoned the working class.

**Criminal Career**

In the 1896 presidential election between Republican William McKinley and Democrat William Jennings Bryan, McKinley represented the wealthy industrialists, and Bryan represented the working poor. Czolgosz believed that money from the wealthy industrialists swayed the election to McKinley. In 1897, the Lattimer Mines Massacre in Pennsylvania occurred during which police killed Slavic miners who were peacefully demonstrating. The police officers were later acquitted, which contributed to Czolgosz's nervous breakdown in the fall of 1897. Czolgosz absorbed the radical literature of his day and was obsessed with the need for radical social change. He was a follower of Emma Goldman, an anarchist and feminist who was a great speaker. Czolgosz heard her speak on a number of occasions and also had brief conversations with her. Anarchists thought that Czolgosz might be a government spy and sent out a warning to others to watch out for him. He often used the alias Fred C. Nieman.

In 1900, King Humbert I of Italy was assassinated by an anarchist named

### Nieman, No Man

*Leon Czolgosz rightly used the alias "Fred Nieman"; the surname means "no man" in German, and it referred to his rejection by the far-left radicals and anarchists among whom he sought acceptance. Suspicious of Czolgosz, Abraham Isaak, the editor of the radical periodical* Free Society, *issued a warning in his paper regarding the possibility that Czolgosz might be a spy in their midst:*

Attention!

The attention of the comrades is called to another spy. He is well dressed, of medium height, rather narrow shouldered, blond, and about 25 years of age. Up to the present he has made his appearance in Chicago and Cleveland. In the former place he remained a short time, while in Cleveland he disappeared when the comrades had confirmed themselves of his identity and were on the point interested in the cause, asking for names, or soliciting aid for acts of contemplated violence. If this individual makes his appearance elsewhere, the comrades are warned in advance and can act accordingly.

Gaetano Bresci. Bresci held that he had killed the king for the sake of the common person. Czolgosz found in Bresci his hero, a man who had the courage to sacrifice himself for a cause. Inspired by Bresci, Czolgosz sought to assassinate President McKinley because he was wealthy and indifferent to the working class. Czolgosz heard McKinley speak in Buffalo at the Pan-American Exposition about the prosperity of the United States, while so many of the working poor suffered. On September 6, 1901, Czolgosz went to the exposition with a pistol concealed in a handkerchief bandaged around his right hand. McKinley was standing in a receiving line greeting people when Czolgosz shot McKinley twice at point-blank range. McKinley died eight days later.

### Legal Action and Outcome

When Czolgosz was arrested, police found a folded newspaper clipping about Bresci in Czolgosz's pocket. Czolgosz pleaded guilty and did not express any regret. He was sentenced to death and executed by electrocution on October 29, 1901.

### Impact

After the assassination, the government sought to eliminate anarchists who were blamed for McKinley's death. While some anarchists condemned Leon Czolgosz, others, such as Goldman, praised him as a brave martyr. Oddly enough, the McKinley assassination provided the United States with a more progressive leader in Theodore Roosevelt, who was more sympathetic to the working class. Roosevelt pushed for the creation of the departments of labor and commerce and also weakened the power of large corporations.

### Further Reading

Clarke, James W. *American Assassins: The Darker Side of Politics*. Princeton, N.J.: Princeton University Press, 1982. Clarke develops a typology for analyzing political assassins throughout American history.

Johns, A. Wesley. *The Man Who Shot McKinley*. South Brunswick, N.J.: A. S. Barnes, 1970. Johns provides a new perspective on the assassin of President McKinley.

MacDonald, Carlos F. "The Trial, Execution, Autopsy, and Mental Status of Leon F. Czolgosz, Alias Fred Nieman, the Assassin of President Mc-

Kinley." *American Journal of Insanity* 58 (January, 1902): 369-386. Provides a contemporary psychological analysis of Czolgosz.

*—Scott P. Johnson*

**See also**: John Wilkes Booth; Charles Julius Guiteau; Lee Harvey Oswald.

# Jeffrey Dahmer

## Serial killer, cannibal, and necrophiliac

**Born:** May 21, 1960; Milwaukee, Wisconsin
**Died:** November 28, 1994; Columbia Correctional Institution, Portage, Wisconsin
**Also known as:** Jeffrey Lionel Dahmer (full name)
**Major offenses:** Murder, cannibalism, and sexual assault
**Active:** June 18, 1978; November, 1987-July, 1991
**Locale:** Bath, Ohio; Milwaukee, Wisconsin
**Sentence:** Fifteen consecutive life sentences; ten years on sixteen counts of murder

### Early Life

Jeffrey Lionel Dahmer (DAH-muhr) had a troubled childhood. He had difficulty making friends and was a loner who was fascinated with death, bodies, flesh, and taxidermy. He had a collection of roadkill and insects preserved in chemicals. Dahmer was also fond of impaling the heads of animals on stakes and mounting the bodies on trees behind his house. By high school, Dahmer had alienated his peers and was shy around female students. He consistently sought attention with his odd behavior and by faking seizures. Dahmer was probably also influenced by the divorce of his parents, Lionel and Joyce. His parents fought over the custody of his younger brother David but not over his custody (mainly because Dahmer was already eighteen and custody was not an issue). Both his father and his mother tried to pressure Dahmer to side with them, pitting Dahmer against each one. His mother eventually received custody of David and moved to Wisconsin, and Lionel moved out of the house shortly thereafter; both effectively abandoned Dahmer.

**Criminal Career**

On June 18, 1978, Dahmer met eighteen-year-old hitchhiker Stephen Hicks and brought him back to the empty home that Dahmer now occupied. The two engaged in sexual intercourse, and afterward, when Hicks tried to leave, Dahmer struck him in the head with a barbell. Dahmer used a sledgehammer to smash Hicks's body, and then he buried the remains in the woods behind the house.

Although Dahmer committed his first murder in 1978, he did not kill again until 1987. Between 1978 and 1981, Dahmer was in the army, from which he was discharged in 1981 because of his alcohol problem. In 1982, Dahmer moved in with his grandmother near Milwaukee and began going to gay bars and bringing men home with him. Dahmer killed again in 1987, when he picked up Steven Toumi in a gay bar. Dahmer took Toumi to a hotel, where the two men got drunk and lost consciousness. According to Dahmer, when he awoke, Toumi was dead, and Dahmer proceeded to take the body to his grandmother's house, where he engaged in necrophilia, dismembered the body, and threw the body parts in the trash. Dahmer continued his pattern of meeting men at gay bars; taking them back to his grandmother's house, where he drugged them; having sex with them (either alive, dead, or both); and then dismembering their bodies.

Dahmer moved from his grandmother's house to his own apartment in

*Jeffrey Dahmer at his preliminary hearing.* (AP/Wide World Photos)

November, 1988. The next day, he brought a thirteen-year-old boy to his apartment, where he tried to drug the boy with sleeping pills. However, the boy escaped, and Dahmer was arrested the next day for sexual assault, to which he pleaded guilty and was given a sentence of five years' probation. However, despite this encounter with the law, Dahmer continued killing men.

In March, 1989, Dahmer picked up a twenty-four-year-old African American male, whom he took to his grandmother's house. There, the two engaged in intercourse, and then Dahmer drugged the man and strangled him. Dahmer disposed of the body but kept the head, boiling it until only the skull remained. As he murdered and dismembered several more men, Dahmer continued this act of keeping a souvenir of his victims. Dahmer eventually transitioned from engaging in necrophilia and collecting skulls and body parts to engaging in cannibalism.

On July 22, 1991, Dahmer picked up another man, Tracy Edwards, whom he took back to his apartment. Edwards managed to escape and was able to notify police. The officers responded to Dahmer's apartment. They smelled a rancid odor and found pictures of dismembered bodies and skulls and a full human skeleton. Dahmer was finally arrested, and his murderous career ended.

### Legal Action and Outcome

After his arrest in 1991, Dahmer pleaded guilty by reason of insanity to the murder charges. The jury found Dahmer sane on all sixteen counts of murder. Wisconsin did not allow the death penalty, so the judge sentenced Dahmer to fifteen consecutive life sentences plus ten years on all counts. Dahmer was sent to the Columbia Correctional Institution to serve his time. However, on November 28, 1994, Dahmer was beaten to death by another inmate.

### Impact

Jeffrey Dahmer's crimes were shocking, not only in number but also in what he did with the bodies. Dahmer had confessed to the murders and admitted to necrophilia and cannibalism, but the question of why he committed these crimes remained, fascinating psychologists and criminal investigators. The crimes also had an impact on the justice system itself. Investigators learned of an incident in May, 1991, during which one of

Dahmer's eventual victims escaped from Dahmer, only to be returned to him by the responding officers, who deemed the event "a lover's quarrel." The fourteen-year-old boy soon became Dahmer's twelfth and youngest victim. Law officers were forced to consider the ways in which they handle such seemingly innocent events. Moreover, Dahmer committed several of his crimes while on probation for his 1988 arrest, calling into question the efficacy of probation and the criminal justice system in general.

**Further Reading**

Dahmer, Lionel. *Father's Story*. New York: William Morrow, 1994. Written by Dahmer's father, who discusses his son's life from the unique perspective of someone who was close to and loved Dahmer, despite his crimes.

Davis, D. *The Milwaukee Murders: Nightmare in Apartment 213, the True Story*. New York: St. Martin's Press, 1991. Discusses in depth the life and crimes of Dahmer, although it was published before Dahmer was killed in prison.

Jaeger, R. W., and M. W. Balousek. *Massacre in Milwaukee: The Macabre Case of Jeffrey Dahmer*. Oregon, Wis.: Waubesa Press, 1991. Discusses the life and crimes of Dahmer, as well as the aftermath of the murders and the consequences of the crimes for the police and the public.

Masters, B. *The Shrine of Jeffrey Dahmer*. London: Hodder and Stoughton, 1993. Discusses the life of Dahmer and his crimes.

—*Jenephyr James*

**See also:** Joe Ball; David Berkowitz; Kenneth Bianchi; Ted Bundy; Angelo Buono, Jr.; Albert DeSalvo; Albert Fish; John Wayne Gacy; Ed Gein; Leonard Lake; Charles Ng; Dennis Rader; Richard Speck; Aileen Carol Wuornos.

# Bob Dalton

## Western outlaw and gang leader

**Born:** May 13, 1869; near Belton, Cass County, Missouri
**Died:** October 5, 1892; Coffeyville, Kansas
**Also known as:** Robert Rennick Dalton (full name)
**Cause of notoriety:** Dalton, along with other members of the Dalton Gang, terrorized the American Old West with bank robberies, train robberies, and cattle theft.
**Active:** c. 1887-1892
**Locale:** California, Kansas, New Mexico Territory (now mostly New Mexico), and Indian Territory (now Oklahoma)

### Early Life

Robert (Bob) Rennick Dalton (REHN-nihk DAHL-tuhn) was one of fifteen children born to James Lewis and Adeline (Younger) Dalton. The Dalton family was constantly on the move, living at one time or another in Missouri, Kansas, Indian Territory (now Oklahoma), and California. The older Dalton children were all law-abiding, respectable citizens. Frank Dalton, for example, was killed in the line of duty while serving as a deputy U.S. marshal under Judge Isaac C. Parker (known as the Hanging Judge because of his preferred sentences). However, four Dalton boys—Bob, Bill, Grattan, and Emmett—eventually became outlaws. It is unclear why the younger Daltons robbed trains and banks while the older siblings minded the law—perhaps the fact that their father had abandoned the family while the younger boys were still in their formative years had an impact. The Dalton brothers also proudly claimed kinship to the infamous James-Younger Gang (with Jesse James and Cole Younger being its most famous members), which might have also played a role in pushing the Dalton boys into criminal activities.

### Criminal Career

After the death of brother Frank, Grattan replaced his fallen brother as a deputy marshal, and he soon appointed brothers Bob and Emmett as his assistants. Bob also served the Osage Nation as chief of Indian police. During the late 1880's, Indian Territory was a raucous and dangerous place where bootlegging, horse theft, and murder reached epidemic levels. Within this world, the Dalton brothers wore badges but also began engaging in crime. Their life of crime began with horse and cattle theft in Indian Territory. However, it soon progressed to murder when Bob shot and killed Charles Montgomery, a man who courted Bob's sweetheart while he was out of town.

By 1890, the Dalton brothers' quasi-law-enforcement careers had ended, and they turned to the more profitable career of full-time horse thieving. With warrants for their arrest in Indian Territory and Kansas, the brothers fled the region. Grattan joined several brothers in California, while Bob and Emmett moved to New Mexico, where they found themselves wanted by the law after robbing men playing a faro game. Emmett retreated to Indian Territory, while Bob joined his brothers in California. Once again, trouble followed Bob. When a train was robbed at Alila, California, by masked gunmen, law officers targeted Bob, Grattan, and Bill Dalton. Although authorities arrested Bill and Grattan, Bob managed to elude capture and returned to Indian Territory. There, he resumed his criminal career by heading a gang of outlaws, which included Emmett Dalton, Bill Doolin, George "Bitter Creek" Newcomb, and Bill Powers, among others. Grattan then rejoined his brothers after escaping from California authorities in September, 1891. For the next year, the Dalton Gang robbed at least four trains within and surrounding Indian Territory and were blamed for dozens of other robberies.

The Dalton Gang made a fatal mistake on October 5, 1892. Five gang members—Bob, Grattan, and Emmett Dalton, along with compatriots Dick Broadwell and Powers—attempted to do what their heroes in the James-Younger Gang had never done: simultaneously rob two banks. The gang chose Coffeyville, Kansas, for the robberies. The robberies, however, were poorly conceived. The Dalton brothers had lived near Coffeyville ten years earlier, and their brother Frank was buried in the town cemetery. As they rode into town, citizens immediately recognized the Daltons, who, by 1892, were well-known criminals. Confident of their abilities, however, Bob and Emmett entered the First National Bank, while Powers, Broadwell, and brother Grattan robbed the Condon Bank across the street. Word quickly spread throughout town that the Dalton Gang was robbing the town banks. Citizens armed themselves, some borrowing guns from local businesses, and began surrounding the banks from concealed positions. Although Bob and Emmett exited the First National Bank with more than twenty-one thousand dollars, they were forced to retreat back into the bank when armed citizens opened fire. They then retreated through a back door, where they were met by the other three robbers.

Trapped in an alley and under heavy gunfire, the Dalton Gang fought tenaciously to escape. Wielding a Winchester rifle, Bob killed three citizens and wounded another, while Grattan reportedly killed Marshal Charles Connelly. One by one, however, the Dalton Gang succumbed to the relentless shoot-out. John Kloher, a Coffeyville liveryman, killed Bob with a bullet to the chest, probably making Bob the first of the gang to die. When Grattan tried to avenge his brother, Kloher fatally wounded him too. Coffeyville marksmen knocked Broadwell and Powers from their horses as they attempted escape. Emmett, the only member of the gang still mounted, perhaps could have escaped, but he returned to the alley and attempted to rescue his dying brother Bob. Armed citizens then fired on Emmett, riddling the twenty-year-old bandit with more than twenty bullets. When the shooting stopped, four Dalton Gang members and four Coffeyville citizens lay dead or dying. Surviving members were soon dead or in prison. Doolin and Bill Dalton, who did not participate in the raid, were later killed by lawmen. Emmett, the sole survivor of Coffeyville, pleaded guilty to second-degree murder and served nearly fifteen years in the Kansas State Penitentiary.

### Impact

The Coffeyville Raid, as it came to be known in history, is perhaps the most famous of the frontier-era bank robberies. During the raid, the Dalton Gang met its end by the quick actions of the citizens of Coffeyville. Historians often point to the failed bank robberies as the point at which the outlaw-driven frontier era began to fade away. Citizens, fed up with criminal activity, sent a message to would-be robbers by killing members of the Dalton Gang.

### Further Reading

Barndollar, Lue Diver. *What Really Happened on October 5, 1892: An Attempt at an Accurate Account of the Dalton Gang and Coffeyville*. 1992. Reprint. Coffeyville, Kans.: Coffeyville Historical Society, 2001. An illustrated history of the Daltons' failed bank robberies.

O'Neal, Bill. *Encyclopedia of Western Gunfighters*. Norman: University of Oklahoma Press, 1979. This valuable collection of 587 gunfighter biographies provides a biography of Bob Dalton, as well as short descriptions of his criminal activity and gunfights. Biographies of Emmett, Grattan, and Bill Dalton are also included.

Smith, Robert Barr. *Daltons! The Raid on Coffeyville*. Norman: University of Oklahoma Press, 1996. A detailed examination of the deadly Coffeyville Raid.

*—Mark R. Ellis*

**See also:** Emmett Dalton; Bill Doolin; Jesse James; Cole Younger.

# Emmett Dalton

## Western outlaw and gang leader

**Born:** May 3, 1871; Kansas City, Missouri
**Died:** July 13, 1937; Hollywood, California
**Also known as:** Em
**Major offenses:** Murder and robbery
**Active:** 1890-October 5, 1892
**Locale:** Northeast Oklahoma and southeast Kansas
**Sentence:** Life in prison; pardoned after fourteen years

### Early Life

Emmett Dalton (EHM-eht DAHL-tuhn) was the eleventh of fifteen children born to James Lewis and Adeline Dalton. Named after an Irish criminal who was hanged on the gallows in England, Emmett was a first cousin of the notorious Cole Younger and his brothers. Dalton received little formal education. He and his older brother Bob developed a close relationship, and Bob protected his younger brother during times of trouble.

For a few months in 1889, Dalton served as a lawman alongside his brothers Bob, Bill, and Grattan in Fort Smith, Arkansas. Later that year, the four brothers served with Indian police on the Osage Indian Reservation. Bored by the lack of action and tired of the meager pay, the brothers turned to cattle rustling but soon discovered ventures that brought more money.

### Criminal Career

In 1890, Emmett and Bob Dalton drifted into New Mexico. After feeling that they were cheated in a faro card game, they held up the players and took back their money—and more. "Wanted" posters were issued for their arrest.

Bob headed to California, while Emmett returned home to his family in Kingfisher, Oklahoma, to spend time with his childhood sweetheart, Julia Johnson.

In the spring of 1891, Emmett joined with his brothers Bob and Grat to form a formidable outlaw gang that included Bill Doolin, George Newcomb, Charley Bryant, Dick Broadwell, and Bill Powers. On May 9, 1891, the gang robbed the Texas Express train near Whorton, Oklahoma, taking about fourteen thousand dollars. A few weeks later, they took nineteen thousand dollars in currency and silver from a train near Lelietta, Oklahoma (then in Indian Territory). Emmett and Bob then left the gang, with hopes of going straight.

After a few months, Grat talked his brothers into rejoining the gang. Their next heist occurred near Red Rock, Oklahoma, where they took eleven thousand dollars from a Santa Fe train. On July 14, 1892, they stopped a train near Adair, Oklahoma, and got away with close to seventeen thousand dollars. On October 5, 1892, Emmett, Bob, and Grat Dalton, along with Bill Powers and Dick Broadwell, attempted to rob two banks at the same time in Coffeyville, Kansas. After they took twenty-four thousand dollars from the banks, an ensuing gun battle led to the death of four Coffeyville citizens and all of the outlaws except Emmett Dalton. He received twenty-three gunshot wounds but survived.

## Legal Action and Outcome

For his participation in the Coffeyville robberies, Emmett was charged with first-degree murder. A preliminary hearing was held on January 16, 1893. The evidence against Dalton was sufficient for him to be held for trial without bail. His trial took place at the Montgomery County Courthouse in Independence, Missouri, in March, 1893. Dalton's lawyer, Joseph Fritch, convinced Dalton to plead guilty to second-degree murder so that he would receive a lighter sentence. The judge unexpectedly sentenced Dalton to life imprisonment in the Kansas State Penitentiary in Lansing, Kansas. Because of his good behavior, Dalton was granted an unconditional pardon on November 2, 1907, after serving fourteen and one-half years.

## Impact

Emmett Dalton is a classic example of a reformed outlaw. He was involved in the first simultaneous double bank robbery in outlaw history. While he was in prison, his model behavior led to his early release. He married Julia Johnson and became an exemplary citizen, living first in Tulsa, Oklahoma, and then in Hollywood, California. He became a real estate agent, author, and actor. With the collaboration of Jack Jungmeyer, Dalton wrote the story of the Dalton gang, *When the Daltons Rode* (1931). The book was made into a film in 1940. Stories of the Dalton gang have been portrayed in magazines, movies, and television shows.

**Further Reading**

Barndollar, Lue Diver. *What Really Happened on October 5, 1892: An Attempt at an Accurate Account of the Dalton Gang and Coffeyville*. 1992. Reprint. Coffeyville, Kans.: Coffeyville Historical Society, 2001. Discusses the outlaw days of Emmett, Bob, and Grat Dalton, with a detailed account of the Coffeyville escapade.

Dalton, Emmett. *Beyond the Law*. 1918. Reprint. Gretna, La.: Pelican, 2002. Dalton recounts his life and memories of the Dalton gang.

_______. *When the Daltons Rode*. Garden City, N.Y.: Doubleday, Doran, 1931. Dalton's memoir. Illustrated.

Pryor, Alton. *Outlaws and Gunslingers: Tales of the West's Most Notorious Outlaws*. Roseville, Calif.: Stagecoach, 2001. Reviews the lives of twenty-seven famous gunfighters of the Old West, including the Dalton brothers.

*—Alvin K. Benson*

**See also:** Bob Dalton; Bill Doolin; Jesse James; Cole Younger.

## Richard Allen Davis

### Sexual predator and murderer

**Born:** June 2, 1954; San Francisco, California

**Major offenses:** Murder, robbery, burglary, kidnapping, lewd act involving a child, and assault with a deadly weapon

**Active:** October 1, 1993

**Locale:** Petaluma, California

**Sentence:** Death

*Richard Allen Davis.*
(AP/Wide World Photos)

## Early Life

Richard Allen Davis (DAY-vihs) was born in San Francisco. His father, Robert, who worked as a truck driver and longshoreman, was an alcoholic who was absent much of the time. His mother, Evelyn, who stayed home with the children, was abusive and emotionally neglectful. Richard's early childhood was unstable, as the family relocated frequently. His parents divorced when he was eleven. Richard began getting in trouble with law enforcement authorities at an early age. His first encounter, at age twelve, resulted in his arrest for burglary. Later that same year, after being arrested for forgery, he was placed in a juvenile detention center, where he remained until his father obtained custody of him. Davis attended school through the tenth grade, when he dropped out and joined the Army. He was enlisted in 1971-1972 but was then discharged after developing a morphine addiction.

## Criminal Career

Through the years, Davis continued his criminal career, with seventeen arrests for various crimes, including robbery, burglary, theft, three separate kidnapping charges, sexual assault, public drunkenness, possession of marijuana, and numerous parole and probation violations. By the time Davis was thirty-nine, he had spent more than fourteen years in prison and had a rap sheet eleven pages long. He was last paroled on June 27, 1993, after serving eight years of a sixteen-year sentence for kidnapping. Only months after his release, on October 1, 1993, he kidnapped and murdered Polly Klaas, a twelve-year-old girl.

In the autumn of 1993, Polly Hannah Klaas was having a slumber party at her home with two friends. While her mother and sister slept in the next room, Davis entered the home, gagged and tied up Polly's friends, and abducted Polly at knifepoint. Later that night, police received a phone call regarding a suspicious man seen near a car in a ditch. Law enforcement officers assisted Davis in pulling his car out of the embankment, allowing him to continue on his way. It is believed that Polly was still alive at that time. The officers at the scene were unaware of the abduction because the appropriate alert had not been dispatched to patrol cars, for fear that the press would hear the information over the scanner.

## Legal Action and Outcome

Polly's disappearance prompted a communitywide search that lasted sixty-five days. At the end of this time, Davis was arrested after forensic evidence—a palm print found in Polly's bedroom—matched his print in the computer network. Four days later, Davis confessed to strangling the child. He led the police to the body, which was located in a shallow grave in a wooded area of Cloverdale, California. On December 7, 1993, Davis was charged with the kidnapping and murder of Polly Klaas. At trial, Davis conceded to all charges except the sexual assault allegation. On June 18, 1996, the jury found him guilty on all counts, and on September 26, 1996, he was sentenced to death. Shortly thereafter, he was sent to San Quentin State Prison to await his execution on death row.

## Impact

Richard Allen Davis's arrest for the kidnapping and murder of Polly Klaas was a catalyst for passage of the "three strikes law" in California, which mandated harsher penalties and longer prison terms for violent repeat offenders. Marc Klaas, Polly's father and an activist for crime prevention programs, lobbied for this law and helped obtain the signatures needed for its passage. Klaas's advocacy was also instrumental in passing the Amber Alert notification system at state and national levels. Klaas formed the KlaasKids Foundation, an organization devoted to protecting children from violent crimes through education and community events. BeyondMissing, another organization founded by Klaas, works to find missing children. The Polly Klaas Foundation, of which Polly's mother was a director, was also established to promote children's safety.

**Further Reading**

Bortnick, Barry. *Polly Klaas: The Murder of America's Child.* New York: Pinnacle Books, 1995. A true-crime book on the Klaas kidnapping and murder.

Filler, D. M. "Making the Case for Megan's Law: A Study in Legislative Rhetoric." *Indiana Law Journal* 76 (Spring, 2001): 315. A review of arguments by legislators regarding the need for sex-offender legislation, including a discussion of Polly Klaas's murder.

Jenkins, Philip. *Moral Panic: Changing Concepts of the Child Molester in Modern America.* New Haven, Conn.: Yale University Press, 1998. Explores the evolution of legislation related to sex crimes against children and how the murder of Polly Klass was a catalyst for predator legislation.

Klaas, Marc. "Sex Offender Registries Protect Our Children." *Corrections Today* 65, no. 1 (February, 2003): 23-24. An article by Polly's father, advocating the monitoring of sex offenders.

Vitiello, M. "'Three Strikes' and the Romero Case: The Supreme Court Restores Democracy." *Loyola of Los Angeles Law Review* 30, no. 1643 (June, 1997). A review of California's "three strikes" legislation, which passed as a result of Polly Klaas's murder.

*—Lisa A. Williams-Taylor*

**See also:** Ira Einhorn; Albert Fish; Gilbert Gauthe.

# Tino De Angelis

## Corporate commodities tycoon

**Born:** 1915; Bronx, New York
**Also known as:** Anthony De Angelis (full name)
**Major offenses:** Conspiracy and transporting forged warehouse receipts across state lines
**Active:** 1957-November, 1963
**Locale:** Bayonne, New Jersey
**Sentence:** Twenty years' imprisonment; paroled in less than seven years

### Early Life

Anthony "Tino" De Angelis (dee AN-jehl-ihs) was born the son of Italian immigrants. While still a teenager, he worked as a butcher in a meat market. In 1938, he started his own slaughterhouse and earned more than $100,000 the first year. At some point, De Angelis began perpetrating a fraud against the National School Lunch Act program by selling spoiled meat. He later began selling substandard vegetable oil products to Europe while its infrastructure was struggling with the aftermath of World War II.

### Criminal Career

Sometime in the late 1950's or early 1960's, De Angelis, through his company, the Allied Crude Vegetable Oil Refining Corporation, began the scam that was to make him infamous: his purported control of the world's supply of soybean oil. However, most of the salad oil he controlled did not exist. To store the salad oil, De Angelis acquired a tank farm in Bayonne, New Jersey, just across the Hudson River from New York City. He filled the forty-two-foot-tall storage tanks almost completely with water and topped them off with vegetable oil. Since oil floats on water, the ingredient at the top of each tank was indeed oil; however, water formed the majority of the tank's contents. Even the small amount of oil on top was pumped from tank to tank via interconnecting pipes. De Angelis then obtained loans using as collateral the valuable salad oil that was supposedly in the tanks. When inspectors and auditors checked the contents of the tanks, all they could see was oil. A subsidiary of American Express, American Express Field Warehousing Company, guaranteed that the oil was really in the tanks.

Lending money on the basis of warehouse receipts is a common banking practice. Banks assume that the receipts prove the existence of the inventory. De Angelis used warehouse receipts to borrow from brokerage companies, and the brokers, in turn, used the same receipts as collateral on loans from banks. Thus, there were many loans but no collateral to support them. In addition to fooling warehouse workers, De Angelis also forged his own warehouse receipts, resulting in the appearance that he owned more salad oil than existed in the entire country.

## Legal Action and Outcome

De Angelis was convicted of conspiracy and transporting forged warehouse receipts across state lines. He was sentenced to twenty years in prison, but he was paroled in only seven years, serving from August, 1965, to June, 1972. However, he apparently did not learn any lessons from incarceration; upon release, he was twice more convicted of similar crimes.

## Impact

The "salad oil swindle" received less publicity than similar scams because it was uncovered during the week that President John F. Kennedy was assassinated, in November, 1963. As a result, the media and American population had more compelling news with which to be concerned than a commodities con in New Jersey. However, at that time, it was one of the biggest frauds in history. The result of Tino De Angelis's scheme for investors amounted to losses of at least $150 million. One brokerage firm, Ira Haupt & Co., was quickly liquidated because of its losses to De Angelis, and another firm, Williston and Beane, was taken over by Merrill Lynch. The American Express Field Warehousing Company also went out of business, but the parent company made good the losses. At least twenty banks that had loaned money to De Angelis also lost money. New procedures for auditing warehoused inventories were subsequently created, thus affecting accountants and auditors. The crime's impact on brokerage firms ultimately led to the passage of the 1971 Securities Investor Protection Act, which provided insurance against losses at securities dealers.

## Further Reading

Eichenwald, Kurt. "Economy and Business: After a Boom, There Will Be Scandal." *The New York Times*, December 16, 2002, p. C3. A retrospective article on how scandals most often occur in boom times.

Miller, Norman C. *The Great Salad Oil Swindle*. New York: Coward-McCann, 1965. This is the complete story of De Angelis, written by a *Wall Street Journal* staff writer who won a Pulitzer Prize for his coverage of the case. Includes an extensive index.

Phalon, Richard. *Forbes Greatest Investing Stories*. New York: John Wiley & Sons, 2001. This volume includes stories with lessons for investors, including a chapter titled "Swindle of the Century: Anthony De Angelis."

*—Dale L. Flesher*

**See also:** John R. Brinkley.

## Albert DeSalvo

### Rapist and suspected serial killer

**Born:** September 3, 1931; Chelsea, Massachusetts
**Died:** November 25, 1973; Walpole State Prison, Massachusetts
**Also known as:** Boston Strangler; Green Man; Measuring Man
**Major offense:** Rape
**Active:** June 14, 1962-January 4, 1964
**Locale:** Boston, Massachusetts
**Sentence:** Life in prison

### Early Life

Albert DeSalvo (duh-SAL-voh) was born in Boston in 1931, where he grew up in an abusive home. His father, Frank DeSalvo, had a history of legal infractions and incarcerations and also physically abused his wife and children. DeSalvo's father was absent for much of his son's childhood, and divorce finally split the family in 1944. Albert compiled a number of juvenile arrests, primarily for property crimes.

DeSalvo joined the Army in 1948 and was first stationed in Germany. While in Germany, he met and married a German woman, Irmgard Beck. He brought her back to the United States with him when he was transferred to Fort Dix, New Jersey, in 1954. At this point, DeSalvo's life appeared stable, with a military career, a wife, and a child who was born in 1955. Later, however, he was charged with molesting a nine-year-old girl in New Jersey. Because the family of the child declined to press charges against DeSalvo, he received an honorable discharge from the Army in 1956 and returned to Boston.

### Criminal Career

Once back in Boston, DeSalvo's involvement in property crime reemerged, and he was arrested several times for breaking and entering over the following years. After arresting DeSalvo in 1960 on suspicion of burglary, police learned of DeSalvo's involvement in repeated predatory sexual behavior. At the time of this arrest, authorities had been searching for a suspect whom they had named the Measuring Man. This suspect had been posing as a talent scout, approaching women's homes and gaining entrance with the hoax. Once inside, this man would take the women's measurements while intimately touching them. DeSalvo confessed to being the Measuring Man and was convicted of breaking and entering and assault and battery, ultimately serving eleven months in prison.

After DeSalvo was released from prison, his sexual offenses turned from perversion and assault to rape. He began breaking into homes across four states over the next few years, tying up his female victims and raping them. The perpetrator of this series of rapes became known as the Green Man, because of the green pants typically worn during the attacks. Overlapping this period was a series of murders that would become known as the Boston Strangler murders. From 1962 to 1964, thirteen women were raped and murdered; most were strangled, and the killer sometimes left the bodies in different poses.

### Legal Action and Outcome

In 1965, nine months after the last of the Boston Strangler murders, DeSalvo was arrested in the Green Man case after a woman identified his picture to police. While awaiting trial, DeSalvo bragged to another inmate that he was the Boston Strangler and then later described the killings to the inmate's attorney, F. Lee Bailey. DeSalvo described the women who were murdered, as well as crime scenes, to Bailey, who gave the information to the police.

The prosecutor's office decided to prosecute DeSalvo for only the Green Man crimes, and he was sentenced to life in prison after being convicted of the rapes. He was stabbed and killed in his prison cell on November 25, 1973. His killer was never identified.

## Impact

The Boston Strangler case was one of the most notorious crime sprees of the 1960's, and it led to a number of books and movies. It brought attention to the deliberate and calculated methods used by some serial rapists and caused a controversy over the credibility and value of confessions in the criminal process. The case also launched the career of attorney F. Lee Bailey, who gained additional fame defending Patty Hearst, Sam Sheppard, and O. J. Simpson.

Although Albert DeSalvo reportedly confessed to the murders, controversy still surrounds the identity of the Boston Strangler. Indeed, a new group of books have been released that challenge the assertion that Albert DeSalvo was the Boston Strangler.

## Further Reading

Junger, Sebastien. *A Death in Belmont*. New York: W. W. Norton, 2006. Junger examines the 1963 slaying of Bessie Goldberg, of whose murder housecleaner Roy Smith was convicted; Goldberg has long been thought to have been a victim of the Boston Strangler.

Kelly, Susan. *The Boston Stranglers: The Public Conviction of Albert DeSalvo and the True Story of Eleven Shocking Murders*. New York: Pinnacle Books, 2002. Follows the life of Albert DeSalvo and contends that he was not the Boston Strangler.

Rae, William. *Confessions of the Boston Strangler*. New York: Pyramid Books, 1967. Focuses on the Boston Strangler case and examines the confessions of Albert DeSalvo.

Sherman, Casey. *A Rose for Mary: The Hunt for the Real Boston Strangler*. Urbana, Ill.: Northeastern University Press, 2003. Like Kelly, Sherman (the nephew of the strangler's last victim) argues in this meticulously researched volume against DeSalvo as the murderer of all eleven women and examines why experts think there was more than one murderer.

*—Brion Sever*

**See also:** Joe Ball; David Berkowitz; Kenneth Bianchi; Ted Bundy; Angelo Buono, Jr.; Andrew Cunanan; Jeffrey Dahmer; Albert Fish; John Wayne Gacy; Ed Gein; Leonard Lake; Charles Ng; Dennis Rader; Richard Speck; Aileen Carol Wuornos.

# Legs Diamond

## Mobster and racketeer

**Born:** 1897; Philadelphia, Pennsylvania
**Died:** December 18, 1931; Albany, New York
**Also known as:** Jack Moran (birth name); Gentleman Jack; Clay Pigeon; John Thomas Diamond; Jack Diamond; John Thomas Noland
**Cause of notoriety:** Diamond, an important figure in Mafia-related bootlegging operations during Prohibition, was referred to as the "clay pigeon of the underworld" because he had been shot and wounded on several occasions.
**Active:** 1920-1931
**Locale:** New York, New York

### Early Life

Raised in Philadelphia by Irish immigrant parents, Jack Moran, who would become infamous under his alias Jack "Legs" Diamond (DI-muhnd), and his younger brother Eddie received a limited public school education. After Jack's mother, Sara, died in 1913, his father, John, a menial laborer, moved the two boys to Brooklyn. However, Jack and his brother soon became involved with a group of hoodlums known as the Boiler Gang. Jack served in the U.S. Army during World War I, but he later went absent without leave (AWOL). He was charged with desertion and spent a year in the military prison at Leavenworth, Kansas. He married Alice Kenny in 1920 and held a series of odd jobs for a short time.

### Criminal Career

Diamond may have received his nickname "Legs" for three reasons. First, Diamond was a good dancer in Philadelphia as a youth. Second, during his early days as a petty thief, he always managed to evade the law. Finally, fellow gangsters dubbed Diamond a liar and a cheat. He earned the reputation among his cohorts as a double-dealer who never maintained a sense of loyalty to the mob family.

Diamond became a member of Hudson Dusters, a small gang in New York City that robbed packages from delivery trucks. He eventually became a bodyguard for Jacob "Little Augie" Orgen, a major racketeer. When Diamond helped in the killing of Augie's main rival, Nathan "Kid Dropper"

> **False Foresight**
>
> The bullet hasn't been made that can kill me.
>
> —*Legs Diamond*

Kaplan, the mob kingpin rewarded him with some of his bootlegging enterprises. Louis "Lepke" Buchalter and Jacob Gurrah Shapiro soon began to attempt a takeover of Orgen's garment district operations.

In 1927, Orgen was killed on the lower East Side in a drive-by shooting. Diamond was severely wounded in the attack, but he survived despite a heavy loss of blood. With money no longer an object, he began to participate in a decadent nightlife, often partying with his mistress, Marion "Kiki" Roberts, and spending many of his evenings in the Hotsy Totsy Club on Broadway. Two years later, on June 13, 1929, he and one of his henchmen, Charles Entratta, killed William "Red" Cassidy after a scuffle in the club. Entratta and Diamond then went into hiding, but for lack of evidence they were never prosecuted. Although twenty-five people had witnessed the crime, none came forward to testify.

Diamond soon began working for Buchalter, a move that put him in conflict with bootlegging mobster Dutch Schultz, who wanted to move his base of operations into Manhattan. Schultz placed a contract hit out on Diamond. In October, 1929, three men stormed into the hotel room where Diamond and his mistress were staying, shooting him five times; he survived.

Diamond decided to travel to Europe and stay there until his safety could be guaranteed, but upon his arrival the authorities in each port city refused to let him off his ship. Diamond returned home; two years later, he was shot again after emerging from a hotel. In December, 1931, his good luck finally ran out; he was in Albany, New York, when two hit men entered the room where he was sleeping and fired three bullets into his head. The men who killed him were never caught.

## Impact

Legs Diamond was a celebrity during his lifetime. Newspaper accounts relished in his underworld exploits during Prohibition, and he achieved legendary status for surviving so many attempts on his life. The criminal career of Diamond reflected the rise of organized crime during the 1920's and 1930's. Gambling, prostitution, and loan-sharking were prominent vices in the late nineteenth century, spurred by alliances between local political machines and gangsters. However, with the passages of the Eighteenth Amendment and the Volstead Act, the outlawing of alcohol caused an increase in liquor trafficking on a national scale. Italian and Irish mobsters began to vie for control of the lucrative bootlegging business during Diamond's era. Diamond proved to be the enforcer between these warring factions until he became a liability for the powerful crime syndicates.

**Further Reading**

Levine, Gary. *Jack "Legs" Diamond: Anatomy of a Gangster*. Rev. ed. New York: Purple Mountain Press, 1995. Levine interviewed known associates of Diamond and policemen who dealt with him in order to produce this biography.

Nash, Jay Robert. *Bloodletters and Badmen: A Narrative Encyclopedia of American Criminals, from the Pilgrims to the Present*. New York: J. B. Lippincott, 1973. Arranged in alphabetical order by last name, a series of entries on memorable gangsters, criminals, and murderers. The author traces their backgrounds, crimes, and prison sentences.

Reppetto, Thomas A. *American Mafia: A History of Its Rise to Power*. New York: H. Holt, 2004. Overview of the rise of organized crime in the United States; the author asserts that the Mafia retained its power in part because of the fragmentation found in law enforcement agencies.

Sifakis, Carl. *The Mafia Encyclopedia*. 2d ed. New York: Facts On File, 1999. Comprehensive overview of organized crime personalities, power clashes, hangouts, hideaways, and rackets.

—*Gayla Koerting*

**See also:** Louis Buchalter; Arnold Rothstein; Dutch Schultz.

# John Dillinger
## Bank robber

**Born:** June 22, 1903; Indianapolis, Indiana
**Died:** July 22, 1934; Chicago, Illinois
**Also known as:** John Herbert Dillinger, Jr. (full name)
**Cause of notoriety:** During the Great Depression, many Americans made heroes of outlaws who took what they wanted at gunpoint. Dillinger was perhaps the most famous of these outlaws, earning celebrity and admiration both for his criminal audacity and for his affable, polite manner.
**Active:** September, 1924-June, 1934
**Locale:** Midwestern United States
**Sentence:** Ten to twenty years' imprisonment for assault and two to fourteen years for conspiracy to commit a felony in 1924; served nine years

### Early Life

Raised in Mooresville, Indiana, John Dillinger (DIHL-ihn-juhr) was born to a farmer who also ran a small grocery. His mother died when he was three, and John was raised by his older sister. A natural athlete and an excellent baseball player, Dillinger nonetheless had no particular life direction, and he quit school in the seventh grade. In 1923, after joyriding in a stolen car, Dillinger was forced to enlist in the navy to avoid punishment. He soon deserted the military and got a dishonorable discharge. He married sixteen-year-old Beryl Hovious in 1924, the same year in which he and an ex-convict tried to rob a grocer by hitting him over the head with an iron bolt. Dillinger pleaded guilty in order to get a reduced sentence; his partner received only a few months in jail. Sentenced to ten to twenty years' imprisonment for assault and two to fourteen years for conspiracy to commit a felony, Dillinger went to a reformatory, and his wife divorced him. He was transferred to the Michigan City Penitentiary in Indiana, where he met bank robbers Harry Pierpont and Homer Van Meter, both of whom agreed to form a gang with him upon release. Dillinger was paroled in May, 1933.

### Criminal Career

In September, 1933, Dillinger robbed his first bank. He also threw guns over the wall of Michigan City to break his friends out of jail but was arrested in Dayton, Ohio, before the reunion. Dillinger was held in a Lima, Ohio, jail, but his gang freed him by killing the town sheriff. The subsequent robbery spree attracted great publicity. The gang walked into the Auburn, Indiana, police station, took police hostage, and stole guns and bulletproof vests. In Peru, Indiana, the gang struck again. Newspapers widely reported it, and the gang was admired for its audacity. There was scant sympathy for banks or for law enforcement among the public during the Great Depression; many Americans rooted for criminals.

Indiana police captain Matt Leach blamed Dillinger for bank robberies throughout his region, inflating Dillinger's notoriety. Dillinger disliked Leach and taunted him through the mail. Although not the gang's leader (a position held by Pierpont), Dillinger became its star. He looked like actor Humphrey Bogart, and he was affable and polite. The public viewed

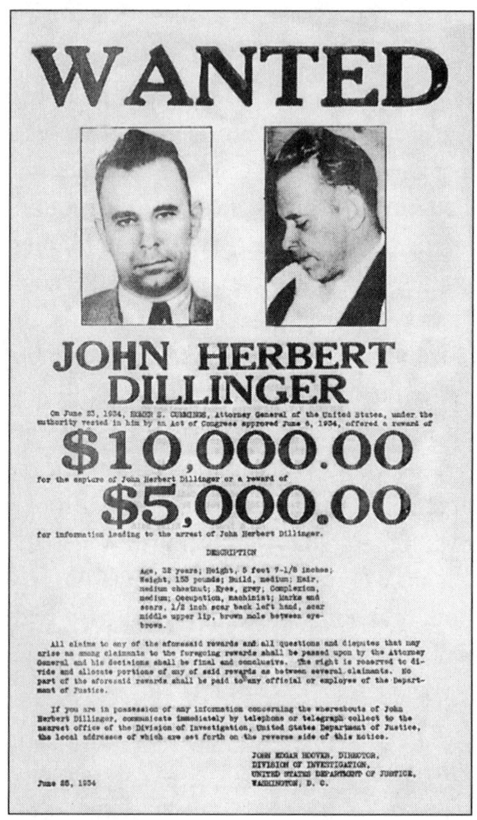

WANTED

JOHN HERBERT DILLINGER

On June 23, 1934, [illegible], Attorney General of the United States, under the authority vested in him by an Act of Congress approved June 6, 1934, offered a reward of

$10,000.00

for the capture of John Herbert Dillinger or a reward of

$5,000.00

for information leading to the arrest of John Herbert Dillinger.

DESCRIPTION

Age, 32 years; Height, 5 feet 7-1/8 inches; Weight, 153 pounds; Build, medium; Hair, medium chestnut; Eyes, grey; Complexion, medium; Occupation, machinist; Marks and scars, 1/2 inch scar back left hand, scar middle upper lip, brown mole between eyebrows.

All claims to any of the aforesaid rewards and all questions and disputes that may arise as among claimants to the foregoing rewards shall be passed upon by the Attorney General and his decisions shall be final and conclusive. The right is reserved to divide and allocate portions of any of said rewards as between several claimants. No part of the aforesaid rewards shall be paid to any official or employee of the Department of Justice.

If you are in possession of any information concerning the whereabouts of John Herbert Dillinger, communicate immediately by telephone or telegraph collect to the nearest office of the Division of Investigation, United States Department of Justice, the local addresses of which are set forth on the reverse side of this notice.

JOHN EDGAR HOOVER, DIRECTOR,
DIVISION OF INVESTIGATION,
UNITED STATES DEPARTMENT OF JUSTICE,
WASHINGTON, D. C.

June 25, 1934

*John Dillinger's "wanted" poster.* (NARA)

**ASPIRATIONS**

All my life I wanted to be a bank robber. Carry a gun and wear a mask. Now that it's happened I guess I'm just about the best bank robber they ever had. And I sure am happy.

*—John Dillinger*

him as a small-town boy gone bad as a result of a too-harsh jail sentence.

The gang robbed banks about twice a month, hiding out in Chicago or St. Paul. Each bank was cased, and getaways were meticulously planned. In January, 1934, the gang robbed a bank in East Chicago, during which Dillinger killed an officer. Someone triggered an alarm, and the robbers walked out with hostages. Officer William O'Malley fired shots into Dillinger's bulletproof vest, but Dillinger killed him with a machine gun.

Several gang members were recognized and arrested in Tucson, Arizona, in January, 1934. Dillinger was sent to jail in Crown Point, Indiana; gang members Pierpont and Charles Makley were sent to Lima, Ohio, for trial. Dillinger escaped in March using a smuggled wooden gun and driving away in the chief deputy's car. Driving over state lines violated a federal law, so Dillinger became a target of the Federal Bureau of Investigation (FBI). Pierpont and Makley got death sentences for killing the sheriff. Dillinger was then declared "public enemy number one." He visited his family in Mooresville, and a photograph of him smugly holding the wooden pistol from his escape was widely distributed.

In April, 1934, the gang—now including infamous robber George "Baby Face" Nelson—hid out at Little Bohemia Lodge in Wisconsin, but they were recognized and surrounded by FBI agents. The FBI opened fire in the dark and killed three innocent men exiting the lodge. The gang escaped out back windows.

In an attempt to avoid recognition, Dillinger and Van Meter had plastic surgery in May, 1934. Their last robbery was in South Bend, Indiana, in June, 1934. A wild shoot-out occurred with police, and civilians were hit; Van Meter was wounded but used his machine gun to kill an officer. Dillinger hid in Chicago with brothel owner Anna Sage.

## Legal Action and Outcome

Sage offered to betray Dillinger in exchange for not being deported back to Romania, to which the authorities agreed. On July 22, 1934, Sage told the FBI that Dillinger was going to take her and a friend to the Biograph Theater to see a gangster film that evening. Dillinger entered the theater at 8:30 P.M., and dozens of agents took their positions outside. As Dillinger exited at 10:35 P.M., agents approached him from behind and either executed him on the spot or shot him as he ran up an alley. Whatever the truth, he died after being shot through the back of his head and in his torso. He was thirty-one years old. Van Meter was killed in St. Paul a month after Dillinger's death, and Pierpont and Makley were executed. Sage was deported to Romania.

## Impact

The death of John Dillinger edged J. Edgar Hoover closer to becoming a national icon. Within two years, G-men (FBI agents) replaced bank robbers as national heroes. Dillinger's photograph became the official target on FBI's firing ranges and remained so into the twenty-first century. It was reported that Hoover hung Dillinger's death mask in his office as a favorite memento.

Dillinger continued to fascinate writers and filmmakers as a smiling "rogue hero," who seemingly was more bad boy than criminal. Bryan Burrough, in his book *Public Enemies: America's Greatest Crime Wave and the Birth of the FBI, 1933-1934* (2004), relates a visit to Dillinger's grave, where he imagined touching his face. Many films have been made about Dillinger, although most were critical failures. *Dillinger* (1945) starred Lawrence Tierney; *Dillinger* (1973) starred Warren Oates and an excellent supporting cast, but its screenplay had little to do with historical reality. *Public Enemy Number One*, a documentary produced for the Public Broadcasting Service (PBS), aired in 2001 on the television network's series *The American Experience*.

## Further Reading

Burrough, Bryan. *Public Enemies: America's Greatest Crime Wave and the Birth of the FBI, 1933-1934*. New York: Penguin Books, 2004. Recounts Dillinger's robberies in exciting detail and in chronological sequence along with discussion of other criminals of the era. The reader comes to understand how short and packed with violence the public enemy era was.

Girardin, G. Russell, with William J. Helmer. *Dillinger: The Untold Story*. Bloomington: University of Indiana Press, 1994. Girardin interviewed Dillinger's attorney and various criminal cohorts in the 1930's, giving an intimate portrayal of Dillinger. The manuscript was unpublished until 1994.

Matera, Dary. *John Dillinger: The Life and Death of America's First Celebrity Criminal*. New York: Carroll & Graf, 2004. Details Dillinger's youth and personal traits but is somewhat speculative about Dillinger's thoughts and motives.

*—Jim Pauff*

**See also:** Ma Barker; Pretty Boy Floyd; Baby Face Nelson; Henry Starr; Willie Sutton.

# Bill Doolin

## Bank robber and gang leader

**Born:** 1858; near Clarksville, Johnson County, Arkansas

**Died:** August 24, 1896; Lawson, Oklahoma Territory

**Also known as:** William Doolin (full name); King of the Oklahoma Bandits

**Cause of notoriety:** Doolin committed his early bank and train robberies in the company of the Dalton brothers; he later headed his own gang, the Wild Bunch.

**Active:** 1891-1896

**Locale:** Indian Territory, Oklahoma, and Texas

### Early Life

Bill Doolin (DEW-lihn) was born to Michael "Mack" Doolin and Artemina Beller in Johnson County, Arkansas, in 1858. His father had had four children from his first marriage and two children with his second wife. The Doolins acquired a small farm in Big Piney Creek, thirty miles northeast of Clarksville, Arkansas, which Doolin helped run after his father's death.

Although illiterate, Doolin was a hard worker and was skilled with tools. He found employment with a ranch owner, Oscar D. Hasell, building corrals and other structures. Hassell also taught Doolin simple bookkeeping.

*Bill Doolin.*

Doolin worked for several ranchers and cattlemen until 1889, when the government vacated the Indian Territory of Oklahoma to make room for homesteaders. On March 14, 1893, Doolin married Edith Ellsworth, a preacher's daughter. The two had one son, whom they named Jay.

## Criminal Career

Doolin's first brush with the law occurred on July 4, 1891, while he was working at the Bar X Bar Ranch. He and some friends had ridden into Coffeyville, Kansas, to celebrate Independence Day with a keg of beer. Kansas was a dry state, and authorities tried to confiscate the beer. A shootout ensued, wounding two police officers and forcing Doolin to flee the area.

Once on the run, Doolin met up with Bob and Emmett Dalton as well as other outlaws. His shooting skills, intelligence, and fairness made Doolin a natural leader among Western bandits. By September of 1891, he was riding with the Dalton gang and participated in train robberies in Leliaetta, Indian Territory; Red Rock, Oklahoma Territory; and Adair, Indian Territory. Doolin did not accompany the Daltons on their fatal attempt to rob two banks simultaneously in Coffeyville, Kansas, on October 5, 1892. On that day gang members, including two Daltons, were shot to death.

With the demise of the Dalton gang, Doolin recruited new men for his own gang, which became known as the Wild Bunch. The gang robbed a passenger train in Cimarron, Kansas, on June 11, 1893, but a posse of lawmen was ready for them and ambushed the gang as they were escaping. Doolin was shot in the left foot and limped for the rest of his life. Three months later, rumors of the Wild Bunch hiding in Ingalls, Oklahoma Territory, were circulating. On September 1, 1893, thirteen sheriffs entered the town and found the gang in a saloon. A shoot-out ensued, later dubbed the Battle of Ingalls, after which three marshals and two innocent bystanders were dead, and many were hurt. Members of the Wild Bunch escaped with minor wounds.

Over the next two years the gang continued its robbery spree. On April 3, 1895, the Wild Bunch ambushed and robbed a passenger train in Dover, Oklahoma Territory. Again, a posse was ready, and a shoot-out began which resulted in "Tulsa Jack" Blake's death. Now infamous, the gang disbanded after the Dover heist. Over the next few months, former members of the Wild Bunch were killed by bounty hunters or in shoot-outs. A realist, Doolin contacted his attorney to arrange a plea bargain in which he would surrender in exchange for a guaranteed short sentence. The authorities would not agree to the terms, and Doolin went into hiding in Eureka Springs, Arkansas.

## Legal Action and Outcome

Deputy Marshall Tilghman, who had long been tracking Doolin, learned of the outlaw's location. There he surprised Doolin and brought him to Guthrie, Kansas, to stand trial for his crimes. While in prison awaiting trial, Doolin and "Dynamite Dick" Clifton, along with twelve other prisoners, escaped.

Missing his family and tired of running from the law, Doolin decided to return home, in order to take his wife and son to an undisclosed location. Deputy Marshall Heck Thomas heard of the plan. When Doolin was seen helping his wife, Edith, load a wagon, Deputy Thomas organized a stakeout. When Doolin later returned to his house, he was met with gunfire. He died on August 24, 1896.

## Impact

Although his crimes instilled fear in Western settlers, Bill Doolin enjoyed a reputation for being reasonable, sincere, and levelheaded. His intelligence and fairness gained him respect among fellow outlaws, members of the community, and—ironically—certain law officials.

When Oklahoma became a state in 1907, its government felt increased pressure to ensure the safety of its citizens. Several laws were passed spelling out police powers and instilling fear among local gangs. Amid rising instances of bank and train robberies, several states enacted rewards and bounties, ranging from one thousand to fifteen thousand dollars, for the capture of Doolin and other criminals, "dead or alive." Civilian vigilantes and sheriffs' posses legally pursued bandit gangs, armed with both muscle and authority. These raids and bounties resulted in the deaths of Doolin and other members of the Wild Bunch. They also served as warnings for other gangs and signified the end of the romantic Western shoot-outs.

**Further Reading**

Drago, Harry S. *Outlaws on Horseback.* Lincoln: University of Nebraska Press, 1998. Focuses on train and bank robbers and provides a riveting account of Bill Doolin's life as a bandit and his associations with other Wild West outlaws.

Lewis, Jon E. *The Mammoth Book of the West: The Making of the American West.* New York: Carroll & Graf, 2001. Lewis offers the reader a comprehensive account of life in the Wild West and mentions all of the key players who were involved. A good reference for Doolin and members of the Wild Bunch.

O'Neal, Bill. *Encyclopedia of Western Gunfighters.* Norman: University of Oklahoma Press, 1991. A factual look at the outlaws who roamed the Old West.

Reasoner, James. *Draw: The Greatest Gunfights of the American West.* New York: Berkley, 2003. Paints a historically accurate picture of the bandits and gunfighters. Reasoner does not romanticize bank robbers and bandits as some writings do but offers an objective look at the West.

Wellman, Paul I. *A Dynasty of Western Outlaws.* Norman: University of Oklahoma Press, 1998. Focusing on the late 1800's and early 1900's, Wellman's book provides a thorough examination of life in the Wild West and its outlaws. Also contains maps and family trees.

*—Sara Vidar*

**See also:** Apache Kid; Tom Bell; William H. Bonney; Curly Bill Brocius; Bob Dalton; Emmett Dalton; John Wesley Hardin; Doc Holliday; Jesse James; Tom Ketchum; Harry Longabaugh; Bill Longley; Johnny Ringo; Belle Starr; Henry Starr; Hank Vaughan; Cole Younger.

# Diane Downs

## Murderer

**Born:** August 7, 1955; Phoenix, Arizona
**Also known as:** Elizabeth Diane Frederickson (birth name)
**Major offenses:** Murder, attempted murder, and assault
**Active:** May 19, 1983
**Locale:** Near Marcola, Oregon
**Sentence:** Life in prison for murder; fifty years for attempted murder and assault

### Early Life

Diane Downs (di-AN downz), the daughter of Wes and Willadene Frederickson, resented her strict Baptist parents dictating how she and her four younger siblings lived. While a junior at Moon Valley High School, she met Steven Downs. After graduation, she briefly attended Pacific Coast Baptist Bible College while he served in the U.S. Navy. The two married in 1973. Downs gave birth to her first daughter, Christie, the following year, then her second daughter, Cheryl, in 1976.

Downs occasionally left, then reunited with, her husband, whom she considered too demanding. She gave birth to a coworker's son, Danny, in 1979. After her divorce in 1981, Downs secured postal employment in Chandler, Arizona, where she met Lew Lewiston, with whom she initiated a romantic relationship despite his disinterest in her children. In February, 1983, Downs was devastated when Lewiston informed her of his decision to remain married to his wife. Downs moved to Springfield, Oregon, where her father was postmaster. She asked Lewiston to relocate there as well.

### Criminal Career

On the evening of May 19, 1983, Downs took her children to visit a friend at Marcola, near Springfield. Returning home on rural Old Mohawk

Road, Downs parked the car and shot her children, then herself, with a pistol. After 10:30 P.M., she blared her horn outside the emergency entrance at McKenzie-Willamette Hospital, screaming that a stranger had attacked her family. While medical personnel focused on saving Downs's children, the hospital receptionist alerted police. Downs's youngest daughter died soon afterward. Physicians performed surgery on Downs's two surviving children.

Police arrived at the hospital and questioned Downs, who told them a disheveled white man had motioned for her to stop driving and demanded her keys. According to her, he had become agitated, shot her children, then her, and ran away. Officers searched the area for the man and the yellow car Downs said she had seen nearby.

### Legal Action and Outcome

Police considered Downs a possible suspect because they observed her erratic behavior at the hospital and believed her wound was self-inflicted. For several months, detectives and Deputy District Attorney Frederick A. Hugi investigated the shooting. Their forensic examinations and interviews provided information that contradicted Downs's claims and suggested she had attempted to kill her children, in the hope of reconciling with Lewiston. Police arrested Downs on February 28, 1984, incarcerating her in the Lane County Jail at Eugene. A grand jury issued indictments for one murder count, two attempted murder counts, and two assault counts.

Downs's trial started on May 10, 1984, at the Lane County Courthouse. Her daughter stated that Downs had shot her and her siblings. Expressing her love for her children, Downs denounced the prosecution's statements. On June 16, jurors unanimously declared Downs guilty of murder, attempted first-degree murder, and first-degree assault. Two months later, Judge Gregory Foote sentenced Downs to life imprisonment extended by fifty years.

Incarcerated in the Oregon Women's Correctional Center at Salem, Downs escaped on July 11, 1987. She was at large for ten days before police apprehended her. A judge added five years to Downs's sentence, transferring her first to New Jersey's Correctional Institution for Women and then to the Valley Prison for Women in California.

## Impact

Because of public fascination with Diane Downs's case, media worldwide focused on Downs during her trial and continued to cover her story after she was convicted. In 1984, a thirty-minute documentary featured her trial. Talk-show host Oprah Winfrey broadcast her interview with Downs in September, 1988. ABC television aired a four-hour movie depicting the murder in November, 1989. Appealing to her supportive fans, Downs published a book in the late 1980's. Hugi, the deputy district attorney, and his wife adopted Downs's children in 1986.

## Further Reading

Downs, Elizabeth Diane. *Diane Downs: Best Kept Secrets*. Springfield, Oreg.: Danmark, 1989. Downs cites information she says authorities overlooked, describing herself as an innocent victim of faulty law enforcement practices.

Meyer, Cheryl L., and Michelle Oberman. *Mothers Who Kill Their Children: Understanding the Acts of Moms from Susan Smith to the "Prom Mom."* New York: New York University Press, 2001. Provides contextual analysis that examines such relevant topics as child abuse, domestic violence, and legal strategies.

Rule, Ann. *Small Sacrifices: A True Story of Passion and Murder*. New York: Signet, 2003. Thoroughly discusses Downs's life and how investigators proved her guilt. Includes excerpts from Downs's journals and letters.

*—Elizabeth D. Schafer*

**See also:** Marie Hilley; Darlie Routier; Susan Smith; Andrea Yates.

# John E. du Pont
## Murderer

**Born:** c. 1939; France
**Also known as:** John Eleuthere du Pont (full name)
**Major offense:** Murder
**Active:** January 26, 1996
**Locale:** Foxcatcher Farms, Newton Square, Delaware County, Pennsylvania
**Sentence:** Thirteen to thirty years in prison or a mental institution

### Early Life

John Eleuthere du Pont (dew-PAHNT) was born into one of the United States' wealthiest families. The great-great-grandson of Eleuthere I. du Pont de Nemours, the founder of the world's largest chemical company, he was born to William du Pont, Jr., and Jean Liseter Austin. For most of his life, he lived with his mother and apparently had a disturbed childhood. His early odd behavior evolved into that of a rather bizarre character: He displayed signs of paranoia and lived in constant fear for his life. In spite of these difficulties, in 1965 du Pont received a bachelor of science degree in zoology from the University of Miami. He became an accomplished ornithologist and published numerous articles about birds, even naming twenty-four new species.

Later in life, du Pont became interested in the sport of wrestling, financially supporting the wrestling program at Villanova University. In 1988, Villanova canceled the program, and du Pont turned his Pennsylvania estate (named Foxcatcher) into a training camp for wrestlers. In spite of his earlier marriage to Gale Wenk, his homosexuality became apparent at about this time.

### Criminal Career

Throughout the 1980's, du Pont's behavior became increasingly bizarre and more troublesome to both his family and his employees. In 1988, a former employee, Andrew Metzger, filed a lawsuit against du Pont for sexual harassment and settled out of court for $555,000. In October, 1995, Dan Chaid, one of du Pont's wrestlers, contacted local police, claiming that du Pont had pointed a machine gun and had made threatening gestures at several people at his Foxcatcher estate while intoxicated. The police took no action. On January 26, 1996, at his Foxcatcher estate, du Pont approached thirty-six-year-old former Olympic wrestler David Schultz while Schultz was fixing his car radio. After a brief exchange of words and for no apparent reason, du Pont fired his gun three times and killed Schultz. Afterward he fled into his mansion and prepared himself for the arrival of police.

## Legal Action and Outcome

The police tried to persuade du Pont to surrender but with no success. Du Pont used his cache of weapons and his skill as a marksman to keep officers at a distance. After a two-day standoff, the police were able to trick du Pont into emerging from his house by shutting off his heat. He was taken into custody without incident.

On January 28, 1996, du Pont was charged with the murder of Schultz. His trial lasted for slightly more than one year and received considerable media attention. Public opinion was that du Pont's great wealth and status would somehow buy him out of serving a long prison sentence. During the trial, it was determined that du Pont was mentally ill, but on February 26, 1997, the court found him guilty of third-degree murder; it also found him to be mentally ill. He was sentenced to between thirteen and thirty years in either prison or a mental institution, whichever best suited his mental state until completion of his sentence. The court recommended that he receive treatment for paranoid delusions. In addition, he was required to pay $742,107 as reimbursement of the court costs. Later, a wrongful death civil suit was filed by David Schultz's widow, Nancy. That suit was settled in 1999 for $35 million.

## Impact

To many people, the conviction of John E. du Pont was a pleasant surprise. As District Attorney Patrick Meehan pointed out in his remarks about the verdict, du Pont was "the wealthiest murder defendant in the history of the United States" to be convicted of third-degree murder. The jury did not accept the defense argument that du Pont should be found innocent on grounds of insanity, despite testimony to his unpredictable behavior with the wrestlers on his estate, his paranoia, and his habit of carrying a sidearm. Nevertheless, du Pont was judged capable of understanding that his actions were wrong. His conviction was hailed as a tribute to justice and to the legal system—in glaring contrast to trials of other notable and wealthy figures, including O. J. Simpson, which many concluded had not served justice.

Schultz's wife Nancy, who witnessed her husband's murder, went on to care for their two children and to oversee the Dave Schultz Wrestling Club, which supports amateur wrestlers. Du Pont's name was removed from Villanova University's wrestling club soon after his conviction.

**Further Reading**

Ordine, Bill, and Ralph Vigoda. *Fatal Match.* New York: Avon Books, 1998. An account of the shooting and subsequent trial.

Palmer, Mark. "The Day Wrestling Died." In *The Life and Legacy of Dave Schultz*, http://www.revwrestling.com/articles. A five-part article details the relationship between du Pont and wrestler Schultz (with emphasis on Schultz), providing the reader with good background information and insight into this tragic murder.

Smith, Carleton. *Blood Money: The Du Pont Heir and the Murder of an Olympic Athlete*. New York: St. Martin's Press, 1996. Traces du Pont's life from his ancestors to his capture and arrest; coverage predates the trial. Considers du Pont's motivations for shooting Schultz to be based in du Pont's disappointed aspirations for a sports career as well as his paranoid delusions.

*—Paul P. Sipiera*

**See also:** Jean Harris.

# Ira Einhorn

## Murderer

**Born:** March 15, 1940; Philadelphia, Pennsylvania
**Also known as:** Ira Samuel Einhorn (full name); Eugene Mallon; Ben Moore; Unicorn
**Major offenses:** Murder and bail jumping
**Active:** September, 1977-January, 1981
**Locale:** Philadelphia, Pennsylvania
**Sentence:** Life imprisonment

## Early Life

Ira Samuel Einhorn (IN-hohrn) was raised in the north Philadelphia Jewish neighborhood of Mount Airy. He attended the academic magnet Central High School, where he was admitted into the advanced curriculum—select curriculum reserved for high-achieving students. After graduation, he attended the University of Pennsylvania, majoring in English. He also received a fellowship to attend the Kennedy School of Government at Harvard.

Einhorn gained local celebrity in the 1960's in Philadelphia as a peace and ecology activist. However, he possessed a tremendous ego, claiming, for example, undue credit for establishing Earth Day. He also was a political gadfly who ran for mayor of Philadelphia in 1971. Einhorn suffered from a degree of megalomania and paranoia, perhaps from excessive drug use in the 1960's. He adopted the nickname Unicorn (literally, "one horn"), which is a translation of his German surname. He often stated that the Federal Bureau of Investigation (FBI) and Central Intelligence Agency (CIA) were persecuting him because of his political views and activities. Einhorn had permitted little toleration for girlfriends who broke off relationships with him. He allegedly strangled one to the point of unconsciousness and beat another.

## Criminal Career

Einhorn's notoriety emerged after the disappearance in 1977 of his girlfriend, Helen "Holly" Maddux, of Texas. Einhorn claimed that Maddux had left him and he had never heard from her again. He even called Maddux's father in Texas shortly after she vanished, asking if he had heard from her.

In fact, Maddux had tired of Einhorn's abuse and left for New York, where she began dating another man. On September 9, 1977, when she informed Einhorn that she was leaving him, he demanded that she return to Philadelphia or he would throw her belongings onto the street. She returned immediately to collect her property; no one saw her again after this point.

Maddux's family became concerned since she usually called several times a month. They notified the Philadelphia police, who then questioned Einhorn. He told them that she had gone shopping sometime before and never returned, and he assumed that she had left him because of the problems they were having. Since he was a well-known figure in the community, the officers believed his story.

However, Maddux's family had not trusted Einhorn since a visit he had made to Texas while dating Maddux; his condescending attitude and boorish behavior had offended them. This unkempt "hippie" seemed an odd match for their neat, former-cheerleader daughter and sister. After Maddux's disappearance, therefore, the family was convinced that Einhorn had harmed her. They hired private detectives, who learned from friends of Einhorn that he had wanted to dispose of a trunk, which was still in his apartment. Neighbors also complained about a foul odor emanating from the apartment. The Philadelphia police again became interested in Einhorn and went to his apartment with a search warrant and a camera to record what they might find. They discovered Maddux's mummified body in the trunk.

### Legal Action and Outcome

At a bond hearing in which a number of prominent Philadelphia citizens testified on Einhorn's behalf, the judge awarded bail at forty thousand dollars, and Einhorn was released on a 10 percent cash bond. Einhorn's lawyer was Arlen Specter, who later became the mayor of Philadelphia and then a senator from Pennsylvania.

Einhorn jumped bail before trial and fled to Europe, first to Ireland and then to France. There, he married Annika Flodin, a Swedish national. Pennsylvania authorities sought his extradition, but the French authorities were unwilling to extradict Einhorn without a guarantee that he would not be executed; France had abolished capital punishment. In the United States, Maddux's family continued to press for the capture of Einhorn. He was found guilty in absentia in a Philadelphia trial in 1993.

Einhorn assumed the alias Eugene Mallon and managed to escape extradition by hiding. He also relied on a technicality in the French-American extradition treaty. The Maddux case gained national attention, and many thought that the French refusal to extradite Einhorn was a political ploy. Several members of Congress sent a petition to French president Jacques Chirac requesting extradition, but Chirac did not have the power to overturn a judicial decision. The Pennsylvania legislature passed a bill in 1998 permitting Einhorn to have a second trial if he returned. Furthermore, he was not eligible for the death penalty, because at the time the crime was committed, Pennsylvania had not legalized executions.

In July, 2000, France agreed to Einhorn's extradition on condition that he receive a second trial and not be subject to the death penalty. Einhorn acted as his own attorney at the trial and alleged that agents had murdered Maddux in order to frame him. However, the jury was not convinced, and after only two hours of deliberation, it found him guilty. He was sentenced to life imprisonment and was sent to the state prison in Houtzdale, Pennsylvania.

## Impact

The Ira Einhorn case was complicated by judicial intricacies based on the difference between French and American law. The question surrounding Einhorn's extradition spurred legislation and legal wrangling in both countries. The bill passed by the Pennsylvania legislature in 1998, which allowed in-absentia defendants to request another trial, was criticized as unconstitutional by many legal authorities, who noted that a legislature should not be able to overrule a final judgment handed down by a court of law. The notoriety of the Einhorn case also led to several accounts in literature and the media. A documentary was aired by the Arts and Entertainment cable network in 1998, and a fictionalized docudrama titled *The Hunt for the Unicorn Killer* was televised by the National Broadcasting Company (NBC) network in 1999.

## Further Reading

Cascio, Michael, et al. *Peace, Love, and Murder: The Ira Einhorn Story.* New York: A&E Home Video, 1998. A film documentary of the case using interviews of friends, witnesses, the Maddux family, lawyers, and police. The documentary was made before Einhorn's extradition.

Levy, Steven. *The Unicorn's Secret: Murder in the Age of Aquarius—A True Story*. 1988. Reprint. New York: Penguin, 1999. The first written account of the case, which appeared while Einhorn was still in hiding and the story had not completely unfolded.

*—Frederick B. Chary*

**See also:** Richard Allen Davis; Scott Peterson; Ruth Snyder; Carolyn Warmus.

# Billie Sol Estes

## Swindler and con man

**Born:** January 10, 1925; near Clyde, Texas
**Major offenses:** Swindling, fraud, interstate transportation of securities taken by fraud, and conspiracy
**Active:** 1950's-1960's
**Locale:** West Texas and Washington, D.C.
**Sentence:** Eight years in prison for swindling, reversed by the U.S. Supreme Court; fifteen years for mail fraud and conspiracy, upheld by the Supreme Court

### Early Life

Born in 1925 near Clyde, Texas, Billie Sol Estes (BIHL-ee sahl EHS-teez) grew up on his family farm. His financial genius was revealed at an early age. While still in high school, he borrowed thirty-five hundred dollars from a local bank to buy government surplus grain to sell for profit. After he married in 1946, he moved to his own farm near Pecos, Texas. When electricity costs for irrigation pumps rose excessively, he formed a company providing natural gas-powered pumps to farmers. Then Estes started a business distributing cheap anhydrous ammonia fertilizer. By 1952, he was a millionaire and was named one of the Outstanding Young Men of the Year by the U.S. Junior Chamber of Commerce.

### Criminal Career

In the late 1950's, the U.S. Department of Agriculture established allotments and quotas for cotton farmers in order to control production. To offset resulting business losses, Estes turned his fertilizer business into a multimillion-dollar scam. In 1958 he owed $550,000 to Commercial Solvents of New York for fertilizer. Estes made a deal with the firm to defer the debt and lend him $350,000, plus $225,000 to build storage facilities. He used money from fertilizer sales to build grain storage facilities, then collected storage fees under federal price-support programs. He assigned the fees to Commercial Solvents to get more fertilizer for distribution. He undercut the prices of competitors until they went bankrupt, then bought the failed firms' assets cheaply and absorbed their businesses. In 1959-1961, Commercial Solvents collected $7,000,000 in grain storage fees paid to Estes by the federal government.

Estes, however, still owed Commercial Solvents $5,700,000. He devised another scheme involving anhydrous ammonia storage tanks. He persuaded a Texas tank manufacturer to let area farmers buy nonexistent tanks, sign bogus mortgages on them, then lease them to Estes. Estes collected $30 million in loans and storage fees and used nonexistent storage tanks and fake mortgages as collateral to borrow an additional $22 million from finance companies in Chicago and New York.

Still in debt in 1960, Estes began yet another scheme using cotton allotments and the eminent domain exception for farmers whose lands were taken by government for public projects. Estes persuaded displaced farmers in Texas, Oklahoma, Alabama, and Georgia to buy Texas farmland from him, transfer their cotton allotments to the new land, and lease the lands and allotments to Estes. The lease default clause virtually ensured that Estes' initial fifty-dollar-per-acre lease payment would effectively transfer ownership of three thousand acres of land and allotments to Estes. He then used nonexistent cotton crops as collateral for bank loans and claimed subsidies from the government for growing and storing the nonexistent cotton. The Agriculture Department finally investigated the deals and found them to

*Billie Sol Estes, as depicted on the cover of* Time *in 1962.* (Courtesy, Time, Inc.)

be fraudulent. Estes was fined for growing cotton under illegal allotments.

Throughout the 1950's and 1960's, Estes made large contributions to the Democrat Party and to candidates for office, including Vice President Lyndon B. Johnson. It was Estes' defeat in a Pecos school board election that led to the exposure of his massive fraud. A local newspaper, the *Independent*, had opposed Estes' candidacy; to get revenge, Estes established a rival paper. The *Independent* investigated Estes and publicly exposed his storage tank fraud. The finance companies immediately sent investigators to Pecos, as did the Federal Bureau of Investigation (FBI).

## Legal Action and Outcome

On March 29, 1961, the FBI arrested Estes on charges of interstate transportation of bogus mortgages. He was released on bond under federal indictment for fraud and state indictment for theft. In March, 1962, the FBI arrested Estes on charges of fraud and theft in a multimillion-dollar swindle involving storage tanks, phony mortgages, and cotton allotments. On April 5, 1962, a federal grand jury indicted Estes and several associates on fifty-seven counts of fraud and conspiracy. Trials were scheduled in Tyler, Texas, for September 24 and in El Paso for December 10, 1962. Estes' trial in Tyler began on October 30, 1962; he was convicted of fraud and sentenced to eight years in prison. The U.S. Supreme Court reversed the conviction on June 7, 1965, because of pretrial publicity.

In the El Paso trial, Estes was charged with twenty-nine counts of mail fraud, interstate transportation of securities taken by fraud, and conspiracy. On December 11, 1962, the judge split the indictment, ordering trial to be held in Pecos on alleged violations that occurred in that jurisdiction. Trial in El Paso was set for March 11, 1963.

On March 28, 1963, the jury found Estes guilty of mail fraud and conspiracy. On April 16, 1963, he was sentenced to fifteen years' imprisonment. After the Supreme Court refused to hear his appeal on January 15, 1965, Estes was committed to the federal penitentiary at Ft. Leavenworth, Kansas, and served seven years. After his release on parole in 1983, Estes and his family settled in Brady, Texas.

## Impact

Congressional investigations revealed widespread political complicity in the Billie Sol Estes scandals. The U.S. Department of Agriculture subsidy programs came under intense scrutiny. Three agriculture officials were forced to resign, as was Assistant Secretary of Labor Jerry Holleman. Secretary of Agriculture Orville Freeman, with his own career in jeopardy, created the first Office of Inspector General, which led to legislation in 1978 establishing twelve federal Offices of Inspector Generals. The Estes scandals became so embarrassing for Democrats that President John F. Kennedy considered dropping Vice President Johnson from the ticket in 1964 because of his close association with Estes.

**Further Reading**

Barmash, Isadore. *Great Business Disasters: Swindlers, Burglars, and Frauds in American Industry*. Chicago: Playboy Press, 1972. Chapter 3 discusses Estes' initial success in agriculture and subsequent turn to illegal activities.

Estes, Pam. *Billie Sol: King of Texas Wheeler-Dealers*. Abilene, Tex.: Noble Craft Books, 1983. A daughter's sympathetic account of Estes' schemes.

Williams, Roger M., ed. and comp. *The Super Crooks: A Rogues' Gallery of Famous Hustlers, Swindlers, and Thieves*. Chicago: Playboy Press, 1973. Places Estes among the foremost scoundrels of the twentieth century.

*—Marguerite R. Plummer*

**See also:** Tino De Angelis; Susanna Mildred Hill; Joseph Weil.

# Albert Fish

## Child molester, serial killer, and cannibal

**Born:** May 19, 1870; Washington, D.C.

**Died:** January 16, 1936; Sing Sing Correctional Facility, Ossining, New York

**Also known as:** Hamilton Albert Fish (full name); Frank Howard; Robert Hayden; Boogey Man; Gray Man; Moon Maniac; Brooklyn Vampire; Werewolf of Wisteria

**Major offenses:** Murder of eleven-year-old Grace Budd; additional child kidnappings and murders

**Active:** June 3, 1928-February 11, 1927

**Locale:** New York City; claimed to have attacked children in twenty-three states

**Sentence:** Death by electrocution for first-degree murder

### Early Life

The father of Hamilton Fish (fihsh), who claimed descent from "Revolutionary stock," was seventy-five years old at Hamilton's birth. When the boy was five, his father died, and his mother sent Albert to St. John's Orphanage, Washington, D.C. There Fish changed his name to Albert; he also began stammering and wetting the bed. Worse, his sadomasochism flowered: "I saw so many boys whipped," he said, "it ruined my mind."

Fish may have been a homosexual prostitute in his teens. At fifteen, he left school to work in a grocery store; soon after, he was apprenticed to a painter and decorator. Fish married an eighteen-year-old woman, Anna, when he was twenty-eight. They had six children, but his wife left him after almost twenty years of marriage in 1917. They were never divorced; Fish raised the children and was a good father. He had three subsequent marriages, short and bigamous, and played quasi-sexual games with a stepdaughter, Mary.

### Criminal Career

The entirety of Fish's crimes may never be known. Detective William King, who tirelessly tracked down Fish, suspected Fish murdered four children in New York City alone; psychiatrist Frederic Wertham believed Fish killed at least five, and the police estimated he killed between eight and fifteen children.

However, Fish attacked perhaps hundreds of children. After Anna left him, he worked around the country; he was never arrested but was often driven off by close calls or attention by police or locals. Many of his victims were poor, including African Americans, whom he said the police were less apt to care about. His activities with them, as with himself, involved inflicting pain more than sexual acts, though Fish's gratification was clearly sexual. Influenced by a religious mania, he became obsessed with castrating boys; in St. Louis in 1911, he left one boy bleeding and fled the city. However, Fish's six arrests by 1930, resulting in one prison term and two mental-hospital stays, were for passing a bad check, embezzling, and continually writing graphic, sadomasochistic letters to women.

His most famous victim was eleven-year-old Grace Budd. Fish pre-

### A Telltale Letter

*Albert Fish was finally caught after he mailed the following anonymous letter to Grace Budd's parents on November 11, 1934, and the authorities traced the stationery:*

My dear Mrs. Budd:

In 1894 a friend of mine shipped as a deck hand on the Steamer Tacoma, Capt. John Davis. They sailed from San Francisco for Hong Kong, China. On arriving there he and two others went ashore and got drunk. When they returned the boat was gone. At that time there was famine in China. Meat of any kind was from $1-3 per pound. So great was the suffering among the very poor that all children under 12 were sold for food in order to keep others from starving. A boy or girl under 14 was not safe in the street. You could go in any shop and ask for steak-chops-or stew meat. Part of the naked body of a boy or girl would be brought out and just what you wanted cut from it. A boy or girl's behind which is the sweetest part of the body and sold as veal cutlet brought the highest price. John stayed there so long he acquired a taste for human flesh. On his return to N.Y. he stole two boys, one 7 and one 11. Took them to his home stripped them naked tied them in a closet. Then burned everything they had on. . . . [They were] roasted in the oven . . . boiled, broiled, fried and stewed. . . .

At that time, I was living at 409 E 100 St. near-right side. He told me so often how good human flesh was I made up my mind to taste it. On Sunday June the 3, 1928 I called on you at 406 W 15 St. Brought you pot cheese-strawberries. We had lunch. Grace sat in my lap and kissed me. I made up my mind to eat her. On the pretense of taking her to a party. You said yes she could go. I took her to an empty house in Westchester I had already picked out. . . . How she did kick-bite and scratch. I choked her to death, then cut her in small pieces so I could take my meat to my rooms. Cook and eat it. How sweet and tender her little ass was roasted in the oven. It took me 9 days to eat her entire body. . . .

sented himself as a wealthy farmer named Frank Howard and received permission to take Grace to a birthday party. When she did not return, all the papers covered her kidnapping. Years later, Fish was caught after he sent a repulsive, detailed letter to Grace's parents, mailed November 11, 1934, and King traced the stationery. Grace's bones were found behind Wisteria Cottage, an abandoned house in Westchester County. Fish then confessed to eating parts of Budd's body as well as to beating, killing, and cannibalizing Billy Gaffney, age four, and to killing Francis McDonnell, age eight.

### Legal Action and Outcome

After his arrest, Fish said he no longer cared for life yet subtly appealed to officials and reporters for sympathy. Tried in March, 1935, Fish pleaded not guilty by reason of insanity. He was convicted; some jurors thought Fish was insane but should be executed anyway. An appeals trial and plea to the governor both failed, and Fish was electrocuted.

### Impact

Albert Fish is known primarily for his bizarre and extreme sexual appetite and for breaking the primal taboo against cannibalism. He also represents the transition of American society from one of trust to one in which strangers became feared. His missing victims, who disappeared around the time that aviator Charles Lindbergh's baby was kidnapped, fueled widespread fear of kidnapping and hence promoted changes in law enforcement.

### Further Reading

"Albert Fish." *World of Criminal Justice*. 2 vols. Farmington Hills, Mich.: Gale Group, 2002. Short, accurate summary of names, dates, and impact of Fish's crimes.

Brottman, Nikita. *Meat Is Murder! An Illustrated Guide to Cannibal Culture*. New York: Creation, 2001. Good exploration of motives for quasi-sexual cannibalism; erroneously implies that Fish had intercourse with Grace Budd.

Martingale, Moira. *Cannibal Killers*. New York: Carroll & Graf, 1994. Slightly inaccurate but provides insight into Fish's crimes and mental abnormalities.

Schechter, Harold. *Deranged*. New York: Pocket Books, 1990. Well-researched coverage of the acts, police investigation, trial, and social context.

Wertham, Frederic. *The Show of Violence*. New York: Doubleday, 1949. A source from which many writers draw, based on interviews with Fish.

*—Bernadette Lynn Bosky*

**See also:** Kenneth Bianchi; Angelo Buono, Jr.; Richard Allen Davis; John Wayne Gacy.

## Pretty Boy Floyd

### Bank robber and murderer

**Born:** February 3, 1904; Bartow County, Georgia
**Died:** October 22, 1934; near Wellsville, Ohio
**Also known as:** Charles Arthur Floyd (full name); Chock; James Warren; Mr. Douglas; Jack Hamilton; George Sanders
**Major offenses:** Bank robbery and murder
**Active:** 1925-1934
**Locale:** Midwestern United States
**Sentence:** Four years in prison for robbery; escaped a subsequent sentence of twelve to fifteen years

#### Early Life

Pretty Boy Floyd (floyd) was born Charles Floyd on a Georgia farm, the fourth of eight children. His family moved to Oklahoma in 1911, to a farm on the edge of the Cookson Hills. The farm was four hundred square miles of wilderness with few dirt roads, in an agricultural area known for its poverty. By the age of fourteen, Floyd was a harvest laborer, fistfighter, and moonshiner. He hated farming but liked clothes and girls. He married sixteen-year-old Ruby Hargraves in 1924; they had a son the same year.

#### Criminal Career

In 1925, Floyd left home for the harvests again; this time he teamed up with an experienced robber. The pair held up Kroger stores in St. Louis. Floyd was described by victims as young, with apple cheeks. The nickname of another criminal, Pretty Boy Smith, was applied to Floyd. Floyd was sentenced to four years in prison, and his wife divorced him before his release in 1929. While in prison he made criminal friendships and after parole went to Kansas City to renew them. He met twenty-one-year-old Juanita Ash,

*Pretty Boy Floyd.* (Courtesy, F.B.I.)

who divorced her husband and became his mistress. He alternated between living with her and with his ex-wife until his death.

As an ex-con, Floyd was harassed by police, for which he grew resentful. In 1929 Floyd's father was shot to death in an argument and his killer acquitted; the man disappeared shortly thereafter—presumably murdered by Floyd. Floyd robbed a bank in Ohio in 1930 and was sentenced to twelve to fifteen years in prison. He jumped from the train taking him to the penitentiary and escaped back to the Cookson Hills. In 1931 he and a partner drove back to Ohio, robbed more banks, and had a gunfight with city police in which Floyd's partner was slain. Floyd killed his first policeman. He again fled to the Cookson Hills.

Floyd went on an Oklahoma bank-robbing spree with a new partner, becoming the most famous bandit in the state. He spent generously to maintain the goodwill of the hill folks among whom he lived. He used his gun more than most professional bank robbers of the era; he also killed for revenge. He was extremely lucky, coming through several shoot-outs unhurt or wounded only superficially. Floyd wore bulletproof vests, sometimes front and back. During his 1931-1932 Oklahoma crime spree, authorities and newspapers blamed him for any large robbery that occurred in the state—which Floyd protested in an interview with a newspaper reporter. Fifty-one bank robberies occurred in Oklahoma in 1931, and Floyd was involved in perhaps half of them.

While home in Oklahoma, Floyd behaved erratically and took odd chances: He visited his mother, robbed a bank in his hometown of Sallisaw, threatened the local sheriff, went to movies, ate lunch in cafés, and attended church. Family members and acquaintances protected him, partly out of loyalty and partly out of fear. In 1932 his partner was killed while robbing a bank without Floyd.

Floyd's final partner was Adam "Eddie" Richetti. In 1933, outlaw Vern Miller contracted Floyd and Richetti to rescue bank robber Frank Nash from being transported to prison by police and the Federal Bureau of Investigation (FBI). The plan went awry as Nash sat inside a police car: The outlaws opened fire with machine guns. Five men, including Nash, died, and two were wounded in what would become known as the Kansas City Massacre. Before Kansas City, Floyd was a regional criminal. Afterward, his name was known nationwide. In 1934, a thousand men raided and searched the Cookson Hills, but Floyd escaped. By August of that year he was the last major outlaw in Oklahoma. He and Richetti, with their girlfriends, drove to Albany, New York, and hid in an apartment.

Several times, Floyd offered to surrender to law enforcement authorities in exchange for life in prison. Oklahoma and the FBI declined the deal. By June, 1934, FBI director J. Edgar Hoover had intensified efforts to find Floyd and ordered him killed on sight. In October, 1934, Floyd and Richetti decided to return to the Cookson Hills. Their car hit a telephone pole in early-morning fog in rural Ohio. Their girlfriends set out for help on foot, while the outlaws hid in the woods. Floyd and Richetti were spotted lying on blankets on the side of a hill, and the police were notified.

### Legal Action and Outcome

In a confused firefight, Richetti was captured, and Floyd ran into the woods. FBI chief Melvin Purvis and two dozen agents hunted him with a hundred local police. Around 3:00 P.M., Floyd walked to a farmhouse, bought a meal of pork chops, and asked for a ride to Youngstown. FBI agents and police suddenly appeared in two cars. Floyd ran across a field toward woods two hundred yards away. Police shot him three times. He died fifteen minutes later, with $122 on his person. His body was shipped home after money to do so was raised by Oklahoma neighbors. About twenty thousand people attended his funeral.

Richetti was executed in the gas chamber in 1938, weeping with fear.

Widows of the Kansas City Massacre received five thousand dollars apiece from Congress. Floyd's wife, girlfriend, and family were not prosecuted after his death.

## Impact

Hoover fired Melvin Purvis for receiving too much newspaper publicity over the death of Pretty Boy Floyd. As a result, Hoover remained the only nationally known personality in the FBI. He stayed on the job until his death in 1972 at the age of seventy-seven. Purvis shot himself in 1960.

Floyd had a significant impact on the public imagination: He was the subject of a ballad by the famous folksinger Woody Guthrie, was mentioned in John Steinbeck's novel *The Grapes of Wrath* (1939), and has been the subject of several films. One, *The Story of Pretty Boy Floyd* (1974), starring Martin Sheen, was introduced by Floyd's mother and included Floyd's younger brother in the cast. Floyd was also the subject of more recent films such as *Public Enemies* (2006), starring Leonardo DiCaprio.

## Further Reading

King, Jeffery S. *The Life and Death of Pretty Boy Floyd*. Kent, Ohio: Kent State University Press, 1998. A well-researched biography based on newspaper and magazine interviews.

Stewart, Tony. *Dillinger: The Hidden Truth*. Philadelphia: Xlibris, 2002. Includes a chapter on public enemies, including Floyd.

Wallis, Michael. *Pretty Boy: The Life and Times of Charles Arthur Floyd*. New York: St. Martin's Press, 1992. Describes Floyd in the context of the social conditions of his day and argues that he was not involved in the Kansas City Massacre.

—*Jim Pauff*

**See also:** Clyde Barrow; John Dillinger; Baby Face Nelson; Bonnie Parker.

# Larry C. Ford

## Physician and suspected bioterrorist

**Born:** September 29, 1950; Provo, Utah
**Died:** March 2, 2000; Irvine, California
**Also known as:** Larry Creed Ford (full name)
**Cause of notoriety:** Ford was allegedly involved with biological warfare in South Africa, Angola, and Zimbabwe.
**Active:** 1970's-1990's
**Locale:** California, South Africa, Angola, and Zimbabwe

### Early Life

Larry C. Ford (fohrd) was born to a Mormon family in 1950. He won first place in the International Science Fair of 1966 for his studies of radiation exposure and received much recognition for that achievement. At the age of eighteen he was invited to work in a government laboratory at an undisclosed location, which started his career with the military and the Central Intelligence Agency (CIA). After graduating from Brigham Young University, he married his childhood sweetheart, Diane, and in 1970 began studying to become a physician at the medical school of the University of California, Los Angeles (UCLA). In 1975, he graduated and pursued postgraduate work in biochemistry and gynecology.

### Scientific Career

In 1987, Ford moved with his family to Irvine, California. He had three children—two boys and one girl—and was described by his children as a good father. He served as a clinical professor and director of research for the Center for Ovarian Cancer at UCLA. He published more than sixty-five articles in the fields of cancer research, antibiotics, and infectious diseases. An international obstetrics/gynecological award was named for him.

In 1997, Ford was fired from UCLA after he was found disposing of blood samples improperly. He developed associations with South African officials and was alleged to have a role in biological warfare programs in South Africa that led to hundreds of deaths there and in the neighboring countries of Angola and Zimbabwe. In the 1980's, he had started a company, Biofem Pharmaceuticals, with an associate, James Patrick Riley. The company's main product was an over-the-counter vaginal suppository contraceptive, Inner Confidence, designed to protect women against HIV/AIDS and other sexually transmitted diseases. The company was waiting for Food and Drug Administration (FDA) approval and never came to the market.

In March of 2000, Riley survived an attempt on his life, a shooting during which the driver of the getaway car, Los Angeles businessman Din D'Saachs, was found to have been a patient of Ford. Ford was being questioned in connection with the attempted murder when he committed suicide by shooting himself on March 2, 2000, leaving a note behind claiming his innocence. A search of his house found C-4 explosives and other weapons buried in his backyard, along with more than 260 bottles of biological materials such as ricin, salmonella, vibrio cholerae, and botulinum.

His autopsy showed he had six antidepressants in his system at the time of his death. Since Dr. Ford committed suicide even before he could be arrested or a trial conducted, questions about his motives could not be established. His life and findings point toward suspicious criminal activities and involvement in developing agents for biological terror and warfare.

### Impact

The sudden suicide of Dr. Larry Ford left many questions unanswered. He had claimed to his colleagues (though not to his family) that he worked for the CIA, and despite being described as friendly, loving to his family, and giving, many also witnessed eccentricities of dress and unusual if not "abnormal" behavior, including his enthusiasm for guns, big-game hunting, and travel. Ford's attorney stated that his client had told him he had worked for the CIA for two decades—including one occasion during South Africa's apartheid days when he parachuted into the country to collect blood samples from dead guerrilla fighters. He had also divulged to colleagues that he worked for the CIA's biological warfare program. Whether these claims were true remains unsubstantiated. However, statements made by CIA agents—as well as Ford's misrepresentations of his credentials (the American College of Obstetricians and Gynecologists, for example, denied his claim to have been a member) and his mysterious suicide—seem to support these claims.

### Further Reading

Hardesty, Greg, and Bill Rams. "Doctor's Suicide Uncovers Skeletons That Shock Family Murder Probe; Arsenal in Yard Tarnishes Image." *Times-*

*Picayune*, April 9, 2000, p. A29. A news account of the events following Ford's suicide. Some intriguing facets of his life are discussed.

Humes, Edward. "The Medicine Man: Involvement of Scientist Larry Ford in Subversive Activities." *Los Angeles Magazine* 46 (July, 2001): 94. A detailed account of the investigation of Ford's suicide, his life, and what was found at his home by investigators.

Klein, Peter, Helen E. Purkitt, Trisra L. Sorrells, and Dan Rather. *"Dr. Death" and His Accomplice*. Video (26 minutes). New York: CBS World Wide, 2002. A program, with the transcript available on videocassette, describes the biological weapons used by Ford and elaborates on his associations in South Africa.

Purkitt, Helen, and Stephen Burgess. "South Africa's Chemical and Biological Warfare Programme: A Historical and International Perspective." *Journal of Southern African Studies* 28 (June, 2002): 229-253. This article includes discussion about Ford and his involvement with South Africa's covert chemical and biological warfare (CBW) program, Project Coast.

—*Manoj Sharma*

**See also:** Linda Burfield Hazzard.

# Antoinette Frank

## Police officer and murderer

**Born:** January 1, 1970; Opelousas, Louisiana
**Major offenses:** Murder and robbery
**Active:** March 4, 1995
**Locale:** New Orleans, Louisiana
**Sentence:** Death by lethal injection

### Early Life

Antoinette Frank (AN-twah-neht frank) was the second of four children born to Mary Ann and Adam Frank. Though born in Opelousas, Louisiana, she spent most of her childhood in New Orleans. The family moved back to Opelousas in 1987. As a youth, Frank became enamored with the idea of becoming a New Orleans Police Department (NOPD) officer. After graduating from high school, she immediately left Opelousas for New Orleans.

Frank applied to the New Orleans Police Department. However, her application failed to disclose that she had been fired from a job in Opelousas and that her brother was wanted for attempted manslaughter. After scoring poorly on two standardized psychological evaluations, Frank was then evaluated by a board-certified psychiatrist, who concluded that she was unsuitable for the job of police officer.

Depressed over this news, Frank disappeared, leaving a feeble suicide note for her father. Adam filed a NOPD missing persons report on her, only to have her turn up the next day. Frank then received another evaluation from a private psychiatrist, who determined she was suitable to be a police officer. Weeks later, Frank was hired by the NOPD.

Rogers LaCaze was a small-time drug dealer and street thug. Frank met LaCaze while investigating a shooting in which he was injured. They began a romantic relationship and were frequently seen together over the next months.

### Criminal Career

On March 4, 1995, around 1:00 A.M., Frank, along with her accomplice, LaCaze, entered the Kim Anh Vietnamese restaurant in eastern New Orleans and shot and killed Ronald Williams and Ha and Cuong Vu during a robbery. Frank had worked off-duty security detail at the restaurant and was aware that the Vu family kept significant amounts of cash around the business. Williams, a young, married father of two, was also employed by the NOPD and worked an off-duty security detail at the restaurant. Ha was the twenty-five-year-old daughter and oldest sibling of the Vu family. She helped run the Kim Anh restaurant with her mother, Bich. Cuong was her seventeen-year-old brother. Cuong played high school football and planned to enter the seminary after graduating. He worked at the restaurant after school.

The criminals left without finding the other two people in the restaurant: Twenty-three-year-old Chau Vu and her eighteen-year-old old brother, Quoc, hid in the restaurant's walk-in cooler when the robbery began. Chau was able to see some of the activity in the front room while she hid. After everything went silent, Quoc called police. Meanwhile, Frank picked up a marked cruiser and drove back to the crime scene and entered it. Chau emerged from the cooler only when she saw uniformed NOPD officers arrive. Detectives arrested Frank at the scene based on Chau's eyewitness report.

## Legal Action and Outcome

Frank's trial began in September, 1995. The state took three days to present its case against her. The defense rested without calling a single witness. It took the jury only twenty-two minutes to convict Frank of three counts of first-degree murder, and forty-five minutes to sentence her to death.

One month into Frank's time on death row at St. Gabriel's Louisiana Correctional Institute for Women, a new crime was discovered. In November, 1995, the new family living in the house that Frank had rented in New Orleans East discovered a bone. Police unearthed a human skeleton from under the house; the skull had a bullet wound. Frank's father had not been seen in more than a year, and many presumed that the skull was his. This case remained unsettled a decade later.

## Impact

Antoinette Frank became the only female on death row in Louisiana and only the second Louisiana woman in one hundred years to be sentenced to death. The sentence's severity, although appropriate for the remorseless Frank, was perhaps more important for the impact it had on the New Orleans Police Department, long considered one of the most corrupt in the nation. As a result of the case, the New Orleans Police Department restructured its recruitment and screening process for hiring new officers, even soliciting the Federal Bureau of Investigation to assist in ethical training. Its officer performance evaluation program was also overhauled.

## Further Reading

Hustmyre, Chuck. *Killer with a Badge*. New York: Berkley, 2004. Describes the crime and the backgrounds of the perpetrators and victims. Also provides insight into the culture of New Orleans East and Vietnamese immigrants.

Treadway, Joan, and James Varney. "Coroner: Bones Beneath Home Appear to Be Human." *Times-Picayune*, November 8, 1995, p. A-1. A newspaper account of the discovery of bones under the home in which Frank once lived.

Varney, James. "Cop Turned Killer Gets Death Sentence, Decision Reached

Within Forty-five Minutes." *Times-Picayune*, September 13, 1995, p. A-1. A newspaper feature detailing aspects of Frank's trial.

—*John C. Kilburn, Jr.*

**See also:** Bambi Bembenek.

# Martin Frankel

## Financier and fraud

**Born:** November 21, 1954; Toledo, Ohio
**Also known as:** David Rosse; Eric Stevens; Mike King; Martin Leon Frankel (full name)
**Major offenses:** Securities fraud, money laundering, and racketeering in the United States; carrying a false passport and evading customs taxes in Germany
**Active:** 1985-1999
**Locale:** Greenwich, Connecticut; Toledo, Ohio; and West Palm Beach, Florida
**Sentence:** Sixteen years, eight months' imprisonment in the United States; three years' imprisonment in Germany

### Early Life

Martin Frankel (fran-KEHL) was born into a well-respected family in Toledo, Ohio. His father, Leon, was an attorney, and his mother, Tillie, worked as a city clerk. Martin was the middle child of three. He was very intelligent but somewhat awkward socially. While Frankel's grades were very good, he had a habit of failing to turn in school assignments, and he experienced a phobia of test-taking. This behavior intensified during his student days at the University of Toledo, where he enrolled in a significant number of courses yet actually completed and passed very few. He left college with nearly two hundred hours of uncompleted coursework. Soon afterward, he received a license to sell real estate but failed to sell a single property.

Frankel lived with his parents until he was past the age of thirty. He spent many hours reading the financial newspapers and visiting Toledo brokerage houses. In 1985, Frankel entered the brokerage office of John F. Schulte, Inc., and announced that he planned to open an account. Though he never funded the account, he continued to visit and befriend John Schulte's wife, Sonia, who was a partner in the brokerage. After many visits, Frankel talked himself into a job with the firm.

In eight months of employment with Schulte, Frankel had only one significant client. Instead of working, he spent numerous hours explaining his system of amassing great wealth through trading securities but never actually placed trades. Similar to his testing phobia, Frankel claimed to have "trader's block" which stopped him from actually making trades, regardless of how passionately he held an investment idea.

### Criminal Career

Frankel later opened a branch office of LaSalle Street Securities, operating it out of his bedroom in his parents' home, with one client he had managed to keep from his previous brokerage job. He created documents that made wild claims about his system of trading commodities, stocks, and bonds for enormous profits. He then teamed up with Douglas Maxwell to recruit investors for the limited partnership Frankel Fund and the Creative Partners Fund. After mismanaging these funds by failing to place trades and using some of the money for his own personal expenses, Frankel was charged with fraud. He accepted a lifetime ban from the securities industry and was fined $200,000 in 1992.

Frankel maintained a relationship with Sonia Schulte, who eventually divorced John Schulte. Because Sonia alleged abuse in her marital relationship, Frankel offered to provide a safe home for her and her two children. With Sonia's assistance, Frankel set up the Donar Corporation, using friends' names as directors because he was banned from trading by the Securities and Exchange Commission.

Frankel then established the Thunor Trust as a corporation to buy insurance companies. His primary idea was to purchase the insurance companies and then steal the cash reserves that were set aside to pay claims. With the assistance of John Hackney, the Thunor Trust purchased the Tennessee-based Franklin American Insurance Corporation, which then bought numerous other insurance companies throughout the United States.

Frankel moved to Greenwich, Connecticut, and lived in luxury with the cash reserves of the various insurance companies his corporation purchased. He hired a large staff, which assisted him in falsifying financial statements for the various firms he controlled under the name Eric Stevens.

Frankel's scheme worked for several years, thanks to the complexity of its transactions: numerous corporations frequently transferring large amounts of money from one to another among banks around the world.

By placing and answering ads in special-interest sex-related magazines, Frankel met women seeking sadomasochistic sex. While many of those who responded to his ads became his sexual partners, Frankel offered others employment in his companies. His rationale was that women interested in a sadomasochistic relationship would be obedient employees. In addition to his large house in Greenwich, he rented a neighboring house so that he could house his partners and business associates.

As his appetite to make larger corporate acquisitions grew, Frankel devised a scheme in which he would acquire insurance companies in the names of charities and claim to give the profits to the charities. Actually, the name of a charity was used to offer a facade of legitimacy to Frankel's fraudulent dealings. He developed the St. Francis of Assisi Foundation with the claim that its funding came from the Vatican. This structure was developed through the nurturing of several politically connected attorneys, business executives, and Father Peter Jacobs.

At this time, several state insurance and banking regulators began to investigate and suspect that Frankel's operations were fraudulent. In May of 1999, Frankel fled to Europe with two women employees and was later arrested in a Hamburg hotel with nine fake passports, 547 diamonds, and an astrological chart drawn up to answer the question "Will I go to prison?"

## Legal Action and Outcome

After serving a brief prison sentence in Germany, Frankel was extradited to the United States in May of 2001. All of his assets were seized and sold. While he was officially charged with insurance fraud, money laundering, and racketeering with $208 million unaccounted for, it is likely that exact figures will never be known. After pleading guilty in a U.S. District Court, Frankel was sentenced to serve sixteen years and eight months in December of 2004.

## Impact

Martin Frankel's case drew substantial attention in the popular press because of his deviant lifestyle. However, his actions are not unique among cases of fraudulent accounting. While deregulation of the insurance and securities industry is often considered helpful to modern trade in the global economy, Frankel's actions illustrate the relative ease with which corporate crime may be perpetrated and millions of dollars stolen. Frankel's story is one of many that justifies frequent and detailed audits of corporations.

**Further Reading**

Johnson, J. A., Jr. *Thief: The Bizarre Story of Fugitive Financier Martin Frankel*. New York: Lebhar-Friedman Books, 2000. Provides a journalistic overview of the events that led to Frankel's rapid financial gains and deviant lifestyle.

Pollock, Ellen Joan. *The Pretender: How Martin Frankel Fooled the Financial World and Led the Feds on One of the Most Publicized Manhunts in History*. New York: Simon and Schuster, 2002. A comprehensive work that details Frankel's personal relationships in building his fraudulent empire.

*—John C. Kilburn, Jr.*

**See also:** Lou Blonger; John R. Brinkley; Tino De Angelis; Billie Sol Estes; Susanna Mildred Hill; Joseph Weil.

# Lynette Fromme

## Cult member and would-be assassin

**Born:** October 22, 1948; Santa Monica, California
**Also known as:** Lynette Alice Fromme (full name); Squeaky Fromme; Red
**Major offense:** Attempt to assassinate President Gerald R. Ford
**Active:** July, 1970-December 23, 1987
**Locale:** Los Angeles, Sacramento, and Dublin, California
**Sentence:** Life in a federal correctional institution

### Early Life

Lynette Alice Fromme (frohm) was born to William Fromme, an aeronautical engineer, and Helen Benzinger Fromme, homemaker and mother of three. Redheaded Lyn, the eldest child, was a star performer in the Westchester Lariats, a children's dance group that became so popular it performed on *The Lawrence Welk Show* and at the White House. Despite having external social success in her early years, Fromme had a troubled home life during her childhood. She was reared by an emotionally cold, detached father who treated her harshly and who parented through fear and intimidation. Fromme's mother was unable to thwart her father's anger toward the family.

When the family moved to Redondo Beach, California, in 1963, Fromme's academic grades plummeted, and she began drinking and taking drugs. After narrowly graduating from high school in 1966, Fromme moved out of her parents' home and drifted until she met Charles Manson in Venice Beach the following year. Eighteen-year-old Fromme was amazed by Manson, an existential philosopher who did not appear to expect anything of her. Their meeting was so provocative, she left with Manson, never to return home.

## Criminal Career

Fromme began living with Manson and his cult of nomadic young people much like her. While with them, she took psychotropic drugs such as LSD and became wholly absorbed with Manson's assertions that racial civil war

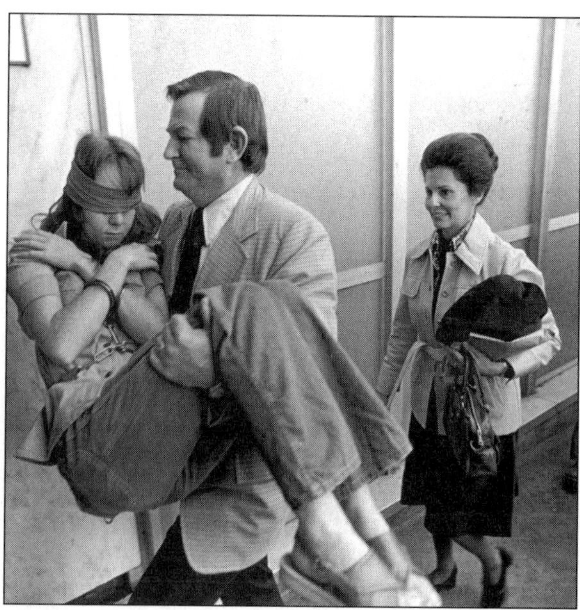

*Lynette "Squeaky" Fromme refuses to walk to her trial.* (AP/Wide World Photos)

> My father had kicked me out of his house at the height of an argument over an opinion difference. He had become so enraged. He told me never to come back, and that was all the severance it took.
>
> —*Lynette Fromme*

was imminent and that the Manson family of followers would ultimately rule the world.

Fromme would come to hold a special place in the Manson family hierarchy. After Manson was arrested in 1969, Fromme (called Squeaky within the Manson family) and fellow Manson family member Sandra Good carved X's in their foreheads to show loyalty to Manson. They also carved the letter to protest Manson's impending conviction for grand theft auto and his concurrent arrest for the Sharon Tate and the Leo and Rosemary LaBianca murders in 1969. Fromme later declared, "We have X'ed ourselves out of this world."

Fromme effectively took control of the family in Manson's absence. Soon after his incarceration, she moved to Stockton, California, with Nancy Pitman, Priscilla Copper, Michael Monfort, James Craig, and a couple, James and Lauren (Reni) Willett. In 1972, when the Willetts were found dead within days of each other, the roommates were taken into custody. However, Fromme was released because of a lack of evidence. Leaving Stockton, she moved to Sacramento with Good. Together, they formed the International People's Court of Retribution, an organization intended to frighten corporate executives into believing that they were on a terrorist hit list for environmental degradation. Using his continued influence, Manson encouraged the two women to wear robes and change their names to symbolize their devotion to his new religion, which Manson called the "Order of the Rainbow." He dubbed Lynette "Red" because of her red hair, while giving her the task of protecting all redwood trees. Good he named "Blue" for her blue eyes.

For several years, Fromme drifted through a life of poverty and petty crimes until she went to Sacramento's Capitol Park in 1975 to complain to President Gerald R. Ford about the destruction of the environment. The Manson "nun," dressed in her red "habit" and armed with a Colt .45 automatic, shot at Ford from a distance of only two feet. Her weapon had four bullets in the clip, but the chamber was empty.

## Legal Action and Outcome

Fromme often claimed she had committed the attempted assassination so that Manson would appear as a witness at her trial and thus give him a worldwide platform from which to talk about his grand vision. However, Judge Thomas J. MacBride refused to give Fromme or Manson a public platform for their views. Serving as her own defense counsel, Fromme boycotted most of the court proceedings. After three days of jury deliberation, she was convicted of attempting to assassinate the president and remanded to the custody of the Federal Bureau of Prisons in Dublin, California.

In 1979, Fromme was convicted and transferred from the Dublin federal prison for striking a fellow inmate in the head with a hammer. After traversing a variety of U.S. federal prisons, she escaped from the Alderson Federal Prison Camp in Alderson, West Virginia, in 1987, in an attempt to meet with Manson, whom she had been told had cancer. She was captured in the nearby woods two days later and sentenced to serve life at the Federal Bureau of Prisons' Carswell Federal Medical Center in Fort Worth, Texas, where she remained in the administrative segregation unit following her arrival in 1998. Although federal law entitled Fromme to a mandatory parole hearing after thirty years, she continued to waive her right to these hearings, and unlike several of Manson's former disciples who remained in prison, she chose not to seek her release. She never renounced Manson.

## Impact

When one reflects on the tumultuous 1960's in the United States, Squeaky Fromme is synonymous with Charles Manson and his cult family. As the emerging counterculture became a national phenomenon, Fromme and her compatriots espoused liberal ideals and defended the right to commit "political" crimes. As self-proclaimed defenders of the First Amendment, they believed it was their duty to create a new moral and political order. The atmosphere of political and social protest during the period exacerbated their susceptibility to influence by charismatic criminals such as Manson. Indeed, Fromme's crimes, like those of many other Manson followers, were clearly criminal acts masked as political activism.

**Further Reading**

Bravin, Jess. *Squeaky: The Life and Times of Lynette Alice Fromme*. New York: St. Martin's Griffin, 1998. An account of Fromme's life from her childhood years, her time with Manson, her attempted assassination of President Ford, and her ensuing trial.

Osborne, John. *New Republic* 173, no. 14 (1975): 9-10. A discussion of the effects of Fromme's attempt to assassinate President Ford and the president's public appearances and security.

Sanders, Ed. *The Family*. New York: Thunder's Mouth Press, 2002. A detailed look at the terror dealt by Manson and his followers with some of the most notorious murders in modern American history.

*—Patricia K. Hendrickson*

**See also:** Charles Manson.

# John Wayne Gacy

## Serial killer

**Born:** March 17, 1942; Chicago, Illinois

**Died:** May 10, 1994; Stateville Correctional Center, Joliet, Illinois

**Also known as:** John Wayne Gacy, Jr. (full name); Killer Clown; Pogo the Clown

**Major offenses:** Sodomy and murder

**Active:** January, 1972-December, 1978

**Locale:** Des Plaines and Chicago, Illinois

**Sentence:** Life imprisonment for twenty-one victims murdered between January, 1972, and June, 1977; death by lethal injection for twelve victims murdered between July, 1977, and December, 1978

**Early Life**

John Wayne Gacy (GAY-cee), Jr., was born on St. Patrick's Day, 1942, and was raised Roman Catholic by his parents, John Wayne Gacy, Sr., and Marion Gacy. His father, who frequently drank alcohol, was physically and psychologically abusive. At age eleven, Gacy was struck on the head with a playground swing, causing periodic blackouts until doctors discovered and treated a blood clot. After dropping out of high school, Gacy drifted to

Las Vegas but eventually returned to Chicago and graduated from business college. At age twenty-two, Gacy married and moved to Waterloo, Iowa, taking a position as manager of a restaurant belonging to his new wife's family.

To the shock and dismay of his family, Gacy was arrested in May, 1968, for coercing a young employee into homosexual acts. He pleaded guilty to sodomy and was sentenced to ten years in prison. After serving only eighteen months of the sentence, Gacy was released on parole. While incarcerated, Gacy's wife divorced him and left with their two children.

Gacy returned to the Chicago area and bought a new home in Norwood Park Township. Shortly thereafter, he established his own business, called PDM Contracting, Inc. Gacy, now a well-respected businessman, held elaborate parties at his home for neighbors and entertained children as "Pogo the Clown." He also held an office in the Democratic Party.

### Criminal Career

Gacy's serial crimes began to surface when he was arrested on February 12, 1971, for disorderly conduct and attempted rape. However, Gacy's accuser, a young male, failed to appear in court, and Gacy's charges were subsequently dismissed. According to Gacy's estimate, his first murder victim was a teenage boy whom he picked up at a bus depot in January, 1972. Between January, 1972, and December, 1978, Gacy killed more than thirty young men. Gacy's primary modus operandi was to troll the streets of Chicago for young boys and prostitutes and bring them (through coercion or by force) to his house, where he would sexually assault, torture, and strangle them. He then buried the corpses around his house.

### Legal Action and Outcome

In early December, 1978, the Des Plaines police department, investigating the disappearance of Robert Piest, confronted Gacy while executing a search warrant at his home. Gacy denied any knowledge about Piest's disappearance. On December 22, 1978, facing mounting physical evidence against him from subsequent searches of his home, Gacy confessed that he had killed thirty-three young men and boys and buried most on his property. Police summoned the coroner, and when digging was finished on Gacy's property, twenty-eight bodies were unearthed from the crawl space, the garage floor, and the patio. Five additional bodies were later recovered from the Des Plaines River. Of the victims recovered between December, 1978, and April, 1979, nine remained unidentified.

Gacy's trial began on February 6, 1980, in Chicago. Gacy pleaded not guilty by reason of insanity. The defense was ultimately unsuccessful when, on March 13, Gacy was found guilty on all thirty-three counts of murder. Gacy was executed by lethal injection on May 10, 1994, in the Stateville Correctional Center in Joliet, Illinois.

## Impact

Dubbed the Killer Clown, John Wayne Gacy lived a double life for years: successful entrepreneur and popular neighbor by day, sexual predator and murderer by night. Gacy's notorious criminal career drew considerable attention. "There's been eleven hardback books on me, thirty-one paperbacks, two screenplays, one movie, one off-Broadway play, five songs, and over five thousand articles," Gacy boasted in one of his last interviews. After his execution in 1994, Gacy's original oil paintings of clowns, made while on death row, were sold at auction to collectors. Author Stephen King reportedly used Gacy as a model for the character of the murderous clown in his novel *It* (1986).

## Further Reading

Cahill, Tim. *Buried Dreams: Inside the Mind of a Serial Killer*. New York: Bantam Books, 1986. A thorough examination of Gacy's many mind-sets and personalities—John the politician, the contractor, and the clown, as well as Jack, the sexual predator and killer.

Linedecker, Clifford L. *The Man Who Killed Boys: The John Wayne Gacy, Jr., Story*. New York: St. Martin's Press, 1993. A factual account of Gacy's serial murders and subsequent trial as portrayed in the local media, official police records, and court documents.

Mendenhall, Harlan H. *Fall of the House of Gacy*. West Frankfort, Ill.: New Authors, 1998. Described as the only authorized biography of the infamous serial killer, Mendenhall's psychological study focuses on the early family abuses that shaped Gacy's personality and his subsequent diagnosis as a psychotic schizophrenic.

Sullivan, Terry, and Peter T. Maiken. *Killer Clown: The John Wayne Gacy Murders*. New York: Kensington, 2000. Sullivan, who was involved in the investigation of Gacy, provides an in-depth and comprehensive look at the complexities of the investigation, prosecution, and conviction of Gacy.

—*Anthony J. Luongo III*

**See also:** Joe Ball; David Berkowitz; Kenneth Bianchi; Ted Bundy; Angelo Buono, Jr.; Andrew Cunanan; Jeffrey Dahmer; Albert DeSalvo; Albert Fish; Ed Gein; Leonard Lake; Charles Ng; Dennis Rader; Aileen Carol Wuornos.

# Carmine Galante

## Mafia boss

**Born:** February 21, 1910; Castellammare de Golfo, Sicily, Italy
**Died:** July 12, 1979; Brooklyn, New York
**Also known as:** The Cigar; Lilo
**Major offense:** Conspiracy to violate narcotics laws
**Active:** 1930, 1939-1962, 1972-1979
**Locale:** New York
**Sentence:** Twelve and one-half years in prison after a shoot-out with police, served nine years; twenty years in prison, served ten years

### Early Life

Regarded by many as one of the more ruthless Mafia bosses in U.S. history, Carmine Galante (CAR-min gah-LAHN-tay), also known as "The Cigar" for the ever-present cigar in the corner of his mouth, was born in Sicily in 1910. In the late 1910's, he relocated with his family to New York and began running with a juvenile street gang in the city's lower East Side at the age of eleven. During the 1920's, Galante made a name for himself by dispatching his Brooklyn-based gang to commit hits (murders), steal liquor, and disrupt legitimate and illegitimate businesses throughout the city.

### Criminal Career

Much of Galante's early criminal activity went undetected by law enforcement authorities. In 1930, however, a New York police officer stumbled across Galante and several others as they were attempting to hijack a truck in the Bronx neighborhood of Williamsburg. A gun battle ensued, leaving the officer and several bystanders injured but still alive. Galante was captured at the scene but refused to reveal the identities of the other men involved in the attempted robbery.

In late 1930, Galante was found guilty of charges stemming from this incident and was sentenced to twelve and one-half years in New York's Sing Sing Prison. After being released on parole in 1939, he began carrying out hits for Vito Genovese, one of New York's most powerful mobsters.

During the 1940's, Galante began working for associates of the Bonanno Mafia family. Starting as a bodyguard for a Bonnano Mafioso named Gaetano Gagliano, Galante was eventually promoted to capo (literally "head," or captain) status. By the 1950's, Galante was a well-known and respected member of the Bonanno family and was handpicked by the family godfather, Joe Bonanno, to expand the syndicate's operations into Canada. Galante was quick to establish contacts and firmly put down foundations of the new Bonanno arm in Montreal, Quebec. Throughout the 1950's, Carmine worked tirelessly to globalize the family's narcotics trade and was successful in establishing illegal networks of producers and distributors worldwide. Galante spent a decade in prison after he was found guilty in 1962 of violating narcotics laws.

Paroled in 1972, he returned to New York and resumed his life of crime. He quickly made his presence felt by blowing the doors off the tomb of Frank Costello, who had died in 1973. Galante was apparently unhappy with Costello for his role in the removal and banishment of his mentor Joe Bonanno.

Galante then set his sights on taking over the Bonanno crime family, whose acting boss, Natale Evola, had recently died. Evola was replaced by Philip "Rusty" Rastelli, but Galante considered this a temporary appointment. Galante soon bullied Rastelli into turning over the leadership of the Bonanno family to him and pushed the syndicate deeper into the drug trade. Relying on his contacts in Canada, he made Montreal the family's main pipeline for heroin from France. The "French Connection" made Galante and his associates millions.

As the family became more involved in the drug trade, Galante began recruiting young, hard Sicilian immigrants to serve as soldiers and bodyguards. These men, who were referred to as "zips" because of the speed with which they spoke their native language, provided Carmine with the necessary muscle to expand and protect his drug operations. Ironically, the zips may have played a critical role in Galante's death. On Thursday, July 12, 1979, while eating lunch with two of his zips, Carmine was approached by several gunmen and was blasted out of his seat. He died with a cigar still clenched in his teeth. Amazingly, both of his bodyguards escaped without a scratch. It is rumored that the murder was arranged by Philip Rastelli, who returned to his position as boss of the Bonanno family after Galante's death.

## Legal Action and Outcome

In 1958, Galante was indicted along with several other Mafiosi, including Genovese, on charges stemming from his involvement in an international narcotics syndication that smuggled cocaine and heroin into the United States from Cuba, Puerto Rico, and Mexico. In 1962, after some time on the run, Galante was found guilty of conspiracy to violate narcotics laws and was sentenced to twenty years in prison. He served his sentence in the federal penitentiary at Lewisburg, Pennsylvania, and kept himself busy by working in the prison's greenhouse and looking after his pet cats.

While incarcerated, he also enjoyed several other luxuries not normally afforded to inmates, such as choice cuts of meat from the prison butcher. As he did on the street, Galante demanded and received great respect behind prison walls. Prisoners and guards alike abided by Galante's informal rules of conduct. In 1972, Galante was paroled after serving ten years of his sentence.

## Impact

Carmine Galante's biggest influence on American organized crime may have been his role in globalizing drug trafficking and establishing the Canadian branch of the Bonanno crime family. The Bonanno family was able to avoid many of the indictments and convictions that have crippled other crime families. The family continued to maintain close ties with the zips, and some believe that the family continued its international drug trafficking into the twenty-first century.

## Further Reading

Abadinsky, Howard. *Organized Crime*. 7th ed. New York: Thomas Dunne Books, 2005. This text provides a detailed analysis of organized crime in New York and Chicago and examines several emerging international groups.

Capeci, Jerry. *The Complete Idiot's Guide to the Mafia*. 2d ed. Indianapolis, Ind.: Alpha Books, 2002. Capeci provides a comprehensive introduction to Italian organized crime.

Lyman, Michael D., and Gary W. Potter. *Organized Crime*. Upper Saddle River, N.J.: Pearson/Prentice Hall, 2004. A comprehensive textbook that covers the essentials of organized crime theory and practice.

*—James C. Roberts and Thomas E. Baker*

**See also:** Joe Adonis; Albert Anastasia; Vincent Coll; Joe Colombo; Frank Costello; Carlo Gambino; Vito Genovese; Sam Giancana; John Gotti; Sammy Gravano; Henry Hill; Richard Kuklinski; Meyer Lansky; Salvatore Maranzano; Carlos Marcello.

# Joe Gallo

## Gangster

**Born:** April 7, 1929; Brooklyn, New York
**Died:** April 7, 1972; New York, New York
**Also known as:** Crazy Joe; Joey Gallo
**Major offense:** Extortion
**Active:** 1961
**Locale:** New York, New York
**Sentence:** Ten years in prison

### Early Life

Joe Gallo (GA-loh) was born in Brooklyn and became involved in organized crime at a young age. When he was seventeen he was arrested for burglary, assault, and kidnapping. He became a "made" soldier for the Profaci Mafia family while still a teenager.

### Criminal Career

Gallo supposedly earned the name "Crazy Joe" for his ruthless and violent behavior as well as his nontraditional ideas about working with African American criminals in Mafia operations—he saw that there was money to be made in neighborhoods like Harlem, and he wanted the Mafia to get some of that money. He may have further cultivated his "crazy" image to assist him in shaking down his extortion victims.

Gallo, along with his brothers Larry and Albert, reportedly served as a gunner for Mafia boss Joseph Profaci and then Joe Colombo. Profaci was an unpopular boss, greedy even by Mafia standards, who dipped heavily into the profits of his "soldiers" for his "tribute." The Gallo brothers rebelled against Profaci, who died of natural causes in 1962. The war waged by the Gallos continued when Joe Colombo took over the family.

Joe Gallo was convicted of extortion in 1961 and sentenced to ten years in prison. Soon after he was freed in 1971, Colombo was shot and subsequently slipped into a coma. Gallo was immediately suspected in the assassination attempt, especially because the shooter was an African American man (who was killed at the scene). Gallo was not tried, however, because of lack of evidence.

Gallo was not a typical gangster. He cultivated relationships among the New York theater crowd and became friendly with actor Jerry Orbach, who comically depicted Gallo in James Goldstone's 1971 film *The Gang That Couldn't Shoot Straight*. After Colombo's death, Gallo continued to operate, moving between high society circles and criminal circles. On April 7, 1972, Gallo, after celebrating his birthday with guests that included the Orbachs, ended his evening at Umberto's Clam House. He was shot and killed by an unknown assailant while seated at the restaurant with his bodyguard and four women friends.

### Legal Action and Outcome

Gallo was not convicted of his most serious offenses. In 1961, however, he received a ten-year prison sentence for extortion.

### Impact

Besides helping to inspire Jimmy Breslin's novel *The Gang That Couldn't Shoot Straight* (1969) and its film adaptation, Joe Gallo was memorialized in the song *Joey* by Bob Dylan and Jacques Levy. Gallo's forward-thinking, albeit criminal, views on crossing racial lines in business enterprise and his intellectual aspirations also make him an important and compelling figure in the study of the American Mafia.

**Further Reading**

Capeci, Jerry. *Jerry Capeci's Gang Land*. New York: Alpha Books, 2003. A compilation of journalist and Mafia expert Capeci's columns in the *New York Daily News* covering organized crime activity in New York City from 1989 through 1995.

Raab, Selwyn. *The Five Families: The Rise, Decline, and Resurgence of America's Most Powerful Mafia Empires*. New York: Thomas Dunne Books, 2005. Recounts the history of the New York crime families; spotlights major figures and events of organized crime in New York.

Talese, Gay. *Honor Thy Father*. New York: World, 1971. Traces Joe Bonanno's career as Mafia boss.

*—David R. Champion*

**See also:** Joe Adonis; Albert Anastasia; Vincent Coll; Joe Colombo; Carmine Galante; Carlo Gambino; Sam Giancana; Vincent Gigante; John Gotti; Sammy Gravano; Henry Hill; Richard Kuklinski; Meyer Lansky; Salvatore Maranzano; Carlos Marcello; Joseph Profaci.

# Carlo Gambino

## Mafia boss

**Born:** August 24, 1902; Palermo, Italy

**Died:** October 15, 1976; Massapequa, Long Island, New York

**Also known as:** Don Carlo; Capo di Tutti Capi; Boss of Bosses

**Cause of notoriety:** Gambino, who worked his way up the chain of command of the American Mafia over several decades, eventually secured the title of Boss of Bosses and ran the notorious Gambino crime family.

**Active:** 1921-1976

**Locale:** New York, New York

### Early Life

Carlo Gambino (gam-BEE-noh) was born in Palermo, Italy, the birthplace of Italian organized crime. Young Gambino needed to go no further than his own well-connected Mafia family to form his early identification with organized crime. Gambino dropped out of high school and started working for

*Carlo Gambino.*
(AP/Wide World Photos)

the Mafia. He earned the respect of his boss by demonstrating his efficient and brutal service to his crime family.

The Italian government's purge of Mafia members forced many young Mafiosi to flee from certain death by using a secret escape route. They eventually found their future destination from various points of entry into Little Italy in New York City. In late 1921, the "secret society" provided an escape route for the nineteen-year-old Gambino; his first destination was Norfolk, Virginia. Eventually, family members smuggled Gambino to New York.

### Criminal Career

Once settled in New York, Gambino, an opportunist, organized illegal truck deliveries of alcohol during Prohibition in the 1930's. During World War II, he became a millionaire in the black market for ration stamps. His criminal endeavors later turned to the New York waterfront and garment industry, as well as labor racketeering and legitimate business fronts.

Gambino always managed to be on the "right side" in Mafia wars, such as the so-called Castellammarese War in 1930-1931, a bloody power struggle between two factions of the Mafia. Eventually, Gambino would rise to power alongside Lucky Luciano. Gambino joined the Mangano crime family, which, by the 1950's, was controlled by Albert Anastasia (also known as the Lord High Executioner). Gambino had earned the rank of *capo*, or captain, while working under the authority of Vincent Mangano. When Anastasia assumed command of the family, he promoted Gambino to *sottocapo*, or underboss. However, in 1957, Anastasia was murdered in a hotel, presumably from a hit ordered by Gambino; he took over the family and renamed it for himself.

Gambino earned the title Boss of Bosses for his murder of Anastasia. His position as the Mafia's top leader was further secured when Vito Genovese, a leading Mafia figure, died in prison in 1969. Despite being the Boss of Bosses, Gambino maintained a low profile, and his crime family became the first family of organized crime. In 1971, Gambino was suspected of ordering the murder of Joe Colombo, the head of the Colombo crime family. Wounded by several bullets, Colombo remained in a vegetative state until he finally died in 1978.

## Legal Action and Outcome

The courts failed to convict Gambino despite sixteen arrests over the course of his Mafia career. He followed the principle of the "lion and the fox": He used force as brutally as a lion and was crafty like a fox when it came to his survival and avoiding arrest. His only successful conviction was for a 1939 liquor tax evasion charge. He received a twenty-month sentence; however, the conviction was reversed on appeal because of unconstitutional wiretapping procedures. Gambino was never convicted or deported for illegal immigration.

Gambino did not attend his racketeering trial in the 1970's because of deteriorating health. During the initial days of the trial, a television reporter tried to interview him, but the old man stood mute: He had learned the benefits of remaining silent. Gambino, the master criminal, once again avoided conviction by hiring competent attorneys. Gambino died in 1976 of a heart attack in his Long Island home while watching a ballgame and still facing illegal racketeering and immigration charges.

## Impact

The Gambino family missed Carlo Gambino's leadership and quiet demeanor. The death of the most commanding Mafia leader left a power vacuum: His cousin, who was also his brother-in-law, Paul Castellano, whom Gambino left in charge of the family, failed to command the same respect.

John Gotti resented Castellano's appointment and eventually ordered the murder of Castellano in 1985, thereby becoming the new boss of the Gambino crime family.

**Further Reading**

Abadinsky, Howard. *Organized Crime*. 7th ed. Belmont, Calif.: Wadsworth/Thomson Learning, 2003. The text is an in-depth analysis of organized crime from a historical and theoretical perspective.

Davis, John. *The Rise and Fall of the Gambino Crime Family*. New York: HarperTorch, 1994. This popular analysis of the Gambino family examines integrated and complex crime and social relationships of America's first family of organized crime.

Lyman, Michael D., and Gary W. Potter. *Organized Crime*. 2d ed. Upper Saddle River, N.J.: Pearson/Prentice Hall, 2000. A comprehensive textbook, covering the essentials of organized crime theory and practice.

*—Thomas E. Baker and James C. Roberts*

**See also:** Albert Anastasia; Paul Castellano; Joe Colombo; Vito Genovese; John Gotti; Sammy Gravano; Lucky Luciano.

## Gilbert Gauthe

### Priest and pedophile

**Born:** 1945; Napoleonville, Louisiana

**Major offenses:** Eleven counts of aggravated crimes against nature; eleven counts of committing sexually immoral acts; eleven counts of taking pornographic photographs of juveniles; and a single count of aggravated rape, sodomizing a child under the age of twelve

**Active:** 1971-1983

**Locale:** Broussard, New Iberia, Abbeville, and Henry, Louisiana

**Sentence:** Twenty years in prison; served ten years

**Early Life**

Born in 1945, Gilbert Gauthe (GO-tay) grew up near Napoleonville, Louisiana. He attended the University of Southwestern Louisiana in Lafayette (now known as the University of Louisiana, Lafayette) before attending Immaculate Junior Seminary for one year. He transferred to Notre Dame Seminary in New Orleans, where he completed his theological studies. While a seminarian, he was active with various youth organizations, including the Boy Scouts of America, and was well liked by the families of children with whom he worked. Gauthe was ordained by the Roman Catholic Church in 1971. He served several churches within the Diocese of Lafayette, where he was popular with both children and adult parishioners.

### Criminal Career

Gauthe's career as a pedophile spans that of his entire priesthood. He admitted that he began having sexual contact with children in 1971, the year of his ordination. While serving as an associate pastor in Broussard, Louisiana, from 1971 to 1973, he molested at least four boys. He was confronted by parents of those boys and, consequently, sought psychiatric help. He received approximately eight sessions of therapy before being transferred in late 1973 to a church in New Iberia, Louisiana, where he admitted to molesting sixteen boys. In 1976 he was once again transferred to another church—this time in Abbeville, Louisiana—where he served until 1977. Gauthe admitted to molesting boys at this church before receiving his final transfer to a church in Henry, Louisiana, where he admitted to molesting twenty-two boys before being suspended from pastoral duties in 1983. Gauthe, unsure of his final victim count, readily admitted to at least three dozen; other estimates place this number closer to one hundred.

### Legal Action and Outcome

Gauthe entered a plea of guilty to thirty-four counts of contributing to the delinquency of a minor and possession of child pornography. At least twenty-five civil lawsuits were filed against the Diocese of Lafayette, claiming that it failed to protect the public. In response, the diocese opted to thwart Gauthe's actions by moving his first-floor bedroom to the second floor of the rectory, so boys could not climb in and out of windows, and instructed Gauthe to make confession and pray. More than twenty-two million dollars were paid to plaintiffs.

### Impact

Gilbert Gauthe's trial marked the first time in U.S. history that the details of a priest's alleged sexual abuse of children were made widely public. His trial served as a test case for prosecuting pedophiliac priests. After his conviction, dozens of other priests in Louisiana and around the United States were accused of child molestation, and various dioceses were sued for alleged cover-ups and gross negligence in handling decades of abuse allegations. In 1986, Gauthe's attorney, along with two priests, drafted a document informing the Roman Catholic Church how best to address allegations of sexual abuse by clergy and estimating its prevalence and potential monetary damage. This document was presented to the U.S. Conference of Church Bishops in 1986 but was not taken up by Church authorities until 2002.

**Further Reading**

Berry, Jason. *Lead Us Not into Temptation: Catholic Priests and the Sexual Abuse of Children*. New York: Doubleday Press, 1992. An authoritative examination of both the Gauthe case and church policy on celibacy and homosexuality.

*Boston Globe* investigative staff. *Betrayal: The Crisis in the Catholic Church*. Boston: Little, Brown, 2002. A chronicle of the events that led up to an international crisis of pedophiliac priests and church officials who were accused of ignoring complaints about sexual predators.

Jenkins, Phillip. *Pedophiles and Priests: Anatomy of a Contemporary Crisis*. New York: Oxford University Press, 1996. An academic and dispassionate review of sex scandals within the Roman Catholic Church and other religious institutions. This book reviews the role of the media in influencing public perceptions about crises.

*—Rachel Kate Bandy*

**See also:** James Porter.

# Ed Gein

## Murderer and necrophiliac

**Born:** August 27, 1906; La Crosse, Wisconsin
**Died:** July 26, 1984; Madison, Wisconsin
**Also known as:** Edward Theodore Gein (full name); Mad Butcher of Plainfield; Plainfield Head Collector; Shy Ghoul; Ghastly Gein
**Major offenses:** Murder and grave robbing
**Active:** December 8, 1954-November 16, 1957
**Locale:** Plainfield, Wisconsin
**Sentence:** Convicted of one count of first-degree murder; judged not guilty by reason of insanity and committed to Central State Hospital for the Criminally Insane in Waupun; later transferred to the Mendota Mental Health Institute in Madison, where he remained until his death.

### Early Life

The father of Edward Gein (geen) was an alcoholic and both verbally and physically abusive to Gein and his brother. However, Gein's fanatically religious mother, Augusta Gein, dominated his early life by teaching him that sex was evil and a contaminating influence to be avoided. In 1914, the Geins moved to a farm near Plainfield. Gein's father died in 1940. His brother died in 1944 while fighting a fire near their home. Some investigators have speculated that Gein killed his brother in the fire, but no one has proven this assertion. Augusta's death in 1945 left Gein alone and appears to be the catalyst that drove his descent into full-blown psychopathic behavior.

### Criminal Career

Mary Hogan, believed to be Gein's first victim, was found dead on December 8, 1954. Although evidence discovered later would implicate Gein in grave-robbing and other crimes, Gein's neighbors suspected nothing, considering him harmless, if eccentric. When police investigated the disappearance of Bernice Worden on November 16, 1957, they discovered her body hanging in a shed on Gein's property, decapitated and disemboweled, with sexual organs removed. Police found her head inside the house, along with the preserved remains of fifteen women. Gein had made a skull into a soup bowl, and he had crafted human face "masks" by carefully peeling the skin away from the skulls of several victims. A "woman suit"—a vest of preserved female flesh, breasts and sexual organs attached—was also found. Police discovered other body parts, including sex organs, noses, and lips, as well as chairs upholstered with skin, all carefully preserved. Gein claimed to have committed more than forty grave robberies beginning in 1947 and admitted using the corpses for sexual gratification but denied having sex with the corpses or engaging in cannibalism.

### Legal Action and Outcome

Initially considered incompetent to stand trial, Gein was committed to the Central State Hospital for the Criminally Insane in Waupun, Wisconsin, on January 6, 1958. A decade later, he was judged fit to stand trial. While convicted of first-degree murder in the death of Worden, during the penalty phase of the trial he was declared not guilty by reason of insanity and returned to Central State. He was later transferred to the Mendota Mental Health Institute in Madison, a minimum-security facility, where he died on July 26, 1984, of respiratory failure at age seventy-seven.

### Impact

The story of Ed Gein's crimes created intense media exposure—reporters from around the world descended on the small town in Wisconsin to cover the story. The public and professionals from the field of psychology were fascinated by a case that combined necrophilia, fetishism, and transvestism. Gein has had an important impact on popular culture: Elements of his story have appeared in films such as *Psycho* (1960), *The Texas Chainsaw Massacre* (1974), *The Silence of the Lambs* (1991), and, most significant, *Deranged* (1974) and *Ed Gein* (2001). A short film, *Ed Gein: American Maniac* (1993), is a graphic, straightforward documentary about Gein's life and crimes.

### Further Reading

Frasier, David K. *Murder Cases of the Twentieth Century: Biographies and Bibliographies of 280 Convicted or Accused Killers*. Jefferson, N.C.: McFarland, 1996. Contains substantial information on its criminal subjects.

Schecter, Harold. *Deviant: The Shocking True Story of the Original Psycho*. New York: Pocket Books, 1989. A somewhat sensationalized recounting of the facts; contains a relatively tame photograph section.

Seltzer, Mark. *Serial Killers: Death and Life in America's Wound Culture*. New York: Routledge, 1998. Briefly but intelligently discusses Gein as an example of "The Face System" within "the Techno-Primitive" culture.

Woods, Paul Anthony. *Ed Gein: Psycho*. New York: St. Martin's Press, 1995. A slightly sensational book that contains explicit crime-scene photographs and an account of Gein's influence on popular culture.

*—Charles Avinger*

**See also:** Joe Ball; Jeffrey Dahmer; Albert Fish; Dennis Rader.

# Vito Genovese

## Mafia boss

**Born:** November 27 1897; Rosiglino, Italy
**Died:** February 14, 1969; U.S. Medical Center for Federal Prisoners, Springfield, Missouri
**Also known as:** Don Genovese; Don Genovesene
**Major offense:** Conspiracy to violate narcotics laws
**Active:** 1917-1959
**Locale:** New York
**Sentence:** Fifteen years in prison; served ten years

### Early Life

Vito Genovese (VEE-toh jihn-oh-VEE-zee), the man described by many as the most powerful organized crime figure in American history, was born in Rosiglino, Italy, in 1897. In 1912, Genovese relocated with his family to the United States and settled in Queens, New York. While his father was busy operating a small contracting firm in Queens, the young Genovese enjoyed the activity and excitement of lower Manhattan. He soon moved to Little Italy to live with relatives and began associating with several multiethnic gangs.

### Criminal Career

In 1917, Genovese was arrested for carrying a gun and spent sixty days in jail. During Prohibition, he worked his way up the ranks of organized crime, graduating from street gang member to professional killer. It was during this time that Genovese became acquainted with Lucky Luciano. By 1930, Genovese and Luciano were working closely with Joe Masseria. Many believe that Genovese helped Luciano arrange the murder of Masseria, who, on April 15, 1931, was surprised and gunned down by several unknown assailants after a lengthy dinner with Genovese. With Genovese at his side, Luciano took over Masseria's operations, eventually expanding them to reach every corner of the country.

In 1937, Genovese fled the United States after being named as a suspect in the murder of a Mafia gangster named Ferdinand "The Shadow" Boccia, a crime that had taken place three years earlier. Genovese settled in Naples, Italy, and quickly established himself as a major narcotics trafficker in the area. When American forces invaded Sicily in 1944 during World War II, Genovese was quick to offer his services as a translator. He also helped American military authorities rid the area of crime and black-market rings for illegal goods. Military authorities did not realize, however, that as drugs and weapons dealers were arrested, Genovese was replacing them with his own men. His plan was thwarted when a military police investigator realized that the helpful Italian was a wanted felon in the United States.

*Vito Genovese.* (Library of Congress)

Genovese was arrested and sent back to the United States to face charges stemming from the murder of Boccia. He was acquitted, however, when the only witness in the Boccia case was found dead.

After the war, Genovese became heavily involved in drug trafficking and began setting up deals with growers in India, Pakistan, and Afghanistan. Mafia leaders, including Luciano, urged Genovese to get out of the drug business. Genovese, however, would not give up the activities that produced most of his income. He soon set his sights on taking over the Luciano crime family. Since Genovese had been away, Luciano had been deported and was no longer the true boss of his family. The only person standing in Genovese's way was the family's acting boss, Frank Costello.

On May 2, 1957, Genovese sent his soldier, Vincent Gigante, to murder Costello in his home. Miraculously, Costello survived the gunshot wound to the head. (He later retired, leaving the syndicate under Genovese's control.) Next on Genovese's list was the removal of Albert Anastasia, boss of the Carlo Gambino crime family. On October 25, 1957, Anastasia was shot and killed by two assailants while sitting in a chair in a Manhattan barbershop.

### Legal Action and Outcome

Eager to establish himself as a leader on the national scene and expecting to be named "boss of bosses," Genovese arranged the ill-fated meeting of U.S. Mafia bosses in Apalachin, New York, on November 17, 1957. The meeting had barely started when several in attendance spotted a police officer outside the home and began to flee. Sixty-three men were apprehended, including Genovese. Charges against the men were later dropped after it was determined that they were taken into custody, detained, and searched without probable cause that a crime had been or was being committed. The Apalachin fiasco, however, was a great embarrassment for the American Mafia and may have cost Genovese his coveted boss-of-bosses title.

On April 17, 1959, Genovese was convicted of conspiracy to violate narcotics laws and was sentenced to fifteen years in prison. However, he continued to control the activities of his crime family through his underlings from his prison cell in Atlanta. Genovese died of a heart attack on February 14, 1969, at the U.S. Medical Center for Federal Prisoners in Springfield, Missouri.

**Impact**

More so than any other individual, Vito Genovese can be credited with keeping the Mafia in the narcotics business, a move that many other Mafiosi of his time opposed. Genovese is also responsible for organizing the disastrous meeting of Mafia bosses in Apalachin, New York, which propelled American organized crime groups into the national spotlight. Before this meeting and the subsequent arrests, Federal Bureau of Investigation director J. Edgar Hoover had boldly stated that there was no such thing as "organized crime." In modern times, the Genovese family is considered one of the richest and most powerful crime families in New York, with an estimated membership of more than 250 "soldiers." It has been reported that, by the twenty-first century, the family had moved into more sophisticated crimes, including computer fraud, stock and securities fraud, and health care fraud.

**Further Reading**

Dickie, John. *Cosa Nostra: A History of the Sicilian Mafia*. New York: Palgrave Macmillan, 2004. Dickie provides a comprehensive history of Italian organized crime in the United States.

Hanna, David. *Vito Genovese: The Godfather Series*. New York: Belmont Tower Books, 1974. Hanna offers an intimate portrait of one of most powerful organized crime figures in American history.

Raab, Selwyn. *The Five Families: The Rise, Decline, and Resurgence of America's Most Powerful Mafia Families*. New York: Thomas Dunne Books, 2005. Provides an in-depth analysis of the Bonanno, Colombo, Gambino, Genovese, and Lucchese crime families.

*—James C. Roberts and Thomas E. Baker*

**See also:** Albert Anastasia; Frank Costello; Vincent Gigante; Lucky Luciano; Joe Masseria.

# Sam Giancana

## Mafia boss and murderer

**Born:** June 15, 1908; Chicago, Illinois
**Died:** June 19, 1975; Oak Park, Illinois
**Also known as:** Salvatore Gilormo Giancana (full name); Mo; Momo; Mooney
**Major offenses:** Murder, extortion, burglary, producing and selling illegal alcohol, operation of illegal gambling, racketeering, and automobile theft
**Active:** 1925-1975
**Locale:** Chicago, Illinois
**Sentence:** Three years in prison for burglary; four years in prison for alcohol violations

### Early Life

Sam Giancana (gee-ahn-KAH-nah) was born in Chicago's Little Italy section to a poor family. His mother died when he was two years old, and his father beat him regularly. At the age of ten, Sam was expelled from elementary school for misconduct and sent to a reformatory school. He eventually dropped out of school and at the age of fifteen was living on the streets of Chicago's West Side. He joined a violent street gang called the 42 Gang. The 42 Gang got its name from the children's story "Ali Baba and the Forty Thieves." Giancana gained the nickname "Mooney," a slang word for "crazy."

### Criminal Career

Giancana developed a reputation for violence and unpredictability, and he was noticed by such Mafia members as Frank "The Enforcer" Nitti, Paul Ricca, and Tony Accardo, for whom he performed robberies and murders. Giancana was also considered an excellent getaway driver and became the "wheel man," or chauffeur, for Accardo, who was a major player on the Chicago crime scene.

While serving time for alcohol violations, Giancana became acquainted with an African American man by the name of Edward Jones from the South Side of Chicago. Jones told Giancana about a lucrative gambling operation, "running numbers." After his release from prison in 1942, Giancana kidnapped Jones and held him for ransom, thus taking over Jones's numbers running with the support of Accardo. In this way Giancana and Accardo gained control of the numbers racket in Chicago.

Giancana gradually gained control of a sizable portion of the labor racketeering, prostitution, and loan-sharking business in Chicago. In 1957, Accardo appointed Giancana to be a Mafia boss. At this time, Giancana moved his wife, Angeline, and his two daughters to Oak Park, a wealthy suburb of Chicago. Giancana eventually became the most senior Mafia figure in Chicago, with all organized crime activity approved solely by him.

### Legal Action and Outcome

Law enforcement authorities were familiar with Giancana from the time he was young. At seventeen, Giancana was arrested for automobile theft and served thirty days in jail. At the age of eighteen, he was arrested twice for murder, although both charges were dropped. After another arrest, Giancana was released because a key witness for the prosecution was murdered. At the age of twenty-one, he served a three-year sentence in a Joliet prison for burglary and theft.

After his release from prison in 1931, Giancana joined his associates from the 42 Gang and began to produce and sell illegal alcohol. In 1939, he was again arrested on several alcohol violations and sentenced to four years in prison.

Because of constant harassment from the federal government, Giancana spent the last years of his life, from 1966 to 1975, in Mexico, paying Mexican officials for his protection. Eventually, Giancana was brought back to the United States and forced to testify before a grand jury about mob-related activities. Soon thereafter, on June 19, 1975, Giancana was murdered in his home at Oak Park when an assailant shot him seven times. Apparently, the organized crime leaders in Chicago feared that Giancana would provide damaging information to the grand jury in exchange for immunity.

### Impact

Sam Giancana's reach extended beyond the mob. During the 1960 presidential election campaign, he struck a deal with Joseph Kennedy to deliver the state of Illinois for his son, John F. Kennedy, by controlling the Chicago wards and labor votes. In exchange, Joseph Kennedy promised Giancana that the federal government would curtail investigations into organized crime and that Giancana would be able to call on the White House for assistance. Some evidence also suggests that Giancana and fellow mobster Johnny Roselli worked with the Central Intelligence Agency during the Kennedy years on a plan to assassinate Cuban leader Fidel Castro.

The removal of Castro would have served both the interests of the U.S. government and the Mafia, who wanted to reopen the casinos in Havana, Cuba. Interestingly, Giancana and John F. Kennedy allegedly shared a girlfriend, Judith Campbell Exner; and J. Edgar Hoover, director of the Federal Bureau of Investigation, apparently used that information as leverage against Kennedy. U.S. attorney general Robert Kennedy, serving in his brother's administration, refused to stop the government's investigation of organized crime, thus angering Giancana, who felt double-crossed by the Kennedys.

Conspiracy theorists have argued that John Kennedy's affair with Giancana's mistress, as well as the federal government's harassment of Giancana, may have caused the Mafia to play a part in the assassinations of John F. Kennedy in 1963 and Robert Kennedy in 1968. In 1978, the House Select Committee on Assassinations concluded that President Kennedy was probably assassinated as a result of a conspiracy and pointed to organized crime as having the means, motive, and opportunity to carry out the murder. In short, although the theory remains unsubstantiated, Giancana may have played a role in the election and assassination of a U.S. president.

**Further Reading**

Brashler, William. *The Don: The Life and Death of Sam Giancana*. New York: Harper & Row, 1977. Brashler focuses upon the rise and fall of Sam Giancana as a Mafia figure, but he also provides a history of organized crime in general.

Giancana, Antoinette, John R. Hughes, and Thomas H. Jobe. *JFK and Sam: The Connection Between the Giancana and Kennedy Assassinations*. Nashville, Tenn.: Cumberland House, 2005. The daughter of Sam Giancana documents the tale of two murders: the assassination of President John F. Kennedy ordered by Giancana and the assassination of Giancana by the Central Intelligence Agency to prevent him from testifying before a congressional committee about the role of the CIA in the plot to assassinate Fidel Castro.

Giancana, Antoinette, and Thomas C. Renner. *Mafia Princess: Growing*

*Up in Sam Giancana's Family*. New York: Morrow, 1984. The daughter of Mafia chief Sam Giancana documents her life growing up in a family whose father controlled the city of Chicago in the 1950's and 1960's.

Giancana, Sam, and Chuck Giancana. *Double Cross: The Explosive, Inside Story of the Mobster Who Controlled America*. New York: Warner Books, 1993. The brother of Sam Giancana, Chuck Giancana, and his nephew Sam provide a profile of Sam Giancana's rise from a low-level hood to a Mafia leader with international influence who may have had a role in the assassination of President Kennedy.

*—Scott P. Johnson*

**See also:** Joe Adonis; Albert Anastasia; Paul Castellano; Vincent Coll; Joe Colombo; Carmine Galante; Carlo Gambino; Vincent Gigante; John Gotti; Sammy Gravano; Henry Hill; Richard Kuklinski; Meyer Lansky; Salvatore Maranzano; Carlos Marcello; Joe Masseria; Bugs Moran; Joseph Profaci; Arnold Rothstein; Dutch Schultz; Bugsy Siegel.

# Vincent Gigante

## Mafia boss

**Born:** March 29, 1928; New York, New York
**Died:** December 19, 2005; Springfield, Missouri
**Also known as:** The Chin; the Oddfather; Gigs; Enigma in a Bathrobe
**Major offenses:** Narcotics trafficking, racketeering, and conspiracy to commit murder
**Active:** c. 1946-1997
**Locale:** New York, New York
**Sentence:** Seven years in prison for narcotics trafficking, of which he served five; twelve years in prison for conspiracy to commit murder, extortion, and racketeering

### Early Life

Vincent Gigante (jih-GAN-tee) was born in 1928 in New York City to Salvatore and Yolanda Gigante, a watchmaker and a seamstress. His parents were Neapolitan by birth, and Vincent had four brothers. His nickname "the Chin" came from a shortened version of Cincenzo, an affectionate version of Vincent used by his mother. Gigante attended Manhattan's Textile High School but quit in ninth grade and became affiliated with crime boss Vito Genovese. He also boxed during this time period, winning twenty-one of his twenty-five bouts. Gigante eventually hung up his gloves and became a full-time member of Genovese's crew around 1946.

### Criminal Career

Gigante was arrested several times as a young man but was convicted only of a gambling charge that resulted in a fine. His early notoriety stems from his alleged involvement in the attempted assassination of rival gangster Frank Costello in 1957. Genovese had ordered Costello's slaying to further his own power, and many observers believe that it was the three-hundred-pound Chin who followed the targeted victim to his apartment building and called out "This is for you, Frank," before firing at Costello's head. It might have been Gigante's words that saved Costello's life, causing him to turn his head enough so that the bullet grazed his head rather than delivering a killing shot. Gigante fled the scene, and Costello stuck to Omerta ("conspiracy of silence"), refusing to identify his assailant. Gigante was identified by another witness and tried for attempted murder, but the case against him fell apart when Gigante appeared in court—after a dramatic weight-loss campaign upstate—svelte and trim, nothing like the huge man originally sought for the murder attempt. Given the confusion over the Chin's physique and Costello's refusal to cooperate with the prosecution, Gigante was acquitted.

Gigante continued his work with the Genovese family and in 1959 found himself the target of a narcotics arrest, reportedly a frame-up engineered by rival gangsters Carlo Gambino, Costello, Lucky Luciano, and Meyer Lansky. Gigante and his boss, Genovese, were arrested after their enemies bribed a narcotics dealer to testify against them. Gigante received a seven-year sentence but was paroled after five years' imprisonment. Soon after his release he was promoted to capo, heading a crew in Greenwich Village.

### The Oddfather

In 1966, when Gigante was being investigated for bribery charges, he began to develop his strategy of feigning mental illness to escape the law. He began a three-decade practice of checking himself into psychiatric treatment centers and thereby avoiding prosecution by being declared mentally incompetent for trial. He produced doctors at his 1969 bribery trial to testify that he was schizophrenic, psychotic, and afflicted with numerous other mental defects. The defense worked, hence Gigante's moniker "the Oddfather." Reports of his demented behavior abounded, even as the power of the Genovese family grew.

Authorities tried to prosecute Gigante for years, but the Chin proved to be an elusive target. In 1987, Gigante was named acting boss of the Genovese family after Fat Tony Salerno was convicted. By then Gigante was wandering the Greenwich Village streets in a bathrobe and muttering incoherently, bolstering his reputation for mental illness. Mentally competent or not, Gigante led the Genovese family to dominate the New York organized crime scene by the 1990's.

## Legal Action and Outcome

Gigante was convicted of narcotics trafficking in 1959 and was sentenced to seven years; he was paroled after five years' imprisonment. He was indicted for racketeering and murder in both 1990 and 1993, both times avoiding trial because he was declared incompetent. Finally in 1997, prosecutors overcame Gigante's tactics, and he was convicted of conspiracy to commit murder, extortion, and racketeering. Convicted on fourteen counts of murder conspiracy and racketeering, he was sentenced to twelve years in federal prison, where some believe he continued to direct the Genovese criminal enterprises. Gigante died in prison in December, 2005.

## Impact

The fact that Vincent Gigante succeeded in evading prosecution for so long made him a compelling figure and the object of public speculation. Gigante's tactics of feigning insanity not only marked him as a colorful character but also highlighted legal issues surrounding the insanity defense. One episode of the television crime-drama series *Law and Order* featured a character based on Gigante. The issues of competence to stand trial and the insanity defense continue to resonate within the criminal justice and public sectors. In 2003, Gigante himself stated in court that his insanity was a ruse, but his attorneys refused to concede the point.

## Further Reading

Capeci, Jerry. *Jerry Capeci's Gang Land*. New York: Alpha Books, 2003. A compilation of *New York Daily News* columns by journalist and Mafia expert Capeci covering organized crime activity in New York City from 1989 through 1995.

Raab, Selwyn. *The Five Families: The Rise, Decline, and Resurgence of America's Most Powerful Mafia Empires*. New York: Thomas Dunne Books, 2005. Recounts the history of the New York crime families; spotlights major figures and events of organized crime in New York.

Talese, Gay. *Honor Thy Father*. New York: World, 1971. Covers the reign of Mafia boss Joe Bonanno.

*—David R. Champion*

**See also:** Joe Adonis; Albert Anastasia; Vincent Coll; Joe Colombo; Frank Costello; Carmine Galante; Carlo Gambino; Vito Genovese; Sam Giancana; John Gotti; Sammy Gravano; Henry Hill; Richard Kuklinski; Meyer Lansky; Lucky Luciano; Salvatore Maranzano.

# Mildred Gillars

## Propagandist and traitor

**Born:** November 29, 1900; Portland, Maine
**Died:** June 25, 1988; Columbus, Ohio
**Also known as:** Mildred Elizabeth Sisk (birth name); Axis Sally
**Major offense:** Treason
**Active:** May 18, 1943
**Locale:** Paris
**Sentence:** Ten to thirty years' imprisonment; served twelve years

### Early Life

Mildred Gillars (GIHL-lahrz) was born to Mary and Vincent Sisk in Portland, Maine. She may have been physically abused by her birth father. After a divorce, her mother married Robert Gillars, and the family moved to Conneaut, Ohio. Mildred Gillars briefly attended Ohio Wesleyan University. She also attended Hunter College, where she met Max Otto Koischwitz, a professor of German literature. They began an affair. Unknown to Gillars, he was married at the time.

**Radio Career**

Gillars was an aspiring actress. Her career from 1926 (when she dropped out of college) to 1940 (when she began working for Radio Berlin) was both colorful and dismal. She auditioned for parts in New York; she made an unsuccessful film, also in New York; she was arrested twice while attempting to promote the film; and she traveled to Algiers with a male friend who was attempting to convince his rich aunt that he was not gay. In North Africa, she worked as a columnist. Moving between the United States and Algiers in the 1930's, she performed in plays and returned to her family in tough times.

In the 1930's she moved between Paris and Berlin, perhaps in an attempt to continue her relationship with Koischwitz. By 1940 he had become a major participant in the German radio propaganda network called the Radiorundfunk. In 1940, Gillars moved to Berlin and accepted a position with Radio Berlin, broadcasting American music and expatriate news. As

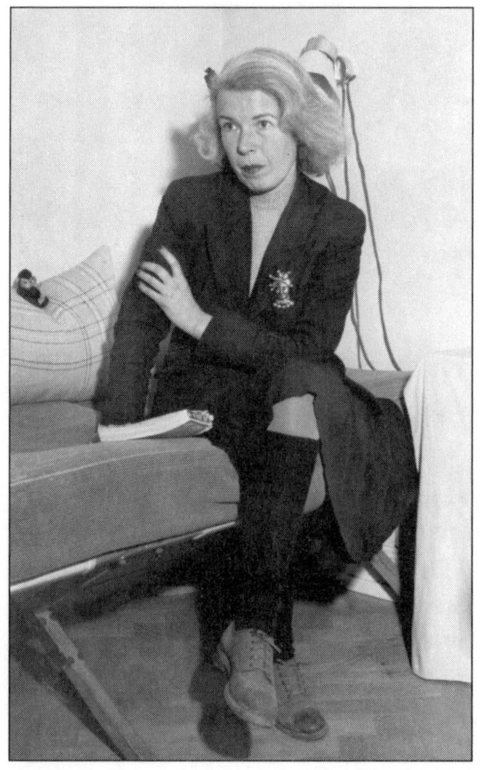

*Mildred Gillars.*
(AP/Wide World Photos)

### Mildred at the Mike

*Although Mildred Gillars was found guilty of treason on only one count, the 1943 "Vision of Invasion" broadcast, her broadcasts were routinely demoralizing to the American soldiers in Europe, as in these typical examples:*

- Good morning Yankees. This is Axis Sally with the tunes that you like to hear and a warm welcome from radio Berlin. I note that the 461st is en route this morning to Linz where you will receive a warm welcome. By the way, Sgt. Robert Smith, you remember Bill Jones, the guy with the flashy convertible who always had an eye for your wife Annabelle. Well, they have been seen together frequently over the past few months and last week he moved in with her. Let's take a break here and listen to some Glen Miller.
- And what are your girls doing tonight, fellows? You really can't blame them for going out to have some fun, could you? . . . You may dislike my repeating this to you, but it's the truth, especially if you boys get all mutilated and do not return in one piece.

"Midge at the Mike," she aired Nazi propaganda. During 1940 the American embassy seized her passport, and in 1941 she signed an oath of allegiance to Germany. Whether this was done freely or under duress is a matter of debate.

At Radio Berlin, Gillars worked with the leading members of the propaganda effort for Hitler's Germany. These included Koischwitz, William Joyce (known as Lord Haw Haw), Fred Kaltenbach, and later Robert Best. With each escalation of the war, Midge added new features to her programming. To her news reports and popular tunes, she added "free interviews" with American prisoners of war. To get these interviews, she posed falsely as a Red Cross representative. During the 1940's she was reviewed by the American press as a mix of Mae West and Marlene Dietrich. At the same time, however, German intelligence felt that her sultry voice was recognized by nine out of ten American soldiers in the European theater, who dubbed her "Axis Sally."

### The Invasion Broadcast

After a 1943 visit to the German fortifications in Normandy, France, Gillars began work on a project to show American military personnel a vision of the outcome of an invasion. At her trial, she would claim that her goal was to delay the invasion until the internal collapse of Germany became apparent to the Allies. However, this broadcast, written by Koischwitz and produced by Horst Cleinow, and like the earlier programs of "Midge at the Mike," called for American troops to lay down their arms and go home. The broadcast, in which Gillars played a mother who dreamed the bloody death of her son on the beaches of Normandy, was an unusually powerful piece of World War II propaganda. It was broadcast from the Nazi studios in Paris and replayed frequently in Europe, Britain, and the United States.

### Legal Action and Outcome

In July of 1943, a U.S. federal grand jury indicted in absentia a number of Radio Berlin personalities charged with treason. Gillars was not among those so charged. Captured in Berlin, she was moved to Frankfurt and then to the United States to stand trial.

After being held without charges for two and a half years, Gillars was charged in the summer of 1948 with giving aid and comfort to the enemy. Tried on eight counts of treason, she was found guilty of only one, the 1943 broadcast of the mother's dream piece. Sentenced to ten to thirty years in prison, Gillars was paroled after twelve years. Whereas German propagandist announcer William Joyce was hanged in his native Britain for treason after the war, Gillars died of natural causes at the age of eighty-seven.

### Impact

Adolf Hilter's radio propaganda was extremely successful. The work of Radio Berlin and other Reichsrundfunk bureaus aided the Nazi cause, and Nazi propaganda was perceived by Britain and the United States as a key ingredient in the collapse of France. This success impelled the Allies to follow suit. Both Britain and the United States established clandestine radio identities which, for the following forty years, broadcast throughout Europe, South America, Africa, and Asia. In 1941, this effort began in the United States as the Office of Foreign Information Services. It continued as the Voice of America.

**Further Reading**

Doherty, M. A. *Nazi Wireless Propaganda: Lord Haw-Haw and British Public Opinion in the Second World War*. Edinburgh: Edinburgh University Press, 2000. A scholarly study of the range and extent of Nazi radio propaganda against the United Kingdom as well as its response in Britain. The book contains a CD of twenty-four broadcasts from Germany to Britain.

Edwards, John Carver. *Berlin Calling: American Broadcasters in Service to the Third Reich*. New York: Praeger, 1991. A study of characters who served in the Nazi U.S.A. Zone. Gillars is not specifically examined; however, the lengthy chapter dedicated to Koischwitz includes much information about Gillars's work for Radio Berlin. In his epilogue, author Edwards questions the motives behind the U.S. prosecution of Americans broadcasting from Hitler's Germany.

Fuller, M. Williams. *Axis Sally: The Most Listened-to Woman of World War II*. Santa Barbara, Calif.: Paradise West, 2004. A fictionalized account of the life and career of Mildred Gillars. Readable and dramatic, the book presents a version of the events that is difficult to assess. Fuller appears to defend Gillars, accepting arguments made at her trial that she was "mesmerized" by her lover Koischwitz and coerced into working for Radio Berlin.

Soley, Lawrence C. *Radio Warfare: OSS and CIA Subversive Propaganda*. New York: Praeger, 1989. Soley examines the initiation and development of U.S. propaganda using airwaves from the period of World War II through the Cold War.

*—Jean Owens Schaefer*

**See also:** Tokyo Rose.

# Gary Gilmore

## Murderer

**Born:** December 4, 1940; McCamey, Texas
**Died:** January 17, 1977; Utah State Prison, Salt Lake City, Utah
**Also known as:** Gary Mark Gilmore (full name); Faye Robert Coffman
**Major offenses:** Robbery and murder
**Active:** July, 1976
**Locale:** Provo, Utah
**Sentence:** Death

### Early Life

When one considers the childhood of Gary Gilmore (GIHL-mohr), it is not surprising that he was to become a career criminal and a remorseless, violent murderer. His father, Frank Gilmore, Sr., was an alcoholic and petty con man who routinely abused young Gary and his siblings and ran from the law for most of their childhood. He forced the family to live under a fabricated surname, Coffman, and routinely shuffled them from town to town throughout the American West, often only a step ahead of the authorities.

By the time Gilmore was fifteen, family turmoil had taken its toll on him. He dropped out of school and within a year was an experienced car thief. His rowdiness and lack of respect for authority eventually landed him in Oregon's MacLaren Reform School for Boys. A second robbery charge shortly thereafter resulted in a conviction and imprisonment in the Oregon State Penitentiary.

### Criminal Career

By age thirty-five, Gilmore had spent more than half of his life behind bars. Released from his first prison stay in 1962, he promptly committed another robbery and returned to prison. Notoriously uncooperative with staff and belligerent toward other inmates, Gilmore spent much of the next ten years in solitary confinement. He was even treated with Prolixin, a strong antipsychotic drug intended to curb his antisocial tendencies. However, Gilmore claimed that the drug caused him to be depressed and suicidal, and treatment was halted. His time in solitary confinement, however, allowed him ample opportunity to develop his high IQ and cultivate a talent for art.

These steps toward rehabilitation earned him early release in 1972 on the provision that he enroll in community college and live in a halfway house in Provo, Utah. Gilmore obtained work in an uncle's shoe shop and a few occasional construction jobs. His family thought this would keep Gilmore out of trouble, but he remained unusually agitated and compulsive.

Despite his family's efforts to help Gilmore readjust to life outside prison, his inherent restlessness and disdain for the law led to tragic consequences in the summer of 1976. Gilmore bought an expensive pickup truck on an impulse, but he could not afford the payments. Then, after his breakup with girlfriend Nicole Barrett, an emotionally distraught Gilmore proceeded to rob a Provo gas station in a convoluted attempt to get the money both to pay off his truck and to lash out at Barrett. The robbery resulted in the point-blank shooting and murder of attendant Max Jensen.

The next morning, Gilmore was still on the run but was having mechanical problems with his truck, which he dropped off at a garage. He robbed the nearby City Center Motel while waiting for the repairs to be finished. Dur-

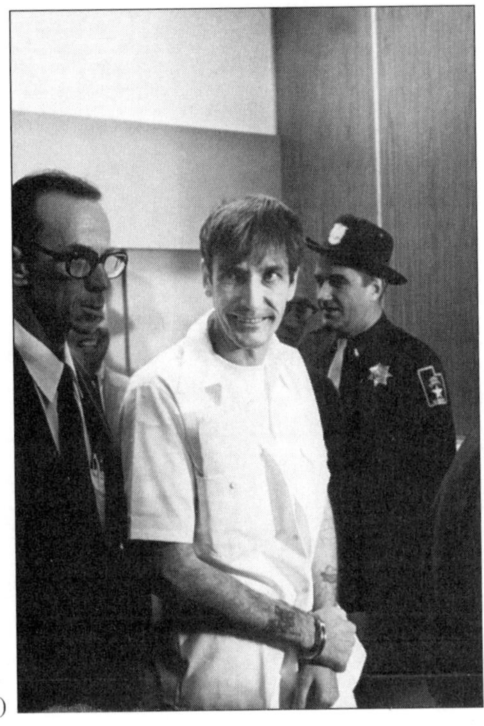

*Gary Gilmore.*
(AP/Wide World Photos)

### Gilmore and the Golden Gloves Girl

"I'm not a nice person. I don't want to cause any more harm. I've harmed too many people and by doing so I've harmed my own soul," Gary Gilmore wrote in 1976 to Amber Edwina Hunt, nicknamed Amber Jim. The eleven-year-old girl had written him to find out why he insisted upon being executed. She thought he might be lonely, and this touched Gilmore. Through the next two months, the two exchanged more letters; their friendship deepened.

Amber Jim was a fifth-grader living in Murray, Utah, the daughter of a janitor. She was a tough girl, too—a sixty-five-pound Golden Gloves boxer who regularly beat boys her own age. When Gilmore learned that she was a boxer, he offered to sponsor her. He sent her two hundred dollars and had a relative of his buy her an eight-millimeter movie camera so that she could film her bouts. His favorite fighter was Rocky Marciano, hers Muhammad Ali, they told each other. She asked about his favorite animal, and he wrote back (quoting William Blake's famous poem), "Tiger, tiger burning bright/ In the forests of the night. . . ." He told her of his favorite musicians—Hank Williams and Johnny Cash—and that he felt close to Native Americans: "Indians like me."

Their friendship was strictly via letters. Prison authorities refused Amber Jim's request to visit Gilmore. He sent her a morose poem of his own about his approaching death, but for the most part his letters contained encouragements: "Amber Jim I believe you are a natural-born winner. You're unique"; "you're the most fantastic little girl I've ever heard of. You have the makings, the heart of a true champion." He had a bank account set up for her and altogether gave some twelve hundred dollars in money and gifts, including a bicycle and a book about Ali. "I will always love you honey. You're a beautiful little girl. . . . Knock 'em all out. For me. Hugs and kisses," he wrote two days before he died. When Amber Jim learned of his execution, she wept.

*Source: Time* magazine, January 31, 1977.

ing the robbery, he shot and killed motel manager Ben Bushnell and accidentally shot himself in the hand while fleeing. He returned to the garage for his truck, and the mechanic, noticing his suspicious wound, reported Gilmore's license number to local police. Gilmore was quickly apprehended and charged with both murders.

## Legal Action and Outcome

Gilmore's trial lasted only two days. A mountain of physical evidence and the testimony of witnesses linking him directly to the killings prompted jurors to convict Gilmore of first-degree murder after only an hour and a half of deliberation. During the penalty phase of the trial, state prosecutor Noall

Wootton sought the death penalty, claiming that the gruesome and arbitrary nature of the killings, combined with Gilmore's extensive criminal record, rendered him incapable of rehabilitation. Gilmore refused to testify on his own behalf during the trial or demonstrate remorse for the crimes during the penalty phase. He was sentenced to death.

Utah had not executed anyone since 1958. In fact, the state's laws regarding the practice remained unusually archaic. One particularly outmoded provision allowed the condemned a choice of execution method—hanging or firing squad. However, Utah had disassembled its gallows and possessed no facility in which an execution by firing squad could officially be conducted. Since Gilmore chose the firing squad, his original execution date of November 15, 1976, was postponed. In the interim, a number of entities, including the American Civil Liberties Union, offered to appeal on his behalf. Gilmore adamantly refused all attempts to prolong his ordeal and was shot to death in a converted cannery at the Utah State Prison on January 17, 1977.

## Impact

Gilmore's execution—the first death sentence to be carried out after the Supreme Court's four-year moratorium on capital punishment—is generally regarded to have ushered in a return to the legitimization of capital punishment in the United States. In 1972's landmark case *Furman v. Georgia*, the U.S. Supreme Court declared unconstitutional capital punishment as then administered in the United States. A series of later revisions to state laws related to execution, however, paved the way for a lift on the ban in 1976. Gilmore made worldwide headlines by refusing all appeals and demanding that his sentence be carried out as soon as possible.

## Further Reading

Gilmore, Mikal. *Shot in the Heart*. New York: Doubleday, 1994. Written by Gilmore's younger brother, this nonfiction work not only focuses on many of the same events as Mailer's book but also seeks to probe into the psychological legacy that contributed to the misfortunes of Gilmore and other family members.

Mailer, Norman. *The Executioner's Song*. Boston: Little, Brown, 1979. A "nonfiction novel" recounting of the events leading up to Gilmore's conviction and execution for capital murder, constructed from interviews and documents relevant to the case. Won the 1980 Pulitzer Prize for fiction.

Philips, Tom. "The Revival of the American Death Penalty." In *Death Penalty*, edited by Hayley R. Mitchell. San Diego Calif.: Greenhaven Press, 2001. Discusses the influence of Gilmore's execution in fostering the growing use of capital punishment in the United States.

—*Gregory D. Horn*

**See also:** Velma Margie Barfield; Andrew Cunanan; Karla Faye Tucker.

# John Gotti

## Organized crime boss

**Born:** October 27, 1940; New York, New York
**Died:** June 10, 2002; Springfield, Missouri
**Also known as:** John Joseph Gotti, Jr. (full name); Teflon Don; Dapper Don
**Major offenses:** Murder, conspiracy, racketeering, robbery, loan-sharking, obstruction of justice, illegal gambling, and tax evasion.
**Active:** 1967-1990
**Locale:** New York, Queens, and Manhattan, New York
**Sentence:** Life in prison without the possibility of parole

### Early Life

John Gotti (GOT-tee) grew up in a large Italian family, one of thirteen children. He emerged in high school as a student who demonstrated above-average intelligence; however, he showed little interest in academic endeavors. His criminal interests developed early when he initiated a high school gambling operation. He eventually organized his own street gang and was involved in several minor crimes after dropping out of school.

### Criminal Career

Gotti eventually sought membership in Italian organized crime, also called among insiders La Cosa Nostra (meaning "this thing of ours"). A high-ranking member of Carlo Gambino's crime family, Aniello Dellacroce, eventually served as Gotti's mentor, sponsoring young Gotti as a member of organized crime. Gotti established himself as a regular at popular mob locales, including Bergin Hunt and Fish Club in Queens and the Ravenite Social Club in Manhattan. Gotti initially became a soldier in the Gambino family, serving as a hit man, among other roles. His first major arrest and conviction took place in 1967 for hijacking trucks at New York's Kennedy Airport, and he served half of a seven-year plea-bargain sentence.

Gotti's use of violence escalated during the 1970's and 1980's. He pleaded guilty to the charge of manslaughter of John McBrantney in 1974 and served two years. The victim was a suspect in the killing of Carlo Gambino's nephew. Gotti then planned several armored-car hijackings during the 1980's. The first robbery netted $300,000; the second, $700,000. Gotti escaped prosecution even though he was recognized by one of the armored-car drivers.

Gotti was charged with assault and robbery in 1984. The victim initially claimed that he was robbed of $325 during an argument over a double-parked car. However, the victim claimed a memory lapse and could not identify Gotti; charges against Gotti were dropped. Next, Gotti was arrested and prosecuted for the murder of John O'Connor; the verdict of not guilty

### "COSA NOSTRA 'TIL I DIE"

*The following is taken from an FBI wiretap of Gotti in 1990 as he spoke to his subordinates in an apartment above Manhattan's Ravenite Social Club on Mulberry Street.*

I'm not in the mood for the toys, or games, or kidding [unintelligible]. I'm not in the mood for clans. I'm not in the mood for gangs. I'm not in the mood for none of that stuff there. This is gonna be a Cosa Nostra 'til I die. Be it an hour from now, or be it tonight, or a hundred years from now when I'm in jail. It's gonna be a Cosa Nostra. This ain't gonna be a bunch of your friends, they're gonna be friends of ours. But at the same time would be friends of ours, it's gonna be the way I say it's gonna be, [unintelligible] a Cosa Nostra. A Cosa Nostra. You might, because a guy's nice to you, and I'm not talking about you, I'm just sayin' you might [unintelligible] makes him a good guy. It makes him a m***f*** to me. It don't make him a good guy. It makes him a good guy if he's one of us and he proves he's part of us. And I'm the best judge of that, I think, right now. . . . I wanna see an effort. I gotta see an effort for [unintelligible] a Cosa Nostra. How many of these guys come, come tell me I feel sorry you got trouble. I don't, I don't need that. I ain't got no trouble, I ain't got no trouble. I'm gonna be all right. They got the f***in' trouble. And I don't mean the cops, I mean the people. The people who coulda made this a joke, you know what I mean. That's not a f***in' joke [unintelligible] guys. Even, even, even some guys, some people downstairs now who I know whose f***ing stomach is rotten. I know whose stomach ain't rotten. You could, I, I could smell it the way a dog senses when a guy's got fear.

enhanced Gotti's moniker, Teflon Don (in reference to Teflon pans because criminal charges did not "stick" to him).

Gotti represented the blue-collar members of organized crime. His cronies viewed mobster activity in the old Mafia tradition (that is, through the use of robbery, extortion, and murder). His faction resented Paul Castellano's appointment as head of the Gambino family in 1976; to Gotti and colleagues, Castellano represented the white-collar faction involved in legal business fronts. In addition, Castellano always demanded a lucrative cut of his members' profits. His disdain for direct involvement in street crimes angered those who earned their living the "old-fashioned" way. Gotti's mentor, Dellacroce, was a restraining figure in any attempt to eliminate Castellano, but when Castellano did not attend Dellacroce's funeral in early December, 1985, his display of disrespect angered Gotti and his blue-collar faction. Later that month, Gotti and his cohorts assassinated Castellano in front of Sparks Steak House. Shortly thereafter, the Gambino family greeted Gotti as their new boss.

Gotti reveled in media attention and wore expensive suits (thus his nickname Dapper Don); many in the crime family felt that his arrogant style drew too much attention to the Mafia. An attempt was made to kill Gotti with a car bomb; however, only his underboss, Frank DiCiccio, was killed. After DiCiccio's death, Sammy Gravano became underboss in the Gambino organization.

## Legal Action and Outcome

In the late 1980's, the Federal Bureau of Investigation (FBI) was determined to prosecute the Mafia. The FBI used electronic surveillance to watch Gotti around the clock and collected a great deal of evidence, including that which implicated both Gravano and Gotti in a number of murders. Authorities arrested the men on multiple counts of violating the Racketeer Influenced and Corrupt Organizations (RICO) Act, as well as loan-sharking, conspiracy to commit murder, and murder.

An exhaustive effort by the federal government during the criminal investigation ensured the conviction of Gotti at trial. Moreover, authorities received the help of Gravano, who violated the Mafia's code of Omerta (silence) by serving as a government witness against Gotti. His damaging testimony assured Gotti's last conviction. On April 2, 1991, he received a sentence of life imprisonment at the Federal Maximum Security Penitentiary in Marion, Illinois. Gotti received consecutive, rather than concurrent, sentences for racketeering and murder. Gotti died of throat cancer at the U.S. Medical Center for Federal Prisoners in Springfield, Missouri, in June, 2002.

### Impact

The death of Paul Castellano and the imprisonment of John Gotti disorganized the Gambino crime family. Gotti appointed his son, John, Jr. (known as Junior) and his brother as his heirs apparent. Gotti tried to maintain control of the family's business from inside federal prison, but Junior never measured up to his father's charismatic leadership.

Senior Mafia leadership was reluctant to step forward and seize power. After the successful targeting and prosecution of Gotti, they feared the limelight and media attention one earns as Mafia boss. While Gotti's imprisonment was an important setback for the Gambino family, his leadership holds lasting impact for modern-day Mafia ventures, whose emerging leadership cannot seem to resist the temptation to seize control and maximize organized crime profits.

### Further Reading

Abadinsky, Howard. *Organized Crime*. 7th ed. New York: Thomas Dunne Books, 2005. An in-depth analysis of organized crime from a historical and theoretical perspective.

Lyman, Michael D., and Gary W. Potter. *Organized Crime*. Upper Saddle River, N.J.: Pearson/Prentice Hall, 2004. A comprehensive textbook, including the essentials of organized crime theory and practice.

Mustain, Gene, and Jerry Capeci. *Mob Star: The Story of Gotti*. Royersford, Pa.: Appha Books, 2002. An insightful, popular book on the life and times of Gotti.

*—Thomas E. Baker and James C. Roberts*

**See also:** Paul Castellano; Carlo Gambino; Sammy Gravano.

# Sammy Gravano

## Mafia underboss and hit man

**Born:** March 12, 1945; Brooklyn, New York
**Also known as:** Salvatore Gravano (full name); Sammy the Bull
**Major offenses:** Racketeering, trafficking, and murder
**Active:** 1960's-2000
**Locale:** New York, New York
**Sentence:** Five years for racketeering; nineteen years for drug trafficking

### Early Life

Salvatore Gravano (grah-VAH-noh) was the youngest of five, born to Sicilian immigrants in Brooklyn, New York. His parents were law-abiding and hardworking, but Gravano would not follow in their footsteps. He had trouble with school and was picked on because of it. Gravano retaliated with violence and would often fight children who were bigger and older than he was. He was nicknamed "the Bull"; his fighting style and his looks were similar to those of a bull. In his teen years, Gravano got involved with gang life and had many run-ins with the police.

Gravano's first arrest was for assaulting an officer, but thanks to a good lawyer, he avoided jail time. In 1964, Gravano was drafted. While in the army, he started a craps circuit and engaged in loan-sharking, which was easy and profitable for Gravano—he even had the military police involved. After two years, he received an honorable discharge and moved back to Brooklyn. There, Gravano joined an old gang called the Rampers, and he continued his shady activities. He and another gang member were shot in a botched car theft. Gravano was shot in the head, his friend in the stomach; both survived.

### Criminal Career

By the time Gravano was twenty-three, he had made a name for himself and soon found himself involved with Tommy Spero, a member of the Colombo crime family. Gravano soon went to work for the Colombos, loan-sharking money out of a club in Brooklyn. Gravano began robbing stores and banks and beating owed money out of people. Soon he would make his first "hit." After the murder, rumors began that Gravano was the workhorse of the group, and he himself said that this first hit was his stepping-stone into the mob. Shortly thereafter, however, Gravano was moved to the Gambino crime family because of problems he had with Spero's brother and nephew.

Gravano was now working for Toddo Aurello, a Gambino family "capo," or leader. As Gravano soon discovered, income from mob life proved sporadic, and he lived from score to score: He would have plenty of money one month and nothing the next. He decided to leave crime and try to make an honest living. Gravano's mob life, however, would come back to haunt him. Roughly a year later, he received a phone call that he was being indicted for murder. Gravano had no choice but to go back to work for the Gambinos. He could not pay his lawyer fees and had to turn again to a life of crime to pay the bills.

Gravano would eventually be acquitted of the murder charges, but he had once again become deeply involved in the Mafia. In 1975, he would become a made member of the Gambino crime family. The Gambino family was run by Paul Castellano, but when Castellano failed to attend his underboss's wake, rumors started that he needed to be murdered. John Gotti, a capo for the Gambinos, asked Gravano to help with the deed. Gravano agreed, and Castellano was killed. Castellano's death put Gotti in charge of the Gambinos. Soon after Gotti took charge, Aurello resigned, and Gravano became capo. Gotti was flashy and drew too much attention to the Mafia. This upset bosses in other families, and an attempt was made to kill Gotti with a car bomb; however, only his underboss, Frank DiCiccio, was killed. After DiCiccio's death, Gravano became underboss in the Gambino organization.

### Legal Action and Outcome

Under Gotti, Gravano's mob activities escalated. He killed increasingly more people. Gravano allegedly had nineteen hits under his belt—eleven under Gotti and eight from before. During Gotti's reign, the Federal Bureau of Investigation (FBI) was moving closer and closer to bringing down the Mafia. Gotti was charismatic and careless and earned the nickname Teflon Don because charges against him never stuck. However, the FBI eventually was able to bug his headquarters, and the government collected a great deal of evidence from its surveillance, evidence that implicated both Gravano and Gotti in a number of murders. This evidence would prove to be too much for the Mafia: The authorities had them on multiple counts of violating the Racketeer Influenced and Corrupt Organizations (RICO) Act, as well as loan-sharking, conspiracy to commit murder, and murder.

Gravano was loyal to the mob, but when he heard some of the tapes in which Gotti was trying to make it sound like Gravano had made the hits on his own, he decided to cooperate with the FBI. Gravano violated Omerta, the Mafia's code of silence, and testified against Gotti. Despite admitting to nineteen murders, Gravano received a much lesser sentence for his cooperation against Gotti. On April 2, 1991, Gotti was found guilty of the racketeering and murder charges and received a life sentence without the possibility of parole. Gotti later died in prison.

## Impact

Sammy Gravano's testimony was responsible for the indictments and convictions of dozens of Mafia figures and the downfall of the Mafia. For his efforts, Gravano received a reduced sentence: five years in prison plus three years of supervised release. Gravano was released early and entered the witness protection program. In 2000, however, Gravano and his son Gerard were charged with distribution of the drug Ecstasy in Arizona. In 2001, they pleaded guilty, and Gravano began serving a nineteen-year sentence. In 2003, while in prison, Gravano was indicted for the 1980 murder of Peter Calabro, a New York police detective. This indictment arose from a plea agreement made by Richard Kuklinski, who was also involved in the detective's death. In June of 2005, Gravano was back in court for a hearing; his current lawyer was stepping down as his representative because of a conflict of interest.

In March, 2006, Kuklinski died of unknown causes at the age of seventy. Medical authorities believe that he died of natural causes, but some view his death as suspicious given that he was scheduled to testify in the Calabro case. A few days after Kuklinski's death, authorities dropped all charges against Gravano because, without Kuklinski's testimony, they had insufficient evidence against him.

## Further Reading

Jacobs, James J., Coleen Friel, and Robert Radick. *Gotham Unbound: How New York City Was Liberated from the Grip of Organized Crime*. New York: New York University Press, 1999. Addresses Mafia realities, the Cosa Nostra's control of New York City, and how the government finally broke down that control.

Maas, Peter. *Underboss: Sammy the Bull Gravano's Story of Life in the Ma-*

*fia*. New York: HarperCollins, 1997. Discusses the innermost sanctums of the Cosa Nostra and Sammy the Bull's place in the underworld of power, greed, betrayal, and deception.

Raab, Selwyn. *The Five Families: The Rise, Decline, and Resurgence of America's Most Powerful Mafia Empires*. New York: Thomas Dunne Books, 2005. Traces the rise of the Genovese, Gambino, Bonnano, Colombo, and Lucchese families and the roles they have played in American crime.

*—Richard D. Hartley*

**See also:** Paul Castellano; Joe Colombo; Carlo Gambino; John Gotti; Richard Kuklinski.

## Charles Julius Guiteau

### Assassin of President James A. Garfield

**Born:** September 8, 1841; Freeport, Illinois
**Died:** June 30, 1882; Washington, D.C.
**Major offense:** Shot President James A. Garfield, who later died of his injuries
**Active:** July 2, 1881
**Locale:** Washington, D.C.
**Sentence:** Hanged on June 30, 1882

### Early Life

Born to Luther and Jane (Howe) Guiteau on September 8, 1841, Charles Julius Guiteau (gee-TOH) was the fourth of six children raised in Freeport, Illinois. His mother died when he was seven, but his father soon remarried. Luther, a banker and local politician who practiced the theological teachings of John H. Noyes, was a strict disciplinarian who physically abused his son to correct a speech impediment. After receiving a small inheritance, the young Guiteau spent the Civil War years in Oneida, New York, in a colony dedicated to Noyes's teaching of Bible Communism, the belief in plural marriages, perfectionism, and the Second Coming of Christ. Guiteau left the community in 1865 for New York City. He tried his hand at journalism and publishing religious tracts, but he soon ran out of money. He moved in with his sister, Frances, who began to notice his erratic behavior, but before she could commit him to a sanatorium, he left for Chicago in 1869. Because of the laxity of the bar exam, Guiteau was admitted to the Illinois bar. He failed to make an effective courtroom attorney and ended up as a debt collector. During his time in the city, he married Annie Bunn, a teenager who worked in the library at the Young Men's Christian Association (YMCA). He became an itinerant preacher for the next three years and sold a series of publications titled *The Truth: A Companion to the Bible*, based largely on Noyes's beliefs. Eventually, meager earnings, poor living conditions, and the emotional strain caused Annie to seek a divorce in 1873.

### Criminal Career

Guiteau had turned his attention to politics by the 1880's. He offered to help James Garfield's presidential campaign in New York City by passing out copies of a speech titled "Garfield Against Hancock" (Winfield Scott Hancock was Garfield's Democratic opponent). Once Garfield assumed the

*A historical composite of images documenting Garfield's assassination by Guiteau.* (Library of Congress)

presidency, Guiteau moved to Washington, D.C. and began appearing at State Department offices saying that he should be given a consulate post in Paris or Vienna. After being spurned by Secretary of State James G. Blaine, Guiteau turned away from the liberal "Half-Breeds" faction of the Republican Party (represented by Garfield) and toward the conservative "Stalwart" faction. The Stalwarts originally backed Ulysses S. Grant for a third term in office, opposed the civil service reform policies of President Rutherford B. Hayes, and opposed his attempts to reconcile with the South. Republican Party divisions increased when New York senators Roscoe Conkling and Thomas C. Pratt resigned in protest of Garfield's nomination for collector of customs in their state. Guiteau began to believe that Garfield's death was a political necessity that would return the Stalwarts, represented by Vice President Chester A. Arthur, to power.

Guiteau bought a .44 British caliber gun with an ivory handle because he thought it would make a good museum exhibit. He began to practice with the handgun in a local park. He made two attempts on Garfield's life, the first being in a church on Vermont Avenue in mid-June. The plan was abruptly halted when the president left the church to go visit his recuperating wife in New Jersey. The next attempt took place in a train depot, but Guiteau took pity on seeing the feeble form of the First Lady.

On July 2, 1881, Garfield, accompanied by Blaine, was about to board a train to attend the twenty-fifth reunion of his college class when Guiteau intercepted him in the ladies' waiting room. He fired two shots; one bullet hit the president in the back and lodged near his spinal column. Garfield lingered for a few months. Doctors were unable to find and extricate the bullet, and the president died on September 19.

### Legal Action and Outcome

Guiteau's trial began on November 14 in the Supreme Court of the District of Columbia with Walter S. Cox presiding. Guiteau's brother-in-law, George Scoville, was his attorney throughout the trial. The defense case relied heavily on the insanity plea, but Scoville also maintained that Garfield died as a result of physician negligence. Guiteau's actions in court led to questions of his mental state. He constantly disrupted court proceedings by making long speeches and reading aloud newspaper accounts of the trial. Nevertheless, the jury found Guiteau guilty, and he was hanged in late June, 1882.

### Impact

The assassination of President James Garfield caused the passage of widespread civil service reform. Charles Guiteau's trial represented one of the most famous cases using insanity as a defense argument; legal ramifications involving such pleas still persist. According to Guiteau, divine inspiration had convinced him that the president must die, but he was found to be a troubled man possessed by an enormous ego who craved recognition and fame.

### Further Reading

Ackerman, Kenneth D. *Dark Horse: The Surprise Election and Political Murder of President James A. Garfield.* New York: Carroll & Graf, 2003. Author recounts the important political figures in the Republican Party, Garfield's presidency, and how his assassination impacted the country and politics.

Clark, James C. *The Murder of James A. Garfield: The President's Last Days and the Trial and Execution of His Assassin.* Jefferson, N.C.: McFarland, 1993. Clark interweaves the lives and events of Guiteau and Garfield, addressing the political climate, legal system, and medical establishment of the late nineteenth century.

Peskin, Allan. "Charles Guiteau of Illinois: President Garfield's Assassin." *Journal of the Illinois State Historical Society* 70, no. 2 (May, 1977): 130-139. The author provides a brief biographical account of Guiteau.

Rosenberg, Charles E. *The Trial of Assassin Guiteau.* Chicago: University of Chicago Press, 1968. Rosenberg examines the public reaction and legal implication of mental illness during the Gilded Age by focusing on Guiteau's trial.

—*Gayla Koerting*

**See also:** John Wilkes Booth; Leon Czolgosz; Lee Harvey Oswald; Giuseppe Zangara.

# Matthew F. Hale

**White supremacist**

**Born:** July 27, 1971; East Peoria, Illinois
**Also known as:** Matt Hale
**Major offenses:** Solicitation of murder and obstruction of justice
**Active:** 1996-2005
**Locale:** Peoria, Illinois
**Sentence:** Forty years in prison at the Administrative Maximum United States Penitentiary, Florence, Colorado

## Early Life

Matthew Hale (hayl) was the youngest son of Evelyn Ackerson Bowshier and Russell Hale, Jr. When he was nine years old, his parents were divorced. His father, a police officer, subsequently raised him. Hale claimed that he experienced a political awakening when he was eleven. A year later, he read Adolf Hitler's *Mein Kampf* (1925-1927; English translation, 1933) and other works by the German leader. Within a year, Hale formed a short-lived group called the New Reich. After graduation from high school, Hale attended Bradley University, where he majored in political science and music. At Bradley, he started an organization called the American White Supremacist Party. Hale dissolved the group after it failed to attract more than seven or eight members. Hale then unsuccessfully attempted to start a chapter of David Duke's National Association for the Advancement of White People. Hale graduated from Bradley in 1993. In 1995, he was a candidate for the East Peoria City Council; however, he received only 14 percent of the vote. He graduated from Southern Illinois University School of Law in 1998.

## Criminal Career

On July 27, 1996, at a meeting in Montana, Hale was elected Pontifex Maximus, or supreme leader, of the World Church of the Creator (WCOTC), a racist and neo-Nazi organization. Ben Klassen, a onetime Florida legislator, founded the WCOTC in 1973. Klassen rejected Judeo-democratic Marxist values and called for a new religion based on race. The so-called Creativity movement considered the white race as nature's highest creation and white people as the creators of all worthwhile culture and civilization. To Klassen, the most dangerous enemy was the Jews. He claimed that Jewish scriptwriters wrote the Bible. Nonwhites were the second most dangerous enemy and, according to Klassen, the laws of nature did not approve of miscegenation or "mongrelization" of the races.

After Klassen committed suicide in 1993, the Creativity movement was left without an effective spokesperson. Hale took over this position in 1996. Hale, who called Hitler the greatest white leader that ever lived, stressed that the Creativity movement was different from German national socialism in several ways. First, the Creativity movement was a religious movement, not a political one. Second, it was concerned with the entire white race, not just the Germans. The Creativity movement recognized the importance of white solidarity, while the Nazis were hostile to their white racial neighbors. Third, Creativity denounced Christianity, while Hitler did not address Jewish Christianity. Finally, Creativity would not form alliances with any nonwhite race, while Hitler allied his movement with the Japanese.

Hale operated the WCOTC out of an office in his parents' home in East Peoria, Illinois. He used an Israeli flag as a doormat and had swastika stickers decorating the walls. He began to publicize his movement through dozens of Internet sites, newsletters, a public cable television program, public meetings, and interviews. One of the most common methods he used was the distribution of racist and anti-Semitic literature on lawns and at libraries.

As his notoriety increased, Hale was interviewed by national media figures, including Jerry Springer, Ricki Lake, Leeza Gibbons, and Tom Brokaw. He was able to attract more members, mostly young men from blue-collar backgrounds, through this publicity. While Hale claimed to have eighty thousand members, the WCOTC had only a few hundred hardcore followers in twenty-two states. He also had nine international contacts. While Hale publicly claimed that his church did not condone violence, he called on his followers to fight a racial holy war.

In 1999, Hale passed the Illinois Bar; however, the Committee on Character and Fitness denied him a law license because of his bigotry. Following this decision, Hale said he could no longer advise his supporters to obey the laws of the United States. Shortly thereafter, one of Hale's followers, Benjamin Smith, went on a shooting rampage in Illinois and Indiana, killing two persons and wounding nine others. All of the victims were African American, Asian American, or Jewish.

In 2002, the WCOTC lost a trademark infringement suit brought against it by the Te-Ta-Ma Truth Foundation. Hale was ordered to stop using "Church of the Creator" as part of both his organization's name and his Internet addresses and to turn over all printed materials bearing that phrase. When he refused, U.S. federal judge Joan Lefkow charged him with contempt.

## Legal Action and Outcome

In January, 2003, Hale was charged with solicitation of murder of a federal judge and for obstruction of justice. The charges were brought after Hale sent an e-mail to his security chief asking for Judge Lefkow's address. The security chief, who was working for the Federal Bureau of Investigation (FBI), later tape-recorded Hale ordering the murder of the judge.

Hale's trial began on April 6, 2004, in Chicago, Illinois. His defense team called no witnesses, gambling that the jury would not convict him; however, on April 26, 2004, Hale was convicted of solicitation of murder and three counts of obstruction of justice. On April 6, 2005, Hale was sentenced to forty years in prison and sent to the Administrative Maximum United States Penitentiary in Florence, Colorado.

## Impact

Following Hale's imprisonment, the Creativity movement split into several factions and virtually ceased to exist. Although he personified the racism of the white separatist movement that continues to be present in the United States in the twenty-first century, he was never able to develop the WCOTC into a significant political movement. While he was college educated and articulate, his two hundred followers were mostly young men from blue-collar backgrounds. Hale garnered media publicity merely because his was a sensationalist story about neo-Nazism.

## Further Reading

Anti-Defamation League. *Poisoning the Web: Hatred Online*. New York: Anti-Defamation League, 1999. This work looks at the use of the Internet by hate groups, including the WCOTC.

Dobratz, Betty A., and Stephanie Shanks-Meile. *The White Separatist Movement in the United States*. Baltimore: Johns Hopkins University Press, 1999. This work is based on interviews with white separatists, including Hale. It provides an excellent analysis of the ideology of the WCOTC.

Swain, Carol M. *The New White Nationalism in America*. New York: Cambridge University Press, 2002. A comprehensive description and analysis of white nationalist groups in the United States, including the WCOTC.

*—William V. Moore*

**See also:** Byron De La Beckwith; Richard Girnt Butler; Joseph McCarthy; Robert Jay Mathews.

# Robert Philip Hanssen

## FBI agent turned traitor

**Born:** April 18, 1944; Evergreen Park, Illinois
**Also known as:** B; Ramon; Ramon Garcia
**Major offense:** Espionage
**Active:** 1979, 1985-2001
**Locale:** New York, New York; Washington, D.C.
**Sentence:** Life in prison without parole

### Early Life

Robert Philip Hanssen (HAN-suhn) was the only child of a police officer who routinely denigrated his son's abilities and occasionally abused him physically. Hanssen grew up in Chicago, where he attended William Howard Taft High School and was remembered by teachers and classmates as bright but socially awkward.

Hanssen excelled in science and won a scholarship to prestigious Knox College in Galesburg, Illinois. He graduated with a degree in chemistry in 1966, but when a hiring freeze prevented his getting a job as a cryptographer with the National Security Agency (NSA), he entered dental school at Illinois's Northwestern University. This step not only accorded with his father's hope that he enter a medical field but also assured him a draft deferment during the burgeoning Vietnam War. However, Hanssen switched programs within a few years and earned a master's degree in accounting and information systems in 1971.

At first, Hanssen worked for the well-known accounting firm Touche Ross & Company but found the job boring. He joined the Chicago police department in 1972 and, ultimately, the Federal Bureau of Investigation (FBI) in 1976. Hanssen's first bureau assignment was to the Gary, Indiana, office, but subsequent assignments moved him back and forth between New York City and Washington, D.C.

## Criminal Career

Over the years, Hanssen's duties gave him access to a variety of highly classified information. He acted as liaison to the State Department Office of Foreign Missions and was responsible for tracking espionage agents working in the United States under diplomatic cover. He was also the liaison to the State Department's Bureau of Intelligence and Research. Nevertheless, he quickly grew disillusioned with the FBI, which he felt underestimated his talents.

In his initial act of betrayal, Hanssen turned over the name of an important Russian double agent in 1979 to the GRU (the Soviet military intelligence agency) in return for twenty thousand dollars. He took a more decisive step in 1985 by approaching agents of the better-known Soviet intelligence agency the KGB (the GRU's rival). For the next sixteen years, Hanssen functioned as a "mole," or embedded double agent, for the KGB, trading yet more secrets for cash, diamonds, and deposits in a Russian bank account. He utilized a system known as the "dead drop," which allowed him to leave documents and agents to leave payment at a prearranged site without the need for face-to-face meetings. In his communications, Hanssen identified himself variously as "B," "Ramon," and "Ramon Garcia."

Although Hanssen eventually collected as much as $1,400,000 for his work, monetary gain does not seem to have been his primary motive. Instead, he seems to have delighted in fooling those closest to him. Moreover, despite being a seemingly devoted family man, a Roman Catholic, and a member of the conservative Catholic organization Opus Dei, Hanssen was obsessed with sex and pornography. Sworn to uphold the ideals of the FBI and the United States, he nevertheless sold his country's secrets with no apparent compunction.

## Legal Action and Outcome

The FBI was finally able to identify Hanssen through information provided by a former KGB officer in return for seven million dollars. Hanssen was reassigned to the Washington office, where he could be kept under closer observation, and was arrested on February 18, 2001, at one of his customary dead-drop sites. In order to avoid the death penalty, he pleaded guilty on July 6, 2001, to fifteen counts of spying and conspiracy. He was sentenced to life in prison without parole on May 10, 2002.

## Impact

Robert Philip Hanssen is regarded as one of the most damaging spies in American history. By the time he was arrested, he had passed on some six thousand pages of documents and twenty-seven computer disks of highly sensitive information to the Russians. The information he sold came from the FBI, the Central Intelligence Agency (CIA), the Pentagon, and the NSA, the last of which probably suffered the most damage.

Among many other secrets, Hanssen revealed the names of Soviet agents actually working for the United States (several of whom were then executed by the Soviets); U.S. estimates of Soviet missile strength; specific Ameri-

### The Worst of Betrayals

*On July 6, 2001, Deputy Attorney General Larry Thompson released a statement regarding Robert Philip Hanssen's guilty plea which reads, in part:*

. . . This case reminds us that the United States remains a target of efforts at home and abroad to undermine our national security, and that our vigilance in defense of our nation's security must be uncompromising. . . . Given the gravity of Hanssen's betrayal, and the strength of the government's case, the decision to forgo the death penalty in this case was a difficult one. In reaching this decision, we determined that the interests of the United States would be best served by pursuing a course that would enable our government to fully assess the magnitude and scope of Hanssen's espionage activities—an objective we could not achieve if we sought and obtained the death penalty against him. The guilty plea that Hanssen has entered today requires him to submit to extensive debriefings by the U.S. Intelligence Community. The information we expect to receive in these debriefings will enable our government to assess fully the scope and consequences of Hanssen's espionage activity.

Today's plea marks the culmination of a lengthy and complex investigation. I want to first commend the FBI for its exemplary work in investigating this extremely sensitive and painful matter. The successful resolution of this case is proof of the FBI's professionalism, skill, and dedication. The men and women of the FBI should be proud of their work in this case, and they have our thanks and gratitude.

I would also like to express my deep appreciation to the many other men and women throughout the United States government who contributed to bringing Hanssen to justice. . . .

can plans for retaliation in case of war and for protecting top U.S. officials; and details of electronic eavesdropping and surveillance techniques. He also provided the Soviets with software used to track intelligence cases—software that, in turn, a Russian agent may have sold to the terrorist organization al-Qaeda. Intelligence officials realized after the fact that they should have recognized signs of danger in Hanssen's often erratic behavior and work habits and consequently tightened their procedures.

The Hanssen case has been the subject of both a made-for-television movie, *Master Spy: The Robert Hanssen Story* (2002), starring William Hurt as Hanssen, and the critically acclaimed feature film *Breach* (2007), starring Chris Cooper as Hanssen and focusing on the role of the young FBI agent Eric O'Neill (Ryan Phillippe) in helping to orchestrate Hanssen's capture.

**Further Reading**

Havill, Adrian. *The Spy Who Stayed Out in the Cold*. New York: St. Martin's Press, 2001. Psychological study of Hanssen and one of the few on its subject to include a bibliography.

Schiller, Lawrence. *Into the Mirror: The Life of Master Spy Robert P. Hanssen*. New York: HarperCollins, 2002. Lightly fictionalized biography based in part on a screenplay by acclaimed author Norman Mailer. Includes a chronology of Hanssen's life and activities.

Vise, David A. *The Bureau and the Mole: The Unmasking of Robert Philip Hanssen, the Most Dangerous Double Agent in FBI History*. New York: Atlantic Monthly Press, 2002. Account by a reporter for *The Washington Post*. Includes a valuable appendix summarizing the secrets that Hanssen sold but no index.

Wise, David. *Spy: The Inside Story of How the FBI's Robert Hanssen Betrayed America*. New York: Random House, 2002. Study by a noted expert on U.S. intelligence services, written with the help of Dr. David L. Charney, a psychiatrist who interviewed Hanssen extensively after his arrest.

*—Grove Koger*

**See also:** Aldrich Ames; Christopher John Boyce; Daulton Lee.

# John Wesley Hardin

## Gunfighter and murderer

**Born:** May 26, 1853; Bonham, Texas
**Died:** August 19, 1895; El Paso, Texas
**Also known as:** James W. Swain; J. H. Swain
**Major offenses:** Robbery and murder
**Active:** 1868-July 23, 1877
**Locale:** Northern Texas, southern Kansas, southern Alabama, and northern Florida
**Sentence:** Twenty-five years in prison; served sixteen years

### Early Life

John Wesley Hardin (HAHR-dihn) was the second of two sons born to Elizabeth and James G. Hardin, a schoolteacher and a Methodist preacher. Events associated with the Civil War embittered young Hardin against Union soldiers and freed slaves. At the age of fourteen, he stabbed a schoolmate during a fight.

As a young man, Hardin worked as a cowboy on a ranch and a schoolteacher in Navarro County, Texas. At the request of his father, Hardin earned a diploma from Landrum's Academy in 1870. In 1871, he participated in a cattle drive along the Chisholm Trail and spent some time in Abilene, Kansas, where he met and reportedly had an uneventful confrontation with U.S. marshal Wild Bill Hickok. Hardin married Jane Bowen in 1872. They had three children.

### Criminal Career

In 1868, Hardin killed a black man and then killed one or more Union soldiers who attempted to take him into custody. He and a friend killed two more soldiers in 1869. Shortly thereafter, Hardin killed a circus worker. During a gambling dispute, he killed gunfighter Jim Bradley in 1870. After escaping from jail and killing a guard, Hardin killed three more Union soldiers who were tracking him.

In August, 1871, Hardin and a friend killed gunfighter Juan Bideno. Near the end of 1871, Hardin killed Gonzales County law officer Green Paramoor. While participating in the Sutton-Taylor range war in DeWitt County, Texas, in 1873 and 1874, Hardin killed lawman J. B. Morgan and was also involved in the killing of Sheriff Jack Helm. On May 26, 1874, Hardin killed Brown County sheriff Charles Webb in a gunfight. As he fled to Florida, he reportedly robbed some trains in Louisiana, Alabama, and Florida.

## Legal Action and Outcome

Hardin was arrested in Longview, Texas, in the spring of 1871 and charged with murder. Shortly thereafter, he escaped and killed a jail guard. In the fall of 1872, he spent time in jail but again escaped.

The law caught up with Hardin again on July 23, 1877, in Pensacola, Florida, where he was arrested on a train by Texas Ranger John B. Armstrong. On September 28, 1877, Hardin was tried and convicted of murder and sentenced to twenty-five years of hard labor at Rusk Prison in Huntsville, Texas. After good behavior, he was pardoned and released from prison on March 16, 1894. He was killed by Sheriff John Selman over a verbal dispute in El Paso, Texas, on August 19, 1895.

## Impact

John Wesley Hardin became known as one of the most notorious gunfighters and vigilante heroes in the Old West. His career paralleled that of Jesse James and William Bonney (Billy the Kid). Hardin killed at least twenty-three men in gunfights. Many historians rank him as having the fastest gun and sharpest eyes of any Old West gunfighter. His criminal activities increased the intensity with which law officers hunted down outlaws.

Hardin has been portrayed in many television and film Westerns. His life was explored on the television series *Death Valley Days* and in the motion picture *Streets of Laredo* (1949). Country musician Johnny Cash wrote and recorded a song about Hardin titled "Hardin Wouldn't Run." The title song of one of folksinger Bob Dylan's albums was also about Hardin. Most of the films and songs include legends and myths that tend to glamorize Hardin or the man who finally killed him.

## Further Reading

Block, Lawrence, ed. *Gangsters, Swindlers, Killers, and Thieves: The Lives and Crimes of Fifty American Villians*. New York: Oxford University Press, 2004. This work includes an account of the life of Hardin, including truths and myths.

Hardin, John Wesley, Jo Stamps, and Roy Stamps. *The Letters of John Wesley Hardin*. Austin, Tex.: Eakin Press, 2001. A collection of 281 letters that were written by Hardin, his wife, and friends between September 8, 1876, and July 28, 1895, which reveal insights about the life and legend of Hardin.

Pryor, Alton. *Outlaws and Gunslingers: Tales of the West's Most Notorious Outlaws*. Roseville, Calif.: Stagecoach, 2001. Explores the lives of twenty-seven of the most famous gunfighters known in the Old West, giving a detailed account of the outlaw life of Hardin.

*—Alvin K. Benson*

**See also:** William H. Bonney; Jesse James.

# Jean Harris

## Murderer

**Born:** April 27, 1923; Cleveland, Ohio
**Also known as:** Jean Struven (birth name); Scarsdale Diet Murderess
**Major offense:** Murder
**Active:** March 10, 1980
**Locale:** Purchase, New York
**Sentence:** Fifteen years to life in prison; received clemency after twelve years

### Early Life

Born Jean Struven in 1923, Jean Harris (HAR-ihs) was the child of a wealthy Cleveland, Ohio, family. Raised in a strict Christian Science household, she was an excellent student and graduated from Smith College. She married Jim Harris, a sales engineer. At first, Jean worked as a schoolteacher, but later she quit teaching to become a full-time homemaker. Her marriage ended in divorce in 1965.

Harris began dating Dr. Herman Tarnower, a high-society cardiologist, well known for his charming and promiscuous ways. He proposed in 1967, but he and Harris never married. Resuming her career as an educator, Harris in 1977 became administrator at Springside, a female academy out-

*Jean Harris.* (AP/Wide World Photos)

side Philadelphia. She later became headmistress of the exclusive Madeira School in McLean, Virginia.

## Criminal Career

In 1980, Harris learned of drug use in a Madiera School dormitory. During the investigation, she telephoned Tarnower, who was her physician. She requested more of the medication he had been prescribing to treat her chronic depression. After promising to send the medicine, he also asked her about some missing books. Harris took this as an accusation of stealing. Tarnower also informed her that she would not be his date at an upcoming banquet in his honor.

Meanwhile, at the Madeira School, drug paraphernalia was discovered, as well as marijuana seeds and stems. Harris called an emergency meeting of faculty, students, and four suspects. The tense meeting resulted in the four students' expulsion from the school.

The campus situation and her depressive state led Harris to thoughts of suicide. Wanting to say good-bye to Tarnower, she drove to his home with a gun, ready to take her own life. Once at his house, she found evidence of another woman, Lynne Tryforos, whom Harris felt was her rival for Tarnower's attentions. What began as a conversation with the doctor escalated into a scuffle, and Harris shot Tarnower four times.

## Legal Action and Outcome

In a high-profile trial, Harris pleaded temporary insanity, saying the shooting was accidental. Her trial raised a number of legal questions and divided public opinion. In 1981, she was found guilty of second-degree murder and sentenced to fifteen years to life in prison. She was sent to Bedford Hills Correctional Facility in New York.

Harris was a model prisoner and became known as an authority on the problems faced by children of incarcerated women. She taught parenting and sex education classes and encouraged pregnant inmates to participate in a program that allowed inmates to keep their infants in the prison nursery. Harris established the Children's Center, where incarcerated mothers could spend time with their children. She also wrote three books about her experiences.

After serving twelve years, Harris was granted clemency on December 29, 1992, on the grounds of ill health. Paroled in 1993, she was in her early seventies. Harris settled in the Northeast and continues to raise money and lecture on behalf of the children of incarcerated women.

## Impact

Jean Harris's crime and conviction took place in the years after the Civil Rights movement swept through the United States. Among the movement's many effects was the more equal treatment of offenders within the criminal justice system. Harris was not a typical murderer. She was upper class, educated, and older than most female offenders. Her trial raised a number of issues, including the fact that her jury was never given the option of determining her crime to be voluntary manslaughter. Harris, then, became emblematic of an offender condemned by a seemingly nondiscriminatory, newly enlightened justice system.

While in prison, Harris was somewhat able to reform her reputation: She contributed positively to the lives of incarcerated women, especially those with children. As an author, she was able to open a window on the world of women in prison. Her legacy at Bedford Hills Correctional Facility remains positive years after her release.

## Further Reading

Alexander, Shana. *Very Much a Lady: The Untold Story of Jean Harris and Dr. Herman Tarnower*. Canada: Simon & Schuster, 2006. Examines the early lives of Harris and Tarnower and the trial following Tarnower's death, including mistakes made by Harris's defense team.

Harris, Jean. *Stranger in Two Worlds*. New York: Macmillan, 1986. The story of Harris's life in and outside of prison, based on her memory and trial testimony.

_______. *They Always Call Us Ladies*. New York: Macmillan, 1988. Provides an excellent discussion of life in prison and the history of women's prisons.

*—Janice G. Rienerth*

**See also:** Bambi Bembenek; Ira Einhorn; Scott Peterson; Pamela Ann Smart; Ruth Snyder; Carolyn Warmus.

## Linda Burfield Hazzard

### Physician and murderer

**Born:** 1868; Carver County, Minnesota
**Died:** 1938; place unknown
**Also known as:** Lana Burfield (birth name); Linda Perry
**Major offenses:** Manslaughter and violating the medical practice acts of California and Washington
**Active:** November, 1902-May, 1935
**Locale:** Minneapolis, Minnesota; Seattle and Olalla, Washington
**Sentence:** Hard labor for two to twenty years at Walla Walla, Washington, penitentiary; served two years before being pardoned

### Early Life

Linda Burfield Hazzard (HAZ-uhrd) was brought up as a vegetarian in rural Minnesota. Her father had his seven children treated annually by a doctor, typical of the era; meat was forbidden as part of her medical treatment. Poorly educated and possessing a limited array of diagnostic techniques, the doctor treated intestinal problems, thought typical of all children, by prescribing blue mass pills. The mercurous chloride in the pills was so toxic that the U.S. Army stopped using it during the Civil War. Memories of the pain and sickness suffered by Hazzard and her siblings made her a lifelong foe of conventional medicine. Burfield attended two schools, training osteopathic nurses and studying with Dr. Edward Hooker Dewey for one term. In her book *Scientific Fasting* (1927), Burfield claimed to "throw new light upon [what Dewey] termed the 'New Gospel of Health.'"

## Criminal Career

In 1898, Burfield opened an office in Minneapolis, Minnesota, and began calling herself Dr. Burfield, D.O., a doctor of osteopathy. Minnesota law allowed the title. She treated hopeless conditions such as diabetes, syphilis, and kidney disease by using a combination of prolonged fasting, frequent enemas, and osteopathic manipulations. This last treatment, generally considered unacceptable, consisted largely of rapping the patient's head, back, stomach, and thighs.

Burfield sought to become the leading authority on "starvation therapy." Medical authorities appear not to have examined her methods until Gertrude Young died in 1902. The coroner, U. G. Williams, M.D., then obtained an autopsy at the University of Minnesota. Although the cause of death was listed as starvation, no charges could be made under the law of the time, and Burfield characterized the outcome of the investigation as a justification of her methods.

In 1903, Burfield met Samuel Christman Hazzard and wanted him both as a husband and as a business manager. Unfortunately, Mr. Hazzard was married to two other women and had fled service in the U.S. Army. While the couple was never married, she adopted the name Dr. Linda Burfield Hazzard for the rest of her life. In 1907, the couple moved to Olalla, Washington, near Seattle, where Dr. Hazzard established her practice and began to develop Wilderness Heights, her sanatorium.

On February 8, 1908, Daisy Maud Haglund died after a fifty-day fast at Wilderness Heights. A number of fatal cures followed, some of which may have involved actual homicide. It also appears that the Hazzards began relieving their victims of money, jewels, and property. The most infamous outcome of Hazzard's treatments, which are described in her book, *Fasting for the Cure of Disease* (1912), was the death of Claire Williamson on May 18, 1911.

## Legal Action and Outcome

Claire's sister, Dorothea, persuaded the local attorney to bring a first-degree murder charge against Hazzard. Dorothea had been rescued from Wilderness Heights by Miss Conway, a lifetime friend. Hazzard was arrested on August 5, 1911, and the trial began on January 15, 1912. The trial involved more than one hundred witnesses and fifteen doctors. Hazzard was found guilty of manslaughter and sentenced to between two and twenty years of hard labor. During her appeal process, the Washington State Board of Medical Examiners revoked her medical license. At least two more persons died of starvation before her appeal was rejected in the fall of 1913. Hazzard served two years in prison at Walla Walla, Washington, and was pardoned by the governor on condition that she leave the United States.

## Impact

Linda Burfield Hazzard was one of many medical "quacks" whose practices undoubtedly contributed to the eventual tightening of educational standards, examinations, and laws governing all aspects of health care. It appears that her story, with two exceptions, has been unnoticed in the extensive literature devoted to women professionals. However, there are still pseudomedical treatments widely available, and excerpts of Hazzard's works can be found readily on the Internet.

## Further Reading

Iserson, Kenneth V. *Demon Doctors: Physicians as Serial Killers*. Tucson, Ariz.: Galen Press, 2002. Chapter 4 relies heavily on Olsen (below) but is clearly written from a knowledgeable doctor's point of view.

Olsen, Gregg. *Starvation Heights*. New York: Warner Books, 1997. Detailed description of the years at Olalla with most attention to the Williamson sisters. The author claims to have consulted "every scrap published about Dr. Hazzard" but was unable to determine either her birth or death dates or places. Many references but phrased very generally. Includes photographs.

*—K. Thomas Finley*

**See also:** Michael Swango.

# George Hennard

## Mass murderer

**Born:** October 15, 1956; Sayre, Pennsylvania
**Died:** October 16, 1991; Killeen, Texas
**Also known as:** George Pierre Hennard (full name); Jo-Jo Hennard
**Cause of notoriety:** Hennard murdered twenty-four people in a crowded restaurant during the noon hour; he committed suicide before being arrested.
**Active:** October 16,1991
**Locale:** Belton and Killeen, Texas

### Early Life

The son of a U.S. Army doctor, George Hennard (HEHN-ahrd) moved frequently as a child, finally settling in Belton, Texas. His parents often had screaming fights, which were heard by neighbors. While Hennard's relationship with his father appears to have been distant, his relationship with his mother was highly contentious. As an adult, he often talked of killing her and drew a picture with her head on a rattlesnake's body.

### Criminal Career

Hennard was convicted of marijuana possession in 1981. On October 17, 1989, he was expelled from the Merchant Marine for flagrant public use of marijuana. He listened obsessively to the Steely Dan song "Don't Take Me Alive," which was about a gunman making a last stand against the police. He also studied every detail of James Oliver Huberty's mass murder at a McDonald's restaurant in 1984. In May, 1991, he was charged with driving while intoxicated and with illegally carrying loaded guns in his car.

On June 5, 1991, he went to a Federal Bureau of Investigation (FBI) office in Nevada, where his divorced mother lived, to complain about a woman's conspiracy against him. That summer, he stalked two teenage girls in his neighborhood, screamed obscenities at women and girls, threw rocks at children, and made threatening phone calls. The Belton police refused to intervene. His request for clemency and reinstatement in the Merchant Marine was denied on October 11.

### Criminal Career

During lunchtime on October 16, 1991, Hennard drove his meticulously maintained Ford Ranger pickup truck through the window of a Luby's Cafeteria in Killeen, Texas. He jumped out of the truck and began killing people. Using a 9-millimeter Glock 17 with seventeen-round magazines and a 9-millimeter Ruger P89 pistol with fifteen-round magazines, he fired ninety-six shots in about four minutes. One patron, chiropractor Suzanne Gratia, had a clear shot at Hennard while his back was turned, but she had left her handgun in her car in compliance with Texas law, which forbade carrying handguns. Gratia's parents were among the twenty-four people whom Hennard killed; Hennard wounded twenty-two more. Five police officers rushed to the scene, began shooting at Hennard, and entered the cafeteria. Wounded, Hennard retreated to a hallway, where he fatally shot himself in his head after a fierce gun battle with the officers.

### Impact

The George Hennard case had important ramifications for legislation passed at the state and national levels. In 1993, Texas substantially strengthened its antistalking laws to help cover cases such as that of Hennard in 1991. In 1992, the National Democratic Party specifically cited the Luby's massacre in its gun-control platform during the presidential election. Democratic congressman Chet Edwards, who represented Central Texas, switched sides on the assault weapon issue, and his support helped the 1994 federal assault weapon ban pass by a one-vote margin. The ban, which ended in 2004, would not have applied to Hennard's guns but did ban the manufacture of new magazines holding more than ten rounds.

Gratia (who married and took the name Gratia-Hupp) was instrumental in helping convince the Texas legislature to pass a "shall issue" bill to allow adults with a clean criminal record and who passed a safety class to obtain a license to carry a concealed handgun for lawful protection. Texas governor Anne Richards vetoed the bill, a move that subsequently played a role in the loss of her reelection campaign to George W. Bush, who, a few months after taking office, signed the "shall issue" bill into law. In 1996, Gratia-Hupp was elected as a Texas state representative on a strong pro-gun platform. She continued to serve in the legislature into the twenty-first century and to speak around the country in support of "shall issue" laws.

**Further Reading**

Cramer, Clayton E. "Ethical Problems of Mass Murder Coverage in the Mass Media." *Journal of Mass Media Ethics* 9, no. 1 (Winter, 1993-1994). Analyzes coverage of mass murders in the periodicals *Time* and *Newsweek* from 1984 to 1991 and shows that mass murders involving firearms receive far more media coverage. Also explores evidence that widespread coverage of mass murders by firearms provides an important motivation for publicity-seeking sociopaths to commit murder.

France, Alan W. *Composition as a Cultural Practice*. Westport, Conn.: Bergin & Garvey, 1994. A writing instructor explains how students reacted to an assignment asking them to analyze the media theme that Hennard's crimes were motivated by his poor relationship with his mother.

Karpf, Jason, and Elinor Karpf. *Anatomy of a Massacre*. Waco, Tex.: WRS, 1994. Excellent analysis of Hennard's failed adult life, his stalking of two teenagers, and information about the Killeen residents and victims.

—*David B. Kopel*

**See also:** James Oliver Huberty; Charles Whitman.

# Henry Hill

## Gangster and government informant

**Born:** June 11, 1943; Brooklyn, New York

**Major offenses:** Extortion and possession of narcotics

**Active:** 1972-2005

**Locale:** New York, New York; Tampa, Florida; and Nebraska

**Sentence:** Ten years' imprisonment for extortion; paroled after six years

### Early Life

Henry Hill (hihl) was born June 11, 1943, in Brooklyn, New York, to an Irish father and Sicilian mother. Hill was fascinated by the power and lifestyles of the local Lucchese crime family "soldiers" and became an associate of the organization at a young age. Still in his boyhood, Hill began to work for Lucchese leaders Paul Vario and Jimmy Burke, as well as other neighborhood gangsters who ran their operation out of Vario's cabstand and pizzeria. As a youngster, Hill helped run credit card scams and other extralegal errands for the older gangsters. After a stint in the U.S. Army as a paratrooper and being stationed at Ft. Bragg (during which time he ran numerous scams), Hill returned to New York in 1963 to continue his criminal career as a mob affiliate with Vario's crew.

## Criminal Career

Hill partnered with Burke and Tommy DeSimone in a variety of criminal enterprises, including truck hijacking, extortion, and other rackets. He was also involved in the infamous 1978 Boston College basketball point-shaving scheme. A 1972 two-million-dollar Air France heist and a six-million-dollar Lufthansa (German airline) robbery in 1978 are two operations in which Hill was reported to have been involved, along with several other crew members. Hill apparently received no money from the Lufthansa scheme and remained the only living member of the six criminals who were involved in the scheme. Hill later noted that he believed that most of the money went to the Mafia bosses.

## Legal Action and Outcome

Hill and Burke were arrested in 1972 for extortion and sentenced to ten years in prison. Hill then became heavily involved in narcotics trafficking and remained so after his release on parole six years later. Hill reportedly had heavy substance abuse problems of his own, and his womanizing and alleged abusiveness strained his family life with his wife Karen and two children, Gregg and Gina. In 1980, Hill was arrested for trafficking and turned government witness to save himself both from prosecution and from vengeful Mafia colleagues. His testimony sent Burke, Vario, and other associates to prison.

Hill continued to find trouble with the law: He was arrested in 1987 for narcotics-related charges, and in the early 1990's he was expelled from the witness protection program; drug-related charges would continue to plague him: In March, 2005, for example, he was convicted of cocaine possession and sentenced to six months in jail; in 2006, actor Ray Liotta encouraged Hill to enter an alcohol-rehabilitation program. Hill later moved to Southern California.

## Impact

Henry Hill was never "made" as a Mafia soldier because of his Irish heritage, but he serves as a good example of the many "connected" associates who work and earn money with the notorious crime families, paying "tribute," extending their own influence, and operating under the boss's protection. Hill achieved wide-ranging fame for the book *Wiseguy: Life in a Mafia Family*, written by Nicholas Pileggi and based on Hill's life. *Wiseguy* was later made into the 1990 film *Goodfellas*, directed by Martin Scorsese and with Liotta portraying Hill. In the 1990's and 2000's, Hill attempted to popularize and cultivate his public persona, appearing on the *Goodfellas* DVD "special features" commentary section, reviving an earlier occupation as a restaurateur, and marketing his own cookbook. However, in 2004, Gregg and Gina, Hill's children, projected a different side of Hill, publishing a book about their tumultuous childhoods with him and excoriating him for his self-centeredness, substance dependence, instability, and violent abuse.

Hill remains an important figure in modern criminal justice lore for his exposition of Mafia life, for making his lifestyle part of popular culture, and for his visibility as a surviving Mafia turncoat.

## Further Reading

Hill, Gregg, and Gina Hill. *On the Run: A Mafia Childhood*. New York: Warner, 2004. Hill's children recount their tumultuous childhood and provide a damning account of their father as a violent, unstable, and self-centered criminal.

Hill, Henry, with Gus Russo. *Gangsters and Goodfellas: Wiseguys, Witness Protection, and Life on the Run*. New York: M. Evans, 2004. Hill reports his version of living as a protected witness and his life since entering the program.

Pileggi, Nicholas. *Wiseguy: Life in a Mafia Family*. New York: Simon & Schuster, 1985. Pileggi recounts Hill's life and provides a story of the American Mafia experience, often in Hill's own words.

*—David R. Champion*

**See also:** Tommy Lucchese.

# Susanna Mildred Hill

## Con artist

**Born:** c. 1880; place unknown
**Died:** Date and place unknown
**Also known as:** Mildred Hill
**Major offense:** Mail fraud
**Active:** 1942-1945
**Locale:** Washington, D.C.
**Sentence:** Five years in prison

### Early Life

Not much is known about the early life of Susanna Mildred Hill (hihl) before her crimes became known to the American public. A mother of ten children living in Washington, D.C., she was in her sixties when she began to deceive men in distant cities with whom she would correspond through the U.S. mail. Sometimes her children would assist her in setting up her scams.

### Criminal Career

Hill, a sixty-one-year-old woman, began sending pictures of her very attractive twenty-one-year-old daughter through the mail to lonely men who were looking for companionship and maybe even a promise of her hand in marriage. These men, thinking that the attractive young woman in the photograph was Susanna, would carry on a long-distance correspondence for some time, assuming that there was a romantic connection between Susanna and themselves. Once a strong bond was in place, Hill would begin asking her "pen pals" for money.

She wrote that she needed funds desperately in order to attain medical attention for her ailing mother. In turn, her lonely victims would send her cash and checks. She took thousands of dollars from unsuspecting men. Hill always chose men who were at least five hundred miles away in order to protect herself and her true identity. If, by chance, one of the victims would show up at her home—and quite a few of them eventually did—she would pose as the "ailing" mother, or she would tell the potential suitor that "Susanna" was not at home at the time. She actually told some of the men that Susanna had left home or that she had eloped with a used-car salesman.

## Legal Action and Outcome

Finally, in Chicago, Susanna's ruse was discovered by a suspicious suitor, and she came under investigation by law enforcement authorities. Hill was quickly arrested, tried, and convicted of mail fraud. She spent five years in prison. Little is known about her time there or what happened to her once she was released.

## Impact

Susanna Mildred Hill's case was made public in the 1940's. Duplicated many times, this type of fraud has since become known as the lonely hearts scam. The case may have influenced present-day computer frauds that are very similar. Today, there are many ongoing cases that involve women or girls who claim via e-mail to be moving from country to country and that they need money to help defray their expenses. They usually prey on lonely men, hoping to part them from their money after spending some time communicating by e-mail. These men believe that they are helping to pay the women's expenses to come to America, or for personal visits or the like. After the scam artists collect the money, they disappear, never to be heard from again.

## Further Reading

Kohn, George C. *Dictionary of Culprits and Criminals*. 2d ed. Lanham, Md.: Scarecrow Press, 1995. Contains interesting facts and short biographies of many criminals in American history.

*—Jerry W. Hollingsworth*

**See also:** Lou Blonger; John R. Brinkley; Tino De Angelis; Billie Sol Estes; Martin Frankel; Joseph Weil.

# Marie Hilley
## Murderer

**Born:** June 4, 1933; Blue Mountain, Alabama
**Died:** February 26, 1987; Anniston, Alabama
**Also known as:** Audrey Marie Frazier (birth name); Audrey Marie Hilley (full name); Lindsay Robbi Hannon; Robbi Homan; Teri Martin
**Major offense:** Murder by poisoning
**Active:** 1975-1979
**Locale:** Anniston, Alabama; Fort Lauderdale, Florida; and Marlow, New Hampshire
**Sentence:** Life sentence for first-degree murder plus twenty years for attempted murder

### Early Life

Audrey Marie Hilley (HIHL-ee) was the daughter of Huey Frazier and Lucille Meads Frazier, who worked at Linen Thread Company near Anniston, Alabama. Her grandmother and great-aunt often cared for her while her parents worked. Marie attended Anniston public schools, familiarizing herself with that community's social elite and aspiring to become wealthy. In seventh grade, she met Frank Hilley, who was four years older. She married him on May 8, 1951. Serving in the U.S. Navy in Guam, Frank sent his paychecks to Marie to deposit while completing her high school education. Instead, she spent the money before her discharged husband returned to Anniston.

### Criminal Career

During the spring of 1975, Frank began suffering nausea and numbness. He died on May 25. Doctors attributed his death to infectious hepatitis and failed kidneys. Marie spent the $31,140 in life insurance benefits. Then, in August, 1979, Marie's daughter was hospitalized with similar symptoms. Blood tests revealed substantial arsenic in her hair and urine. The county coroner ordered the exhumation of Frank's body on October 3, 1979. The state toxicologist said his body contained deadly amounts of arsenic. Police arrested Marie on October 8 for attempting to murder her daughter, for whom she had bought life insurance.

## Legal Action and Outcome

A Calhoun County, Alabama, grand jury indicted Marie of attempted murder of her daughter on October 25, 1979. After friends posted her fourteen-thousand-dollar bond on November 16, the freed Marie vanished. While she was missing, a Calhoun County grand jury, on January 11, 1980, indicted her of murdering her husband.

As a fugitive, Marie reinvented herself. Traveling to Fort Lauderdale, Florida, she met John Homan and introduced herself as Lindsay Robbi Hannon. The couple moved to Marlow, New Hampshire, where they married on May 29, 1981. Marie then concocted a bizarre story: While traveling alone to Texas, she telephoned Homan and identified herself as Lindsay's twin sister, Teri Martin. Teri told Homan that Lindsay had died. Then, pretending to be Teri, Marie traveled back to New Hampshire to comfort Homan. However, coworkers investigated items in Lindsay's obituary that Marie (as Teri) had written and discovered that it was fraudulent. They alerted authorities, who arrested Marie on January 12, 1983.

Marie's nine-day trial began on May 30, 1983. Her two children, sister-in-law, and cellmate testified against her. The state toxicologist confirmed that bottles seized from Marie's home had contained arsenic. After deliberating for almost three hours, the jury declared Marie guilty, convicting her of first-degree murder and attempted murder. Judge Sam Monk sentenced her to life imprisonment plus twenty years in Julia Tutwiler State Prison for Women in Wetumpka, Alabama.

Marie received a three-day pass from prison on February 19, 1987, and disappeared. On February 26, police found her seeking shelter from heavy rain on a porch near her birthplace. Suffering from hypothermia, she died en route to the hospital.

## Impact

Marie Hilley's criminal activities shocked the people in Anniston who knew her. Nationwide, her case received a great deal of media attention, and Americans were dismayed that a seemingly normal housewife could act so lethally against her family. Marie's evasive techniques, elaborate lies, and years as a fugitive mystified many people. Some, including her second husband, remained in denial about her murderous nature. Marie's actions influenced the way in which many physicians interpreted possible poisoning situations, while criminal analysts studied her case to profile other females who kill using poisons. Marie defended her innocence, refusing to offer reasons for her behavior. In 1991, a television film titled *Wife, Mother, Murderer: The Marie Hilley Story* depicted Marie's bizarre behavior and multiple identities.

**Further Reading**

Douglas, John, and Mark Olshaker. *The Anatomy of Motive*. New York: Scribner, 1999. Douglas profiled Hilley when she was a fugitive to help Federal Bureau of Investigation (FBI) agents find her, describing her as a complex psychopathic personality motivated by control, anger, and greed.

Ginsburg, Philip E. *Poisoned Blood: A True Story of Murder, Passion, and an Astonishing Hoax*. New York: Charles Scribner's Sons, 1987. In-depth depiction of Hilley, her victims, case investigators, and people associated with her. Includes photographs of Hilley and her family.

Kelleher, Michael D., and C. L. Kelleher. *Murder Most Rare: The Female Serial Killer*. London: Praeger, 1998. Categorizes Hilley as an unexplained serial murderer, noting that she was sane and that she never clarified the motives for her murderous behavior.

McDonald, R. Robin. *Black Widow: The True Story of the Hilley Poisonings*. Far Hills, N.J.: New Horizon Press, 1986. A detailed account written by an *Anniston Star* reporter, providing background information concerning Hilley's family and the Anniston community.

*—Elizabeth D. Schafer*

**See also:** Velma Margie Barfield; Susan Smith; Andrea Yates.

# John Hinckley, Jr.
## Would-be assassin of President Ronald Reagan

**Born:** May 29, 1955; Ardmore, Oklahoma
**Also known as:** John Warnock Hinckley, Jr. (full name)
**Cause of notoriety:** Hinckley was found not guilty by reason of insanity in the attempted assassination of President Ronald Reagan, a verdict that subsequently had important impact on the criminal justice system.
**Active:** March 30, 1981
**Locale:** Washington, D.C.

### Early Life

John Hinckley (HIHNK-lee), Jr., was born into a wealthy family. His father was the chairman and president of the Vanderbilt Energy Corporation. His mother was a homemaker. Hinckley was the youngest of three children. He grew up in Texas, and later his family moved to Colorado. As a young child, he excelled in football and basketball, and he was elected president of his seventh- and ninth-grade classes.

During high school, Hinckley became reclusive. In 1973, after graduating from high school, he enrolled in Texas Tech University, which he attended intermittently until 1980; he never received a college degree. In 1976, he traveled to Los Angeles to pursue his dream of becoming a songwriter. However, his efforts were not successful. During his stay in Los Angeles, he saw the film *Taxi Driver* (1976) several times and became obsessed with Jodie Foster, a child actor who played a prostitute in the film. After living in Los Angeles for a few months, he became disillusioned with Hollywood and returned to his parents' home in Colorado. In 1979, Hinckley bought his first gun, and in 1980 he bought another gun, which was later used in the assassination attempt.

### Criminal Career

In 1980, Hinckley read an article about Foster's enrollment at Yale University, and he decided to enroll in a writing course at Yale so that he could be near her. He slipped poems and messages under her door and repeatedly tried to contact Foster by telephone. However, Hinckley failed to develop any meaningful contact with Foster. He then decided that he could gain her respect and love if he achieved notoriety by assassinating the president.

In the fall of 1980, Hinckley decided to stalk President Jimmy Carter. He traveled to two locales during Carter's campaign trips; during his second trip, he was arrested at the airport when security officials detected handguns in his suitcase. Hinckley returned home, and his parents convinced him to see a psychiatrist in order to receive treatment for depression.

Hinckley's mental health failed to improve, and he decided to target the newly elected president, Ronald Reagan. He boarded a bus and checked into the Park Central Hotel in Washington, D.C., on March 29, 1981. On Monday, March 30, 1981, Hinckley wrote a letter to Foster describing his plan to assassinate Reagan, and on that same day he took a cab to the Washington Hilton Hotel, where Reagan was scheduled to speak to a labor convention. Hinckley fired a Rohm RG-14 revolver six times at Reagan as he left the Hilton Hotel. The bullets from Hinckley's gun struck Reagan in the left chest; stray bullets also wounded Press Secretary James Brady in the left temple, as well as police officer Thomas K. Delehanty and Secret Ser-

*John Hinckley, Jr.*
(AP/Wide World Photos)

### Hinckley's Other Victims

*The six shots that John W. Hinckley fired at President Ronald Reagan on March 30, 1981, wounded three other people as well:*

- **James Brady,** the president's press secretary, received the most damaging wound. Shot in the head, Brady was erroneously reported dead at first. Surgeons were able to save him, but he was left partially paralyzed for life. Even though he never again was able to perform the job, he kept the title of press secretary until the end of the Reagan presidency. In the meantime, he was far from idle. With his wife, Sarah, he launched the Brady Campaign to Prevent Gun Violence and the Brady Center to Prevent Gun Violence, both dedicated to gun control. He lobbied relentlessly for it, and after a fierce political fight in Congress the Brady Handgun Violence Prevention Act, now known as the Brady Bill, passed and was signed into law by President Bill Clinton in 1993. Three years later, President Clinton awarded Brady the Presidential Medal of Freedom for his advocacy.
- **Thomas K. Delehanty** had been a District of Columbia police officer for seventeen years when one of Hinckley's bullets hit him in the back and he fell to the sidewalk beside James Brady. He recovered from his wound but later retired on a disability pension.
- **Timothy J. McCarthy** was a Secret Service agent assigned to guard the president. (That day, however, he was not originally scheduled for duty; he was added to the entourage at the last minute after losing a coin toss with another agent.) The job description requires an agent literally to throw himself or herself between the president and danger—even if that means "taking the bullet" for the president. McCarthy is the only agent ever to do precisely that, and he was shot in the stomach. After surgery he made a full recovery and returned to duty, directing the Secret Service's Chicago Division until retiring in 1993. He then became chief of the Orland Park Police Department in Illinois. He ran unsuccessfully as a Democrat for Illinois secretary of state in 1997 and then returned to school and earned a master's degree in criminal and social justice in 1999. In 2005, the Illinois State Bar Association awarded McCarthy its Law Enforcement Award, for service that brings honor to the profession.

vice agent Timothy J. McCarthy. Hinckley was immediately arrested. Surgeons successfully operated on Reagan at George Washington University Hospital; however, Brady was permanently disabled by the bullet lodged in his brain.

## Legal Action and Outcome

The trial of Hinckley took place in 1982. Hinckley claimed the defense of not guilty by reason of insanity. At the time that Hinckley shot Reagan, the law of insanity in the District of Columbia provided that a person was not criminally responsible for his or her acts if, at the time of the commission of the crime, the defendant, as a result of mental disease or defect, lacked substantial capacity to appreciate the wrongfulness of his or her conduct or to conform conduct to the requirements of the law.

The word "appreciate" became a critical issue in the trial of Hinckley. The defense argued successfully that "appreciate" not only meant cognitive awareness but also included an emotional understanding of the consequences of his actions. The defense maintained that Hinckley did not have the capability to emotionally understand the consequences of his actions at the time of the shooting. The defense utilized medical experts at trial who could testify in support of Hinckley's mental condition. They also presented writings that Hinckley had generated in the months preceding the shootings, including the letter to Foster, in order to portray him as a man who was totally without the mental capacity to appreciate the wrongfulness of his conduct or to conform his conduct to the requirements of the law. The prosecution also presented medical experts as witnesses who testified that Hinckley did indeed know what he was doing at the time of the shootings and was therefore legally sane. However, on June 21, 1982, the jury found Hinckley not guilty by reason of insanity.

Although Hinckley was found not guilty, the court ordered him to St. Elizabeths Hospital for treatment of his mental illness. Beginning in 1999, Hinckley was permitted to leave the hospital for brief periods of time in order to have supervised visits with his parents in the Washington area, as well as to take day trips to local places. In 2005, a federal judge granted his request to make several overnight visits to his parents' home.

## Impact

The acquittal of John Hinckley, Jr., by reason of insanity sparked public concern about the abuse of the insanity defense and created pressure for reform. At the federal level, Congress passed the Insanity Defense Reform Act of 1984. The act's provisions included changing the phrase "lacks substantial capacity to appreciate" to "unable to appreciate," thereby raising the standard of proof. It further specified that the mental disease or defect in a defendant must be severe. Moreover, the Insanity Defense Reform Act of 1984 required defendants to plead insanity as an affirmative defense. This meant that the act shifted the burden of proof to the defense, which must prove that the defendant is insane. In addition, the standard of proof that the defense must meet is the standard of "clear and convincing" evidence—a standard of proof in between the standard of preponderance of the evidence (more likely than not) and beyond a reasonable doubt (a reasonable certainty). While the prosecution must prove the defendant's guilt using the standard of beyond a reasonable doubt, the act requires that the defense must prove a plea of not guilty by reason of insanity with clear and convincing evidence.

At the state level, as a result of the Hinckley case, thirty-four states made some type of alteration to their insanity defenses between 1982 and 1985. The changes to the defense of insanity at the state level were similar to the ones made under the Insanity Defense Reform Act of 1984. In addition, in some states, "guilty but mentally ill" became a possible verdict in addition to "not guilty by reason of insanity."

**Further Reading**

Bonnie, Richard, Joseph Jeffries, and Peter Low. *A Case Study in the Defense of John W. Hinckley, Jr.* New York: Foundation Press, 2000. Provides a thorough analysis of why the Hinckley defense was successful.

Caplan, Lincoln. *The Insanity Defense and the Trial of John W. Hinckley, Jr.* Boston: David R. Godine, 1984. Discusses the history of the case and pays special attention to the relationship between law and psychiatry.

Simon, Rita, and David Aaronso. *The Insanity Defense: A Critical Assessment of Law and Policy in the Post-Hinckley Era.* New York: Praeger, 1988. Provides a review of the insanity defense in other countries, how the defense has been treated in literature and the theater, and the results of a survey of legal and mental health experts.

Steadman, Henry, et al. *Before and After Hinckley: Evaluating Insanity Defense Reform.* New York: Guilford Press, 1993. Examines insanity defense reform by focusing on the states of California, New York, Georgia, and Montana.

*—Patricia E. Erickson*

**See also:** Arthur Bremer; Samuel Joseph Byck; Mark David Chapman; Lynette Fromme; Richard Lawrence; Lewis Powell; Yolanda Saldívar.

# Alger Hiss

## Lawyer and U.S. State Department appointee

**Born:** November 11, 1904; Baltimore, Maryland
**Died:** November 15, 1996; New York, New York
**Major offense:** Perjury
**Active:** Late 1930's-1940's
**Locale:** United States, mainly Washington, D.C.
**Sentence:** Five years in prison; served forty-four months

### Early Life

Born the fourth of five children into a financially stable family, Alger Hiss (AL-juhr hihs) experienced emotional trauma throughout his early years. His father committed suicide when Hiss was only three. When he was twenty-five, his sister committed suicide, and his older brother died later from alcoholism.

Despite his emotionally troubled youth, Hiss became successful at an early age. In 1926, he graduated from the Johns Hopkins University, where he had been an outstanding student, both academically and socially. He was voted most popular student by his peers, was a cadet commander in the Reserve Officers' Training Corps (ROTC), and was a member of Phi Beta Kappa. He graduated from Harvard Law School in 1929. At Harvard, he had become acquainted with U.S. Supreme Court Justice Felix Frankfurter, who recommended him as a private law clerk to U.S. Supreme Court Justice Oliver Wendell Holmes. Hiss later credited Holmes with having the most profound influence on his career. In 1929, Hiss married Priscilla Hobson, a divorced editor and writer. Unlike many women of the time, she continued to work.

### Political Career

An intelligent, well-educated, and handsome man, Hiss quickly made an impact as a lawyer and government employee. After working in law firms in Boston and New York, he began his government career in 1933, working as an attorney for the Agricultural Adjustment Administration, for the Nye Committee investigating the munitions industry, and for the Justice Department. In 1936, he joined the State Department. Hiss later played major roles in creating the United Nations and in serving as a member of the American delegation at Yalta in 1945, during the meeting of the "Big Three" Allied powers at the end of World War II. In 1947, he became president of the Carnegie Endowment for International Peace.

Hiss had gained prominence during a tumultuous time in American history. After World War II, another Red Scare exacerbated fears that communists had infiltrated U.S. government agencies at the highest levels and resulted in government investigations of suspected radicals. In this volatile climate, Hiss was accused of being a member of the Communist Party by Whittaker Chambers, a writer and journalist who, by his own admission, had been a member of the Communist Party. In 1942, Chambers met with the Federal Bureau of Investigation (FBI) regarding his membership in the Communist Party. He contended that he had recanted his membership in the late 1930's, having become disillusioned by the purges in the Soviet Union orchestrated by dictator Joseph Stalin. During the questioning, Chambers accused Hiss of being a Communist, but the FBI did not pursue the matter immediately. However, after interviewing Chambers again in 1945 and following other tips, the FBI tapped Hiss's phones and put him under surveillance. When Hiss met with FBI officials, he denied any connection with the Communist Party.

### The HUAC Hearings

Chambers appeared at congressional hearings held by the House Committee on Un-American Activities (HUAC) in 1948, and he again accused Hiss of being a member of the Communist Party.

Hiss demanded an appearance before the HUAC and unequivocally denied being a member of the Communist Party or knowing Whittaker Chambers. HUAC members, including a young Richard Nixon, continued to harbor suspicions regarding Hiss's denials. Chambers continued supplying committee members with additional information, such as describing receiving a car from Hiss and identifying Hiss as an avid bird-watcher. Although some of the information was inaccurate—for example, that the Hisses did not drink—the new information convinced the HUAC to continue its investigation.

At a face-to-face meeting, Hiss admitted knowing Chambers but by a different name. Later, Chambers accused Hiss of espionage activities and supplying him with secret State Department documents, some of which Chambers kept to protect himself. These new revelations escalated the charges from Hiss being a Communist to being a spy and incriminated Chambers, as he earlier had denied espionage activities. Chambers gave these documents—all dating from 1938 and some containing Hiss's signature and notes—as well as the infamous Pumpkin Papers (microfilm rolls), to the HUAC. Hiss declared the documents were fraudulent.

## Legal Action and Outcome

A grand jury indicted Hiss in December, 1948, for perjury. His trial began in New York City in May, 1949, and lasted six weeks. The prosecution produced the typewriter, which was owned by Hiss, on which State Department documents had been copied. The defense argued that Hiss had disposed of the typewriter, after which others copied the documents. The defense also called several notable character witnesses, including two U.S. Supreme Court justices, a governor, and diplomats, as evidence of Hiss's impeccable loyalty to the United States. Chambers was portrayed as a liar and a person of ill repute. The trial ended in a hung jury—eight jurors for conviction, four against—and a second trial began in November.

At this trial, lasting only three weeks, Hiss was found guilty on two counts of perjury. The prosecution produced another witness who corroborated Chambers's accusations. Additionally, Hiss had less public support, resulting from enhanced Red Scare fears at home and the Cold War intensifying abroad.

Hiss continued to proclaim his innocence by using documents he acquired through the Freedom of Information Act (1966) and requesting Russian authorities to search their archives for documents. Indeed, in the 1990's a former Soviet general declared he found no evidence of Hiss's espionage in Soviet archives, but he later withdrew his statement. Further released archival documents, including the valuable Venona Papers, seem to weaken Hiss's denials.

## Impact

The case of Alger Hiss became emblematic of the 1950's "witch-hunts" against Communist sympathizers that threatened to undermine civil liberties in the United States. The trial of and denials by Alger Hiss reflect the hysteria of the Red Scare and Cold War attitudes in post-World War II America. Hiss's opponents and supporters remain divided on whether he was a guilty as charged or a victim of this era that witnessed attacks on political and civil rights.

**Further Reading**

Chambers, Whittaker. *Witness*. New York: Random House, 1952. In his best-selling autobiography, Chambers discusses his turbulent life and defends his accusations against Hiss.

Hiss, Alger. *In the Court of Public Opinion*. New York: Alfred A. Knopf, 1957. Hiss presents his side of the story, claiming complete innocence. In 1988, he published another book, *Recollections of a Life*, which presented additional information on his life and career.

Tanenhaus, Sam. *Whittaker Chambers: A Biography*. New York: Random House, 1997. A highly favorable account of Chambers, who the author believes is a significant American intellectual.

Weinstein, Allen. *Perjury: The Hiss-Chambers Case*. New York: Alfred A. Knopf, 1978. Weinstein originally set out to prove that Hiss was innocent, but based on evidence he uncovered, he concluded that Hiss was guilty as charged.

White, G. Edward. *Alger Hiss's Looking-Glass Wars: The Covert Life of a Soviet Spy*. New York: Oxford University Press, 2004. A study that examines and interprets Hiss's struggle to deny accusations made against him.

*—Sharon Wilson and Raymond Wilson*

**See also:** Aldrich Ames; Whittaker Chambers; Joseph McCarthy; Ethel Rosenberg; Julius Rosenberg.

# Doc Holliday

## Gambler and gunfighter

**Born:** August 14, 1851; Griffin, Georgia

**Died:** November 8, 1887; Glenwood Springs, Colorado

**Also known as:** John Henry Holliday (birth name); Tom Mackey

**Major offenses:** Assault and battery and murder

**Active:** January 2, 1875-August 19, 1884

**Locale:** Northcentral Texas, southwestern Colorado, and southeastern Arizona

**Sentence:** Jailed October, 1880; March, 1881; October to November, 1881; May, 1882

*Doc Holliday.*

## Early Life

John Henry Holliday (HAHL-ih-day) was the second child of Alice Jane and Henry Burroughs Holliday. John's father was a pharmacist who became a wealthy planter and lawyer in Georgia. John's beloved mother died of tuberculosis on September 16, 1866.

In 1870, Holliday attended dental school in Pennsylvania and earned the degree of doctor of dental surgery in March, 1872. Later in 1872, he started a dental practice in Atlanta. After developing tuberculosis, he moved to Dallas, Texas, where he practiced dentistry for a short time prior to taking up gambling. A man with a quick temper, "Doc" became very proficient with a gun and a knife.

## Criminal Career

After killing a prominent citizen in Dallas in 1875, Holliday fled to Jacksboro, Texas, and worked as a faro dealer. In the summer of 1876, Holliday killed a U.S. soldier from nearby Fort Richardson. In order to avoid the law, Holliday headed for Denver, Colorado, where he dealt faro. After a fight with a prominent gambler in Denver, Holliday eventually wound up in Fort Griffin, Texas, where he met the love of his life, Kate Elder Haroney.

While in Fort Griffin, Holliday also met U.S. marshal Wyatt Earp, who was in Texas tracking an outlaw. After stabbing a man over a gambling dispute in Fort Griffin, Holliday was jailed. Haroney helped him escape. The two headed to Dodge City, Kansas, where Holliday dealt faro at the Long Branch Saloon. While in Dodge City, Holliday saved Earp from a band of Texas ruffians. The two became lifelong friends.

Holliday killed gunfighter "Kid" Colton in 1879 in Colorado. He drifted to Tombstone, Arizona, in 1880. Earp and his brothers had also moved there. The Earps and Holliday became fierce enemies of the lawless group of cowboys in Tombstone, which led to the famous gunfight at the O.K. Corral on October 26, 1881. Holliday killed two men in the battle.

## Legal Action and Outcome

In October, 1880, Holliday was arrested and charged with assault with a deadly weapon for a brawl in the Oriental Saloon in Tombstone. In 1881, he was arrested for a stagecoach robbery but later released when witnesses testified that he was elsewhere when the stage was robbed. After the gun battle at the O.K. Corral, Holliday and the Earps were arrested and tried for murder. They were later freed when it was determined that they had acted within the law.

In May, 1882, Holliday was accused of murder, arrested, and jailed in Denver for the killing of Tombstone outlaw Curly Bill Brocius. The governor of Colorado refused to honor a request for extradition from Arizona, and Holliday was set free. In August, 1884, he was acquitted of shooting charges during a gunfight in Leadville, Colorado, since he had acted in self-defense.

## Impact

Known as one of the most fearless men on the Western frontier, Doc Holliday became a close personal friend of Earp and the Earp brothers. Doc and the Earps helped clean up the lawless element in Tombstone, Arizona. Doc was a primary participant in the gunfight at the O.K. Corral, one of the most famous gunfights in the history of the Old West. He killed two of the three men who were slain in the battle.

Earp claimed that Doc was the fastest six-gun that he ever saw. Beginning in the 1940's, Holliday's fame grew as a result of numerous Western novels and magazines, television Westerns, and at least eight films. He is also featured in computer games, particularly the "Fallout" series.

**Further Reading**

Brooks, L. T. *The Last Gamble of Doc Holliday*. Raleigh, N.C.: Pentland Press, 2004. Biography that investigates the truths and myths about Holliday's life.

Pryor, Alton. *Outlaws and Gunslingers: Tales of the West's Most Notorious Outlaws*. Roseville, Calif.: Stagecoach, 2001. Explores the lives of twenty-seven of the most famous gunfighters known in the Old West, giving a detailed synopsis of the life of Holliday.

Tanner, Karen Holliday. *Doc Holliday: A Family Portrait*. Norman: University of Oklahoma Press, 2001. Tanner reveals many intriguing insights into the life, times, and experiences of Holliday.

*—Alvin K. Benson*

**See also:** Apache Kid; Clyde Barrow; Tom Bell; William H. Bonney; Curly Bill Brocius; Bob Dalton; Emmett Dalton; Bill Doolin; John Wesley Hardin; Jesse James; Tom Ketchum; Harry Longabaugh; Bill Longley; Johnny Ringo; Belle Starr; Henry Starr; Hank Vaughan; Cole Younger.

## H. H. Holmes

### Serial killer

**Born:** May 16, 1861; Gilmanton, New Hampshire

**Died:** May 7, 1896; Moyamensing Prison, Philadelphia, Pennsylvania

**Also known as:** Herman Webster Mudgett (birth name); Henry Howard Holmes (full name); H. M. Howard; O. C. Pratt; Harry Gordon; Monster of Sixty-Third Street; Torture Doctor; Modern Bluebeard

**Major offenses:** Fraud, bigamy, and murder

**Active:** c. 1890-1895

**Locale:** Chicago, Illinois; Philadelphia, Pennsylvania; Toronto, Canada; and Irvington, Indiana

**Sentence:** Jailed for stock fraud; death by hanging for murder

*Holmes, H. H.*

## Early Life

Herman Webster Mudgett, later known as H. H. Holmes (hohmz), was born to a religious mother who could not protect him from his strict, harsh father. A bright child, he was harassed by bullies; once they chased him into a doctor's office, terrifying him with a skeleton. He also performed experimental operations on neighborhood pets before he was eleven years old.

In 1878, Holmes married Clara Lovering. After working as a schoolmaster, he attended the University of Michigan Medical School in Ann Arbor; then he ensconced his wife and son with her parents in New Hampshire. He practiced medicine briefly in Mooers Falls, New York, then moved to Chicago, using the name Henry Howard Holmes. Holmes became partner in a pharmacy in Englewood, then a suburb and later incorporated into the city. In 1887, he bigamously married Myrta Belknap.

## Criminal Career

How many people Holmes murdered remains a mystery. His multiple and unreliable confessions vary widely in their facts. Contemporary newspapers speculated that he had murdered as many as two hundred; modern historians estimate the number to be between nine and about fifty.

Holmes's first murder victim was probably Mrs. E. S. Holton, Holmes's partner in the Englewood pharmacy. Her disappearance in 1890 left him the business's sole owner. Ned Conner managed a jewelry counter in Holmes's store; in late 1891, his wife Julia disappeared with their daughter, Pearl. Other likely victims were his fourth simultaneous wife, Minnie Williams; her sister Nannie; and Holmes's mistress, Emeline Cigrand. He may have sold some of his victims' remains to medical schools.

When the Chicago World's Columbian Exposition opened in 1893, Holmes rented out rooms in a huge building he had erected on Sixty-Third Street. The building, called The Castle, had three stories with hidden passageways; an insulated, room-sized vault; gas jets in some rooms; and peepholes in all. In 1895, police discovered that the basement held a dissection and a torture table, mysterious wooden tanks, and an iron stove—eight feet tall by three feet wide—containing remains such as jewelry, clothing, and bones. Holmes may have murdered many visitors; he imprisoned guests and spied on them, gaining a sense of power and sexual thrills. He may have used the gas to incapacitate women and molest them.

Holmes clearly also murdered for financial reasons. Under many names, he committed various swindles, from defaulting on credit to selling faked inventions. His motive in the 1894 murder of longtime assistant Benjamin Pitezel seemed to be insurance fraud; he received ten thousand dollars in Pitezel's benefits. Holmes murdered three of Pitezel's children, perhaps to prevent discovery of their father's death.

### Legal Action and Outcome

In 1894, Holmes was jailed for stock fraud. In 1895, Pinkerton detectives arrested Holmes for insurance fraud. Tireless and clever work by Detective Frank Geyer proved Holmes's culpability for the Pitezel deaths. In an internationally publicized trial, Holmes—primarily serving as his own lawyer—presented his defense but was convicted on four counts of murder; he was hanged.

### Impact

Arguably America's first well-documented serial killer, H. H. Holmes represents the dark side of the Gilded Age, when commerce and invention boomed and Americans admired the self-made tycoon. Chicago, especially, was growing from the ashes of its great fire and offered local opportunity and the glamour of the World's Fair. Moreover, Holmes's crimes eerily mirrored the burgeoning technological sophistication of the United States as it prepared to enter a new century, both in his killing "factory" and in the "mass production" of his crimes. His exploits scandalized post-Victorian America, receiving far more publicity than his English contemporary, Jack the Ripper. He also inspired a reporter to coin the term "multimurderer," a forerunner of the current concept of the serial killer. Many books on the Holmes case were published, including Holmes's own self-serving autobiography. For a time, Holmes was largely forgotten, but attention to his story was revived during the 1970's and 1980's with a concomitant rise in interest concerning serial killers.

### Further Reading

Franke, David. *The Torture Doctor*. New York: Hawthorn Books, 1975. Well-researched and detailed discussion about Holmes.

Geary, Rick. *The Beast of Chicago: The Murderous Career of H. H. Holmes*. New York: NBM Comics, 2003. A graphic novel, impeccably researched both factually and visually.

Holmes, H. H. *Holmes' Own Story*. Philadephia: Burk & McFetridge, 1895. Holmes's autobiography.

Larson, Erik. *The Devil in the White City: Murder, Magic, and Madness at the Fair That Changed America*. New York: Vintage, 2004. Well-researched and well-written analysis, with a useful index, that places Holmes within the context of the Chicago World's Columbia Exposition and turn-of-the-century Chicago.

Schechter, Harold. *Depraved: The Shocking True Story of America's First Serial Killer*. New York: Pocket, 1994. Another accessible, detailed account of Holmes's criminal career.

Wilson, Colin. "H. H. Holmes: The Torture Doctor." In *The Mammoth Book of Murder*, edited by Richard Glyn Jones. New York: Carroll & Graf, 1989. Brief but useful, with minor errors.

_______. *The History of Murder*. New York: Carroll & Graf, 2000. Contains a slightly revised version of the essay in the book edited by Jones.

—*Bernadette Lynn Bosky*

**See also:** Joe Ball; Albert Fish.

# James Oliver Huberty

## Mass murderer

**Born:** October 11, 1942; Canton, Ohio
**Died:** July 18, 1984; San Ysidro, California
**Cause of notoriety:** Huberty entered a busy McDonald's restaurant and shot and killed twenty-one people before being killed by law enforcement officers.
**Active:** July 18, 1984
**Locale:** San Ysidro, California

### Early Life

When James Oliver Huberty (HEW-buhr-tee) was seven, his mother abandoned the family to become a Pentecostal missionary. He was frequently teased by other children for coming from a broken home and for having spastic paralysis from polio. After graduating from the Pittsburgh Institute of Mortuary Science, Huberty got a job in a funeral home. Although his embalming skills were good, he was fired because of his unsympathetic demeanor toward the bereaved. Around 1976, Huberty began hearing disembodied voices.

A successful career as a welder in Ohio ended in 1982, when he was laid off by the Babcock and Wilcox Company. Huberty, his wife Etna, and his children moved to Mexico briefly and then to San Ysidro, California (near the Mexican border), where Huberty earned a meager income as a security guard. He sometimes hit his wife, who did her best to shield the increasingly reclusive and hot-tempered Huberty from the rest of the world.

### Criminal Career

On July 17, 1984, after being fired from his security guard position, Huberty called a mental clinic, and an employee promised to get back to him in two days to schedule an appointment. Worried that her husband might kill someone in the interim, Etna called every mental clinic in the area in an attempt to determine which clinic Huberty had called and to plead for an immediate appointment. However, because the clinic had misspelled Huberty's name, there was no record of his call. Etna ignored one clinic's suggestion that she call the police.

The next day, Huberty told Etna that his life was over and that he was "going to hunt humans." Etna did nothing. A little before 4:00 P.M., Huberty entered a McDonald's in a Mexican American neighborhood. Huberty had expressed his hatred for children and for Mexicans; he felt that Mexicans were to blame for the loss of some of his jobs. Using a 9-millimeter Browning pistol, a 9-millimeter Uzi pistol, and a Winchester 12-gauge shotgun, he began killing people. An assistant manager at the McDonald's called the operator and reported a shooting in progress. The operator told her to dial 911; only after extensive pleading from the manager (noting that if she reached for the wall phone to dial 911, she would be killed) did the operator connect her to the police. Several officers finally arrived but did not enter the restaurant. The commander of the Special Weapons and Tactics (SWAT) team took almost an hour to arrive because of rush-hour traffic, and the SWAT officers would not act without a commanding order. Finally, at 5:17 P.M., a SWAT sniper, following orders, took a clear rifle shot at Huberty's head and instantly killed him. In 77 minutes, Huberty had fired approximately 150 shots, murdered 21 people, and wounded 19. Many of those who died bled to death while the police officers remained outside the building.

## Impact

James Oliver Huberty's life and murders were later carefully studied by George Hennard, who would commit a similar but deadlier mass murder in a restaurant in Killeen, Texas, in 1991. Gun control groups attempted to use the McDonald's Massacre, as the event came to be called, to promote their cause; they met with little success. Furthermore, no changes occurred in the law enforcement policies of refusing to enter a building in order to confront an "active shooter" or of not allowing police snipers to act except in response to a command.

In 1987, several survivors filed a lawsuit, *Lopez v. McDonald's Corporation*, accusing McDonald's of failing to provide adequate security within the restaurant, but their litigation efforts failed. Also in 1987, Etna Huberty sued McDonald's and Babcock and Wilcox Company, claiming that a combination of the monosodium glutamate in the restaurant's food and Huberty's long years of working with poisonous metals contributed to his delusions and episodes of rage. Her lawsuits were also unsuccessful.

## Further Reading

Foreman, Laura, ed. *Mass Murderers*. Alexandria, Va.: Time-Life Books, 1993. Chapter 4 serves as an excellent survey of Huberty's childhood, lifelong interest in guns, and descent into mental illness. Also provides extensive information about the victims, as well as the police department's response to the killings.

Kohl, James. "Foreseeing One's Duty to Protect." *Security Management* 33, no. 9 (September, 1989). Analyzes the unsuccessful lawsuit, *Lopez v. McDonald's*, that a few San Ysidro victims brought against McDonald's for allegedly failing to provide adequate security.

Salva-Ramirez, Mary-Angie. "The San Ysidro Massacre, Ten Years Later: McDonald's Actions Spoke Louder than Words." *Public Relations Quarterly* 40, no. 1 (1995). Explains how the reaction of the McDonald's Corporation to the massacre focused on providing all possible assistance to the victims and their families without regard for possible legal liability and how the compassionate approach left the positive corporate image of McDonald's as strong as ever.

*—David B. Kopel*

**See also:** George Hennard; Charles Whitman.

# Jesse James
## Western outlaw and gang leader

**Born:** September 5, 1847; near Centerville (now Kearney), Missouri
**Died:** April 3, 1882; St. Joseph, Missouri
**Also known as:** Jesse Woodson James (full name); Dingus James; Thomas Howard; Ed Everhard; Dave Smith; J. T. Jackson; John Davis Howard; J. D. Howard
**Cause of notoriety:** James, leader of the James-Younger Gang, led a sixteen-year lawless rampage and was suspected of robbing banks, trains, omnibuses, stagecoaches, and a state fair, as well as causing the deaths of ten people.
**Active:** February 13, 1866-September 7, 1881
**Locale:** Alabama, Arkansas, Iowa, Kansas, Kentucky, Minnesota, Missouri, Texas, and West Virginia

### Early Life

Jesse James (JEHS-ee jaymz) began his life as the third child of Robert James and Zerelda James. Robert James was a slave-owning, well-to-do, educated minister who cofounded William Jewell College in Liberty, Missouri, and several churches in Clay County, Missouri. When Jesse was three, his father left his family for the goldfields of California, where he died and was buried in an unmarked grave. Zerelda, a mother of three children, married Benjamin Simms but divorced him after a few months. Dr. Reuben Samuels became her third and last husband and stepfather to her children.

Little else is known of James's childhood. His teen years were marked by the bloodshed of the Civil War and its devastation of Missouri. He followed the exploits of William Quantrill's guerrillas, who roamed under the Black Flag, indiscriminately plundering and killing both Union and Confederate sympathizers. Frank James, Jesse's older brother, joined the guerrillas, and Jesse followed when he turned seventeen. He participated in the Centralia (Missouri) Massacre, where twenty-five unarmed Union soldiers were lined up and killed. From his days with Quantrill and Quantrill's lieutenant William "Bloody Bill" Anderson, Jesse James learned guerrilla tactics that would later serve him well as the leader of an outlaw gang. His outlawry did not hamper his marriage to his first cousin, Zerelda Mimms, with whom he had two children, Jesse Edwards James and Mary Susan James.

## Criminal Career

Following the Civil War, James and Frank, who refused to take the loyalty oath demanded by the United States government, were not granted amnesty for their guerrilla activities. The James brothers gathered their old wartime comrades and formed a gang. Their first target, the Clay County Savings Association in Liberty, is considered the first bank in the United States to experience a daytime robbery during peacetime. Over the following fifteen years, the gang netted more than $175,000 from nine banks, seven trains, two stagecoaches, two omnibuses, and one state fair. Rewards for the arrest and conviction of James ranged from three thousand to five thousand dollars. Although the Pinkerton's National Detective Agency and hundreds of posse members chased James and his gang through eight states, he was never captured. Only after Robert and Charles Ford, members of James's gang, met with Missouri governor Thomas T. Crittenden and agreed to kill James did his outlawry end. The Ford brothers waited until James was unarmed and shot him in the back of the head on April 3, 1882.

*Jesse James*. (Library of Congress)

### The James-Younger Gang

*At various times during Jesse James's criminal career, forty-one men rode with the James-Younger Gang. The most famous were:*

- **Frank James:** He surrendered to Governor Crittenden five months after his brother was murdered. He explained, "I have been hunted for twenty-one years, have literally lived in the saddle, have never known a day of perfect peace. It was one long, anxious, inexorable, eternal vigil." He was indicted for only one of his crimes and found innocent in court. Before he died of a heart attack in 1915, he worked as a shoe salesman, theater guard, and betting commissioner and toured briefly with the Cole Younger and Frank James Wild West Company in 1903.
- **Cole Younger:** After serving twenty-five years for the Northfield, Minnesota, robbery, he was paroled in 1901. He joined with Frank James in a Wild West show and wrote a memoir claiming he was a Confederate diehard rather than an outlaw. In 1912, he espoused Christianity and apologized for his violent past. He died in 1916.
- **Jim Younger:** He was also paroled in 1901 after a twenty-five-year jail sentence for the Northfield robbery. He committed suicide a year later.
- **Bob Younger:** He died of tuberculosis in Stillwater Prison while serving out his sentence for the Northfield robbery.
- **John Younger:** He was shot dead by Pinkerton agents in Missouri in 1874.
- **Robert Ford:** He was "the dirty little coward who shot Mr. Howard and laid Jesse James in his grave" (according to the song "Jesse James"). He died in a barroom brawl in Colorado in 1892.
- **Charlie Ford:** He committed suicide in 1882.

## Impact

For more than one hundred years, Jesse James has been the subject of newspaper and magazine articles, dime novels, ballads, biographies, plays, poems, television series, movies, documentary footage, and an operetta. James, the Missouri farmboy with the alliterative name, became known as an American Robin Hood, an outlaw hero known far beyond his boyhood home. Historians, journalists, and sociologists have pondered how such a man gained such renown.

In post-Civil War Missouri, devastated by guerrilla warfare and Union military actions, James's outlawry resonated with people who had southern sympathies. They believed that James was forced to become an outlaw and that he was merely robbing the rich to give to the poor. Nationally, James appealed to America's sense of individualism, the little man taking on larger forces and escaping to rob another day. James's post-Civil War exploits evidence sociological arguments that societal upheavals are breeding grounds for outlaw hero adulation. In 1927, efforts failed to erect a monument to commemorate James's life, but the number of markers and festivals bearing his name ensure he will not be forgotten.

The violence of the way James lived has been largely forgotten. Beginning with the 1927 film *Under the Black Flag*, the quasi-historical treatments used by Hollywood have served to anchor James more firmly in a world of fiction than reality, where he remains today.

**FURTHER READING**

Brant, Marley. *Jesse James: The Man and the Myth.* New York: Berkley Books, 1998. Historical treatment that attempts to separate the legend from the reality of James's life.

Dyer, Robert L. *Jesse James and the Civil War in Missouri.* Columbia: University of Missouri Press, 1994. A historian documents the role James played in the Civil War and its influence on his outlaw career.

Kooistra, Paul. *Criminals as Heroes: Structure, Power, and Identity.* Bowling Green, Ohio: Bowling Green State University Popular Press, 1989. A sociologist notes the effect societal crises had on the lawless careers of Frank and Jesse James, Billy the Kid, Butch Cassidy, John Dillinger, Bonnie Parker, Clyde Barrow, Charles Arthur "Pretty Boy" Floyd, and Al Capone.

Settle, William A. *Jesse James Was His Name: Or, Fact and Fiction Concerning the Careers of the Notorious James Brothers of Missouri.* Columbia: University of Missouri Press, 1966. The first scholarly treatment of James's life traces his outlawry through newspapers, ballads, plays, dime novels, and movies.

Stiles, T. J. *Jesse James: Last Rebel of the Civil War.* New York: Alfred A. Knopf, 2002. Well documented, this account depicts James as a nineteenth century terrorist and a public relations hound who politicized and maneuvered his way into infamy.

*—Cathy M. Jackson*

**SEE ALSO:** Apache Kid; Tom Bell; William H. Bonney; Curly Bill Brocius; Bob Dalton; Emmett Dalton; Bill Doolin; John Wesley Hardin; Doc Holliday; Tom Ketchum; Harry Longabaugh; Bill Longley; William Clarke Quantrill; Johnny Ringo; Belle Starr; Hank Vaughan; Cole Younger.

# Jim Jones

## Minister turned cult leader

**Born:** May 13, 1931; Crete, Indiana

**Died:** November 18, 1978; Jonestown, Guyana

**Also known as:** James Warren Jones (full name); the Reverend Jim Jones

**Cause of notoriety:** The founder of a cultlike church called the People's Temple, Jones led its members in a mass murder-suicide in Guyana.

**Active:** 1952-1978

**Locale:** Indianapolis, Indiana; Redwood Valley, California; and Guyana

### Early Life

James Warren Jones (commonly known as the Reverend Jim Jones) was born into an impoverished family in rural Indiana during the Great Depression. He was the only child born to his parents, James and Lynetta Jones. His father was a disabled military veteran. His mother supported the family and was primarily responsible for rearing Jones.

During high school, Jones was employed as an orderly at a hospital, where he met his future wife, Marceline Baldwin, who was a nursing student. They married on June 12, 1949. The marriage produced one child, Stephan, who was born in 1959. When Jones married Marceline, he was a freshman at Indiana University. However, he did not complete college until 1961, when he obtained a bachelor's degree in education from Butler University.

### Ministry Career

Jones's career in the ministry began as a student pastor at Sommerset Southside Methodist Church in 1952 in Indianapolis, Indiana. His ministry emphasized racial integration at a time when the United States was still racially segregated, and he sought to bring African Americans into his all-white church. His differences with the Sommerset church over segregation led to his dismissal. Afterward, he became involved with several Pentecostal churches before founding the People's Temple Full Gospel Church in 1955 in Indianapolis. In 1959, the People's Temple became an affiliate of the Disciples of Christ denomination, but Jones was not ordained as a minister for the Disciples of Christ until 1964.

*Jim Jones.* (AP/Wide World Photos)

Jones's ministry included staged faith healings and other faked miracles. His theology emphasized socialist political views and racial integration. He encouraged his followers to practice communal living and communal rearing of children. In 1964, Jones relocated the People's Temple to Redwood Valley, California, where he believed his political and social views would be more welcomed. Jones's ministry grew in California, and additional People's Temple churches opened in San Francisco and Los Angeles in the early 1970's. In 1974, the People's Temple leased a plot of land in the South American nation of Guyana. Jones's stated intention was to create a socialist and racially integrated community, free of what he saw as the evils of modern American capitalist society. The community came to be called Jonestown and was later the site of the mass murder-suicide for which Jones became infamous.

### Tragedy in Jonestown

As the congregation of the People's Temple grew in California, so did Jones's political influence and media presence. While media attention toward the People's Temple was initially positive, several exposés of the organization alleged financial misconduct, faked faith healings, and abusive practices toward members. In the wake of these exposés, as well as a potential tax problem, Jones relocated to Jonestown in July, 1977; his followers were encouraged to relocate as well. By September, 1977, more than one thousand members lived in Jonestown. The majority of the residents of Jonestown were African American, more than a quarter of the residents were children, and many were senior citizens.

The factors that ultimately led Jones to advocate suicide among his followers may not ever be fully understood, but biographers have noted that Jones perceived himself as persecuted by the media and that he had developed an addiction to prescription narcotics, both of which intensified in Jonestown.

In November, 1978, a delegation from the United States led by Congressman Leo Ryan arrived in Guyana to investigate allegations that People's Temple members were being abused and held in Jonestown against their will. Fifteen members opted to leave with the delegation but were attacked along with members of the delegation as they boarded a plane to leave. Five people were killed, including Ryan. Ten people were wounded.

After the attack, Jones called a meeting of the entire Jonestown community, where he announced that their community would be destroyed because of the attack on the delegation. He argued that they must commit an act of "revolutionary suicide," by taking their own lives before the military and police could launch a counterattack. Jonestown's medical staff distributed fruit punch containing a mixture of cyanide and sedatives to the People's Temple members. More than nine hundred of Jones's followers, including Jones's wife

### Death Rehearsal

*On June 15, 1978, Deborah Layton Blakey, a Jonestown survivor, recorded a sworn affidavit about her experience:*

[Jones] convinced black Temple members that if they did not follow him to Guyana, they would be put into concentration camps and killed. White members were instilled with the belief that their names appeared on a secret list of enemies of the state that was kept by the CIA and that they would be tracked down, tortured, imprisoned, and subsequently killed if they did not flee to Guyana. . . .

During one "white night," we were informed that our situation had become hopeless and that the only course of action open to us was a mass suicide for the glory of socialism. We were told that we would be tortured by mercenaries if we were taken alive. Everyone, including the children, was told to line up. As we passed through the line, we were given a small glass of red liquid to drink. We were told that the liquid contained poison and that we would die within forty-five minutes. We all did as we were told. When the time came when we should have dropped dead, Reverend Jones explained that the poison was not real and that we had just been through a loyalty test. He warned us that the time was not far off when it would become necessary for us to die by our own hands.

*Source*: "Affadavit of Deborah Layton Blakey," Rick A. Ross Institute, http://www.rickross.com.

and several of their adopted children, were forced to drink or voluntarily drank the poisoned punch. Jones was killed by a gunshot wound to the head. It is unclear if he fired the fatal shot himself or if one of his followers fired the shot.

### Impact

Jim Jones is less well known for his ministry than for the tragedy in Jonestown, which remains the largest mass murder-suicide in American history. The Jonestown tragedy was widely reported in the national and international media and spurred debate about the dangers of cults and other extremist organizations. Subsequent study of Jones and the People's Temple by academicians, as well as memoirs by former members, has provided insights into how cults and other extremist organizations control their followers and how these members can make destructive choices that they may have never considered prior to their involvement in the group. The lingering impact of Jonestown on American popular culture is reflected in the expression "drink the Kool-Aid," a phrase that indicates an individual has conformed to the demands of a larger social group without considering the consequences of his or her conformity.

### Further Reading

Hall, John R. *Gone from the Promised Land: Jonestown in American Cultural History*. New Brunswick, N.J.: Transaction, 1987. Contains a biography of Jones and a history of the People's Temple; compares People's Temple practices to those of other religious movements.

Kilduff, Marshall, and Phil Tracy. "Inside People's Temple." *New West*. June, 1977. The original exposé that drew critical attention to Jones's ministry.

Lalich, Janja. *Bounded Choice: True Believers and Charismatic Cults*. Berkeley: University of California Press, 2004. Discusses a theory, Bounded Choice, to explain how cult members come to make destructive and irrational decisions that diverge from their behavior prior to cult membership.

Maaga, Mary M. *Hearing the Voice of Jonestown: Putting a Human Face on an American Tragedy*. Syracuse, N.Y.: Syracuse University Press, 1998. Focuses on the female leadership of the People's Temple; analyzes the causes of the Jonestown tragedy from a sociological perspective.

*—Damon Mitchell*

**See also:** Marshall Applewhite; Bonnie Nettles.